Thinking Through
PROJECT-BASED LEARNING

Thinking Through

PROJECT-BASED LEARNING

Guiding Deeper Inquiry

JANE KRAUSS • SUZIE BOSS

CORWIN
A SAGE Company

CORWIN
A SAGE Company

FOR INFORMATION:

Corwin

A SAGE Company

2455 Teller Road

Thousand Oaks, California 91320

(800) 233-9936

www.corwin.com

SAGE Publications Ltd.

1 Oliver's Yard

55 City Road

London EC1Y 1SP

United Kingdom

SAGE Publications India Pvt. Ltd.

B 1/I 1 Mohan Cooperative Industrial Area

Mathura Road, New Delhi 110 044

India

SAGE Publications Asia-Pacific Pte. Ltd.

3 Church Street

#10-04 Samsung Hub

Singapore 049483

Acquisitions Editors: Debra Stollenwerk and
                       Arnis Burvikovs

Associate Editor: Desirée Bartlett

Editorial Assistant: Mayan White

Permissions Editor: Adele Hutchinson

Project Editor: Veronica Stapleton

Copy Editor: Kim Husband

Typesetter: C&M Digitals (P) Ltd.

Proofreader: Dennis W. Webb

Indexer: Sheila Bodell

Cover Designer: Karine Hovsepian

Printed in the United States of America

A catalog record of this book is available from the Library of Congress.

ISBN: 9781452202563

This book is printed on acid-free paper.

13 14 15 16 17 10 9 8 7 6 5 4 3 2 1

Contents

Preface

When Jane was a high school student, her history class took a field trip to a historical Western town located about 50 miles from her school. At the local museum, she and her classmates followed a docent from exhibit to exhibit. They wandered among Native American artifacts, a display about Chinese miners and gold prospecting, and collections of 19th-century housewares, toys, and farming implements. After the tour, students were free to stroll the city's wooden boardwalks, visit tourist shops, and buy treats at an old-time soda fountain. The day stands out as a fond high school memory when Jane looks back, but not because of any academic content she learned. The field trip was disconnected from what was happening back in the classroom.

As an adult and veteran teacher, Jane happened to revisit the same town. This time, she and her friends wandered off the beaten path and found themselves at the local pioneer cemetery. Many aspects of that place piqued their curiosity. They noticed how graves were organized into separate sections depending on religious affiliation, with one particular section sporting the largest and most ornate headstones. They wondered why so many gravestones were inscribed with 1918 as the year of death. Even though Chinese laborers made up a large part of the population in the town's early years, there was a dearth of Chinese graves. Why was this so?

Wearing her project-based learning hat, Jane couldn't help but imagine what a different experience she and her classmates might have had if they had started their tour at that cemetery. They would have been full of questions by the time they arrived at the museum. Chances are they would have ended their visit with a deeper understanding of pioneer history and a desire to learn more. They would have been primed for an engaging and academically meaningful project-based learning experience.

LEARNING THAT STICKS

At the start of workshops we lead on PBL—project-based learning—we often ask teachers to recall a significant memory from their school days. As you launch into this book with us, take a moment to conjure up your own recollections. Think back to your school days and quickly (without filtering!) focus on an especially vivid, "sticky" memory.

How would you classify your memory—was it academic, social, extra-curricular, or interpersonal in nature? Perhaps it involved a field trip, guest speaker, performance, or other novel event? Maybe it was purely social. In hindsight, can you tell whether this experience contributed to any enduring understanding? What did you take away from it?

Take another moment to imagine your current students, years from now, looking back on their K–12 education. Which of today's experiences do you expect will have staying power for them? Will they remember events that were fun because they were a break from the regular school day or experiences that whetted their curiosity and engaged them as thinkers and learners? Can you imagine any of their experiences becoming a springboard for lifetime of curiosity about the world around them?

FINDING AND FILLING THE GAPS

We know from experience that project-based learning has the potential to create powerful—and memorable—learning experiences for students. We also recognize that it can be hard to extract the full benefits of PBL. In our previous book, *Reinventing Project-Based Learning,* we focused on helping teachers *prepare* for projects that connect to real-world issues and integrate technology to maximize learning. Since that publication in 2007, our interactions with many educators—in the United States and internationally—have convinced us that there's a need to go deeper with advice about *doing* projects.

This book is designed to support teachers, school leaders, and professional learning communities that are looking for strategies to guide the implementation of projects. We know this is a fast-growing audience, including both PBL veterans and newcomers to the project approach.

A number of factors are helping PBL to gain traction as a key teaching and learning strategy, including:

- New standards that set more challenging learning goals than those of the "inch-deep, mile-wide" traditional curriculum. In the United States, Common Core State Standards present learning objectives that address "big ideas" in a more holistic and interdisciplinary way. This new approach to standards aligns with the philosophy and best practices of project-based learning.
- Continuing call for students to develop 21st-century skills that will prepare them for college, careers, and future life challenges. The Framework for 21st Century Skills calls for students to develop mastery in the 4 Cs: communication, collaboration, creativity, and critical thinking. We can't expect students to master these essential skills for

the future if they don't start gaining experience with them during their K–12 years. PBL offers arguably the best way to develop these 21st-century skills.

- Growing networks of schools that are adopting PBL as a wall-to-wall strategy for teaching and learning. These schools have been serving as laboratories for developing best practices in PBL. Many are eager to share field-tested resources and classroom success stories, paving the way for others to get a faster start with project-based learning.

- New networks of educators driving their own professional learning. Connecting via Twitter, Skype, and a host of other tech tools, teachers are coming together around shared interests, including project-based learning. Many meet weekly on Twitter for a #PBLChat, while others focus on subject-area innovation. Across these contexts, teachers are stepping into new leadership roles as influencers and experts. Many are natural collaborators who bring good thinking to project design teams.

WHY WE EMPHASIZE INQUIRY

A central feature of this book is our focus on developing students' inquiry skills during projects so that they can make deep investigations into big and enduring ideas. The double entendre of our title—*Thinking Through Project-Based Learning*—is deliberate. We want to help you think through all the aspects of planning and implementing projects so that you can guide your students to the deeper thinking that PBL affords.

Inquiry is the engine that drives learning in PBL. By understanding more about how inquiry works, teachers can engage and sustain students' curiosity across the arc of a project. We will offer suggestions to help educators retool how they teach so that they can harness the full power of inquiry with their students. We'll also suggest ways to redesign classroom environments (without extensive resources) and create new traditions so that students learn more deeply.

We also recognize the challenge of getting at and shaping covert acts of thinking. That's why we take readers into an exploration of new research in cognitive science and brain-based learning. By applying insights from these fields, educators can improve questioning strategies and make students' thinking less mysterious—and more effective.

One of the appealing promises of PBL is the opportunity to engage students in authentic, real-life projects (hence, the subtitle of our previous book: "Your Field Guide to Real-World Projects in the Digital Age"). Unless teachers are career changers from fields outside education, however, they are unlikely to have had much exposure to other professions. How are they expected to guide real-world inquiry into fields that they have never explored? To help readers think outside the classroom, we offer insights from experts in a variety of professions for whom inquiry is central to their work. By knowing more about the thinking strategies of scientists, authors, artists, and mathematicians, teachers will be in a better position to help students tackle projects from diverse perspectives.

A development we have followed with interest is the potential for projects to "take off," having an impact that spirals far beyond the classroom in which they started. For instance, when compelling student work is shared publicly or published online, it can engage much larger audiences than students (or teachers) ever expected to reach. Don't be surprised if other teachers or schools ask to join your efforts, turning a single-class project into a connected learning experience.

WHAT TO EXPECT

The book is organized in two sections.

Section One, Inquiry: The Engine of Deep Learning, builds a foundation to help readers see how theory and concepts translate to better thinking in PBL. It includes five chapters:

Chapter 1, The Whys and Hows of PBL, offers an overview of project-based learning, distinguishes the project approach from other instructional strategies and explains the critical role of inquiry in PBL.

Chapter 2, The Inquiring Human Animal, turns to human development, cognitive science, and brain-based education to draw lessons about learning, particularly the deep kind that has students inquiring to construct their own meaning.

Chapter 3, Making the World Safe for Thinking, explores critical factors that influence inquiry, including features of the learning environment, design of learning experiences, and interactions that maximize children's development toward mature inquiry.

Chapter 4, The Thinking-Out-Loud-and-in-View Classroom, focuses on PBL teaching methods, including discussion and questioning techniques and "thinking routines" that can be applied across grades and subject matter.

Chapter 5, Designing Rich Learning Experiences, summarizes our approach to effective project planning with a step-by-step guide for developing inquiry-rich projects.

Each chapter in Section One is illustrated with project examples and advice from teachers.

Section Two, Taking a Page from the Experts, makes connections between core content areas and the ways in which experts in affiliated professions approach problem solving. In each chapter, we contrast how subject matter is typically approached in school with "real-world" applications of knowledge by historians, scientists, journalists, community activists, and other capable people. We consider the language, tools, and methods professionals use in their investigations and draw lessons for classroom practice.

Chapter 6, Thinking Across Disciplines, sets the stage for this section by comparing disciplinary and interdisciplinary thinking.

The next four chapters focus on PBL in core content areas:

- Chapter 7, Language Arts
- Chapter 8, Social Studies
- Chapter 9, Science
- Chapter 10, Math

Because chapters are organized by traditional content areas, a reader might be inclined to focus on the subject matter he or she teaches. We encourage readers to read beyond their subjects to become familiar with the big ideas and real-life applications of other disciplines. With this familiarity, they will be better able to plan interdisciplinary projects that more closely mirror authentic work. Each subject-area chapter includes an assortment of interdisciplinary project examples. Readers might be inspired to collaborate with teachers from other disciplines, a practice we repeatedly recommend.

The main text concludes with Chapter 11, The Project Spiral. Here we describe how projects can expand in scope, complexity, and impact as teachers and students gain familiarity with PBL. We close with suggestions for building traditions for PBL that can lead to stronger connections between school and local community and, perhaps, connect students with the wider world.

At the back of the book, we include a Discussion Guide to help teacher teams, school leaders, instructional coaches, and others use the text to guide teacher learning. The guide summarizes key concepts from each chapter and advises on facilitating group and individual activities. It also helps facilitators know what to look for and respond to during class visits to encourage high-quality PBL.

The Appendices include a Project Library, with more than 80 short descriptions of all projects featured in the book, plus a few more projects we admire, too. There is also a companion Professional Development Guide, with suggestions for using the Project Library as a resource for professional learning or discussions by professional learning communities. Finally, we include a Resources Guide with suggestions of books, videos, and websites to round out your learning of PBL.

SPECIAL FEATURES

Whether you are reading alone or reading along with colleagues, whether you are new to project-based learning or a PBL veteran, we hope the book inspires you to reflect deeply on your own practice.

These special features are included throughout the book to encourage deeper engagement and reader interaction:

- *Project Signposts:* These just-in-time tips alert readers to try out tools and strategies that are useful at key points during the PBL process.
- *Exercises:* These do-it-yourself suggestions in Section One are intended to help readers connect what they are learning to their own practice. Mini-exercises are building blocks for the ultimate exercise, which is planning a standards-based, inquiry-rich project that causes students to operate as experts would when tackling a challenge or investigation.
- *Tech Spotlights:* Technology spotlights are presented in the subject-specific chapters of Section Two, highlighting useful technologies teachers and students can adopt to maximize learning opportunities in PBL.
- *Project Library:* Appendix A features a library of project sketches, including projects featured throughout the book. You can scan them quickly to find ones that match your grade level or subject area and then borrow or adapt them to meet your context and learning goals. Project sketches can also be useful in professional development to give teachers a wide range of project ideas to discuss and consider for their own classrooms.
- *Discussion Guide:* Appendix B supports shared reading, summarizing key concepts, and advising on group and individual activities.
- *Professional Development Guide:* Appendix C is a resource for facilitated professional development or professional learning community (PLC) work, this guide outlines five discussion starters for teachers or instructional leaders.
- *Resources Guide:* Appendix D supports further exploration. As noted before, this book is not a PBL primer but instead delves deep into project implementation. For those new to PBL, we include a resource guide with a wealth of books, readings, websites, and experts to help you understand and get started with PBL.

BETTER WITH PRACTICE

This book is intended to appeal to a wide range of readers.

If you are new to project-based learning, you will find examples and teaching strategies to give you a strong foundation. The many project illustrations will help you envision PBL so that you can plan and manage projects more effectively. Guided exercises will help you apply new ideas to your own practice and develop a more critical eye for quality projects.

If you are already somewhat familiar with PBL, we hope the book will challenge you to reflect on your previous project experiences and imagine how you might guide your students into deeper inquiry. After all, revision and reflection are important aspects of the project experience. That's equally true for students and for educators.

Wherever you are starting, we hope you will be inspired to take project-based learning in new directions. That might mean planning your first interdisciplinary project, connecting your students with community experts, or planning for projects that spiral out of your classroom and into the local neighborhood—or into the wider world.

For school leaders, instructional coaches, and other decision makers who are interested in project-based learning as a route to school improvement, we hope you will come away with a clear understanding of how to support teachers—and students—as they make the shift to PBL. Developing your critical eye for quality projects will help you know what to look for when you visit PBL classrooms or offer feedback on projects. Understanding the right environment for inquiry projects will help you plan for changes that will allow PBL to flourish in your learning community so that teachers and students alike can do their best thinking.

Acknowledgments

In the main, this book is built on the stories and experiences of teachers and school leaders who fulfill the promise of project-based learning every day. We are grateful to these exemplary educators for their contributions to students and to our book: John Burk, Cherisse Campbell, Kathy Cassidy, Teresa Cheung, Richard Coote, Diana Cornejo-Sanchez, Vicki Davis, Jenna Gampel, Andrew Gloa, Mike Gwaltney, Heather Hanson, Amy and Randy Hollinger, Laura Humphreys, Maggie Johnston, Diana Laufenberg, Julie Lindsay, George Mayo, Lisa Moody, Frank Noschese, Jeff Robin, Julie Robison, Terry Smith, and Neil Stephenson.

We appreciate these educators who, as they reflect on their practice in blogs and other publications, teach us so much: Jackie Ballarini, Sue Boudreau, Jenna Gampel, Dan Meyer, Margaret Noble, John Pearson, Lacey Segal, Sarah Brown Wessling, Shelly Wright, and many others who regularly share their thinking.

Many schools, districts, and educational organizations have informed our thinking. We wish to acknowledge: Birkdale Intermediate School, Buck Institute for Education, Conservatory Lab Charter School, Edutopia, High Tech High, High Tech High Media Arts, Manor New Technology High School, National Writing Project, New Tech Network, Science Leadership Academy, Teach 21-West Virginia Department of Education, Technology High School, and TESLA, the Technology Engineering Science Leadership Academy.

A chief intent of this book was to relate the mindsets and practices of accomplished people for whom inquiry is central to their work. We are grateful to these experts for the personal stories and advice they shared that inform authentic practices in school: historian H. W. "Bill" Brands, chemist Catherine "Katie" Hunt, author Rebecca Skloot, and computer scientist Jeannette Wing.

It all starts and ends with kids. Thank you to Grace, Zoe, Eli, and especially Michael Greenberg for your exemplary project work. A+.

PUBLISHER'S ACKNOWLEDGMENTS

Corwin wishes to acknowledge the following peer reviewers for their editorial insight and guidance.

Patricia Allanson, Math Teacher/Department Chair
River Springs Middle School
Orange City, FL

Tania E. Dymkowski, Instructional Support K–8
Hays CISD
Kyle, TX

Jeanne R. Gren, Principal
Anna Jarvis Elementary School
Grafton, WV

Susan Harmon, Teacher
Neodesha Jr./Sr. High School
Neodesha, KS

Telannia Norfar, Technology Coach/Math Teacher
US Grant High School
Oklahoma City, OK

Lisa Parisi, Teacher
Denton Avenue Elementary School
New Hyde Park, NY

About the Authors

Jane Krauss is coauthor with Suzie Boss of the bestselling book *Reinventing Project-Based Learning*. A long-time teacher and technology enthusiast, Jane is currently a curriculum and program development consultant to organizations interested in project-based approaches to teaching and learning. Among others, she works with NCWIT, the National Center for Women & Information Technology, paving the way for inclusive practices that encourage the meaningful participation of girls and women in computing. In addition, Jane teaches online courses in project-based learning, speaks at conferences, and presents professional development workshops in the United States and internationally. In her free time, Jane enjoys dabbling in glasswork and mosaics and keeps fit running and hiking on woodland trails just outside her door in Eugene, Oregon.

Suzie Boss is a writer and educational consultant who focuses on the power of teaching and learning to improve lives and transform communities. She is the author of *Bringing Innovation to School: Empowering Students to Thrive in a Changing World* and co-author with Jane Krauss of *Reinventing Project-Based Learning*. She contributes regularly to Edutopia.org and the *Stanford Social Innovation Review* and has written for a wide range of other publications, including *The New York Times*, *Educational Leadership*, and *Principal Leadership*. She is a member of the National Faculty of the Buck Institute for Education and has worked with educators internationally to bring project-based learning and innovation strategies to both traditional classrooms and informal learning settings. An avid tennis player, she enjoys exploring the great outdoors near her hometown of Portland, Oregon, and spending time with her husband and two sons.

SECTION 1
Inquiry
The Engine of Deep Learning

1

The Whys and Hows of PBL

"The educator's part in the enterprise of education is to furnish the environment which stimulates responses and directs the learner's course."

—John Dewey

In Diana Laufenberg's 12th-grade social studies class, students learn about government functions managed by the executive branch. How would you go about teaching this topic? Where one teacher might have students read and discuss Article II of the U.S. Constitution and move on, Laufenberg sees an opportunity for deeper learning. Laufenberg's students interact with federal functions as anyone might who navigates a bureaucratic process. They "apply" for federal student aid or a green card. They make a request permitted by the Freedom of Information Act. Along the way, they analyze each process, present it in a diagram or infographic, and recommend ways the process might be improved. As students share their investigations, the class comes to understand the myriad ways in which citizens interact with government.

Laufenberg's project exemplifies many of the features of high-quality project-based learning:

- It deals with real-world concerns and gets at essential understandings.
- It is personalized; students choose the bureaucratic process they study, often based on issues they are dealing with in their own lives.

Figure 1.1 Green Card Application Flowchart

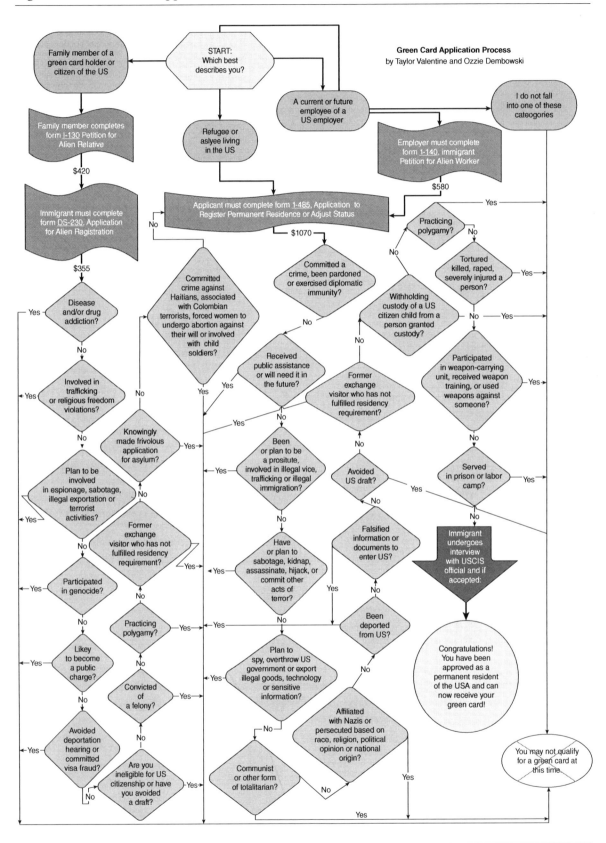

- It causes them to inquire, and their investigations require that students grapple with complexity.
- They learn together and from one another, and their learning is meaningful to people beyond school.
- Students are personally affected by what they learn and are likely to remember it.

A student named Grace, for instance, examined the process of getting a green card for permanent residency in the United States. She and her project partner found the process to be so convoluted that they created a flow chart to be able to visualize the many steps (and opportunities for confusion) between application and approval (see Figure 1.1). Let's listen to Grace reflect on what she learned:

> This bureaucratic function has become so complicated because over the years, United States immigration standards have become more exacting. Many believe that if a person cannot complete the process, they do not deserve to be in the U.S.

> The most upsetting realization I had was that immigrants go through this process. If my partner and I, both English-speaking seniors, had this much confusion during the process, it must be nearly impossible for a person just learning English to do.

GAIN FAMILIARITY WITH PBL

Beginning with this chapter, you will examine many projects that exemplify the qualities of project-based learning. Before digging into teaching with projects, it helps to establish an understanding of what project-based learning (PBL) is—and isn't. Having a clear definition in mind will help you navigate the PBL process (without the need for a flowchart!).

Project-based learning has been a subject of professional interest for more than 40 years. You're likely familiar with the project approach. Let's begin with your understanding. How would you describe PBL to someone? What opinions would you share about its value as an approach to teaching and learning? Jot down some notes before reading on.

Now, read the description we have crafted (through a process of multiple revisions, informed by our observations) to capture the essential ingredients of PBL:

In project-based learning, students gain important knowledge, skills, and dispositions by investigating open-ended questions to "make meaning" that they transmit in purposeful ways.

Does your characterization of PBL share common elements with ours? Let's unpack the ideas that define PBL.

	Meaning	*So*
In project-based learning,	*The emphasis is on the student experience—learning*	*The teacher does less direct instruction. He or she designs, prepares, and guides projects and learns alongside students.*
students gain important *knowledge, skills,* and *dispositions*	*Projects **are** the curriculum—not an add-on—and through them, students develop important capabilities*	*The teacher designs toward and assesses growth in all three areas.*
by investigating open-ended questions	*Questions activate, arousing curiosity and driving students to inquire*	*The right question at the start leads to more questions—ones that students can investigate.*
to "make meaning"	*The learning is important, unique, and holds value for the student and others*	*Projects elicit higher-order thinking: theorizing, investigating, analyzing, creating, and drawing unique conclusions.*
that they transmit in purposeful ways.	*The form the project takes matches the function it's meant to serve (inventing, entertaining, persuading, motivating, or inspiring)*	*A "loose" project structure allows for creative expression, and transmission of knowledge makes the learning "stick."*

Teachers like Laufenberg use the project approach deliberately and skillfully, with the intention of helping their students develop into knowledgeable, autonomous, and life-long learners. In the brief description of her project, you can see how she helps students investigate questions that matter in their lives. Their research helped them develop a better understanding of how government works. In fact, as students like Grace demonstrate, they are able to think deeply about how bureaucratic processes could be improved. Through PBL, these students are not just studying civics but are developing the skills, knowledge, and dispositions of good citizens.

→Project Signpost 1: Sum It Up

Take a moment to sum up what you think projects accomplish. Capture your thinking Twitter-style—that is, in 140 characters or less. (Example: *Kids learn by doing in content-rich PBL.*)

Sharing a headline or tweet that succinctly captures your thinking is an assessment of your own thinking. In classroom practice, you will want to check in on student understanding frequently during projects, using a variety of formative assessment tools. Mix it up by using exit slips at the end of class, on which students answer a specific question. Or ask them to share a headline or tweet that succinctly captures their thinking (and will quickly reveal any misunderstanding).

What Distinguishes PBL

As you delve into PBL, it helps to be alert to differences between PBL and other forms of activity-based or experiential learning. Two variations worth distinguishing from PBL are thematic teaching and *problem*-based learning.

PBL and Thematic Teaching

Thematic teaching is a practice that organizes learning activities within a theme. Dinosaurs, seasons, survival, Roman times, probability, famous authors, China, and other topics might organize assignments across subjects.

PBL and thematic teaching share common features. A central idea organizes each. Both are meant to be of high interest. Both involve longer-term study—a "unit" of connected learning activities. Thematic teaching and PBL often span multiple subjects.

Occasionally, we have encountered a hybrid approach in which teachers plan successive projects that relate to an overarching theme, such as power or identity. This approach of unifying a course of study under a theme or master question has value. In an Advanced Placement government course design that integrated PBL, for example, several projects related to a single "master question": *What is the proper role of government in a democracy?* Yet each project retained the features of high-quality PBL with inquiry at the core (Boss et al., 2012).

The biggest differences between thematic instruction and project-based learning come down to control, relevance, rigor, and enduring understanding.

Control. As the term suggests, thematic *teaching* is teacher centered. The teacher selects the topic or theme, presents activities for students to do, and makes decisions about the course of study. Students follow their teacher's lead.

In contrast, PBL is student centered. Students have a degree of control over what they learn, how they learn, and how they express their learning. Does student control sound like out-of-control to you? Fear not; with good project design, students achieve the learning aims their teachers intend and, likely, even more.

→Project Signpost 2: Watch Your Step(s)

Be wary of project plans that call for too many scripted steps. Overplanning is a symptom of teacher-directed instruction that's likely to lead to predictable—and possibly mediocre—results. Step-by-step projects leave little room for students to wrestle with uncertainty, raise new questions, or solve problems in novel ways. They are unlikely to challenge students to reach their full potential as capable, creative learners. (In Chapter 5, you will learn more about where to focus your attention for the most effective results in project planning.)

Relevance. When a project is relevant, it touches a student deeply and personally. PBL causes students to look at the world—and their place in it—differently. Thematic projects are interesting, sometimes entertaining, but not necessarily life changing in the way that PBL can be.

Two examples illustrate distinctions of *control* and *relevance* when comparing PBL and thematic projects.

Thematic Project: Insects!

A second-grade class studies insects. Students draw, read, and write about insects. They watch insect movies and do insect math. They learn that insects have defining characteristics and visit insect websites. Each child researches a particular insect, then writes, creates a digital slide show, or dictates a report about it. Students present their reports to the class and celebrate by constructing marshmallow and pretzel insects. They're busy with many hands-on activities, most of which are orchestrated by the teacher. It's thematic teaching with a science focus. Everyone learns a bit of science, but the activities do not add up to truly essential learning outcomes.

Project-Based Learning: The Square of Life

Now let's look at the same topic but with a project-based approach. Imagine a teacher presenting students with a world map and specimens of monarch butterflies and Australian stick insects. He poses a challenging question: *Why here and not there? Why there and not here? How can we find out?* He has registered his class in the Square of Life, an Internet-based collaborative project in which students investigate their local environment and share information with students from around the world. Students select a square meter of local ground to examine. They organize what they find into categories, which they define, such as living and nonliving, plants and animals. Through close examination (facilitated by their teacher but driven by student interest), they organize small creatures into groups by shared characteristics, and learn to discriminate between classes of creatures including insects, isopods, and annelids (segmented worms!). Students theorize about and investigate the role of habitat and niche in species distribution, eventually reaching defensible conclusions that feel like "theirs." They share their findings through Skype with Australian students and report their conclusions about, *Why here and not there? Why there and not here?*

Rigor. These two examples also demonstrate a difference in rigor. In thematic projects, rigor can be wanting. Students often research factual information and report it back as a summary. Activities are connected by the theme but, as we saw in the first case, do not necessarily add up to fundamental understanding greater than the sum of the parts. In contrast, through *Why Here?*, students learn interconnected concepts about classification and habitat that they will return to and build upon as they study science in years to come.

At times, a lack of rigor in thematic projects is masked by digital wizardry. Students may create appealing brochures, slideshows, podcasts, and other media to transmit information, but the content is often the same as can be found in a reference book, on the Internet, or in a traditional report.

In quality PBL, students use technology to investigate and construct new meaning. Technology helps them reach beyond the classroom to a community of learners. Projects like the Square of Life are "Google-proof." Students could not have searched for the right answer online; they had to actively investigate to figure out their own answer to the intriguing question, "Why here and not there?"

Two more examples help illustrate the difference in *rigor*.

Shopping on a Budget

Middle-school students research the question, *How does someone get the greatest bang for the buck when grocery shopping?* With a partner, students devise a healthy 1-week meal plan for four based on USDA guidelines. Next, each partner selects a store, and they comparison shop to find the best price per unit for each ingredient or menu item. Based on their per-item and per-grocery basket comparison, teams reach a conclusion about the most affordable place to shop. They get bonus points if they figure out how to put coupons to work to lower their grocery bill.

This is a good project—relevant to students' lives and connected to core content. But it could be better if it challenged students to think more critically about broader issues. The next project, similar in its intention of having kids use math, understand nutrition, and explore personal economics, is more rigorous and builds civic understanding to boot.

Deserts in Rainy Seattle?

In a project called Deserts in Rainy Seattle?, students ponder the fundamental question, *Is healthy food a right or a privilege?* After examining USDA nutrition guidelines, students discuss how easy or hard it is to meet them. Their teacher helps them arrive at this open-ended driving question: *What are the barriers to good nutrition?* Students discuss, defend their reasoning, and settle on three major barriers: knowledge about nutrition, interest in healthy eating, and access to nutritious foods. For this project, their teacher encourages them to tackle the latter. Pairs identify local "food deserts," neighborhoods where fresh and affordable food is lacking (USDA, n.d.), in which to "shop" for a week's menu using the price-indexed USDA "thrifty" food budget (USDA, 2012). Using Google Maps, spreadsheets, phone calls, grocery advertisements, and actual visits to "desert" neighborhoods, students analyze food availability and affordability, interview residents, draw conclusions about issues of food access, and recommend ways to solve them.

Compared to Shopping on a Budget, the food deserts project challenges students to think more critically about underlying problems affecting healthy food choices, develop possible solutions, use technology for research, and explain their reasoning with evidence. The first project may sound interesting, but the second involves rigorous thinking and deeper learning.

> *"When you DO something, not only do you learn it better, but it just affects you in a way that I think is a lot more influential in the long term."*
>
> —High school student reflecting at the end of a project

Enduring Understanding. Both grocery projects teach useful, real-world skills. In the food deserts project, however, students are more likely to develop awareness and lasting curiosity about issues of equity and social justice. Not all projects will have this impact, but designing a project with an eye toward enduring understanding is a good aspiration. Imagine your students learning through projects that have staying power because you have used their curiosity as a catalyst for deep investigations. Throughout the book, we will look at ways that social, interpersonal, and extracurricular elements can boost the academic experience and enduring nature of projects.

Project-Based and Problem-Based Learning

Project-based learning overlaps with *problem*-based learning, too. Problem-based learning emerged in medical schools during the 1950s. Finding that medical students struggled to make the leap from academic work to effective clinical practice, teaching physicians at McMaster University in Canada developed the problem-based approach (Barrows & Tamblyn, 1980). Instead of memorizing medical textbooks, future doctors were now learning through clinical scenarios set up to mirror the problems physicians might encounter in daily practice. This shift from knowledge acquisition to problem solving proved effective, and the approach has since become standard not only for medical schools but also in economics, engineering, and many other fields.

There are more similarities than differences between the two PBLs. For starters, similar pedagogic concerns influenced the development of both. Education and social reformer John Dewey advised that treating students as receptacles of knowledge left true intellectual engagement to chance. In 1916, in *Democracy and Education,* he declared, "Education is not an affair of 'telling' and being told, but an active and constructive process" (Dewey, 1997). Both problem- and project-based learning press students beyond knowledge acquisition, causing them to engage in critical thinking in order to construct their own meaning by applying what they have learned.

Both project- and problem-based experiences launch from an open-ended question, scenario, or challenge. Neither states the steps to a solution; instead, they cause learners to interpret and plan an approach they may repeatedly revisit and revise. In the best sense, both PBLs require problem refinement on the way to problem solving.

Both methods ask students to operate in the manner of professionals. In problem-based learning, this has students approaching problems in the way that scientists, mathematicians, economists, computer scientists, and other "pros" do.

In project-based learning, students adopt the "mantle of the expert," too, but even more broadly. Depending on the project, they might function as scientists or mathematicians, travel agents or museum curators, citizen advocates or manufacturing consultants, documentary filmmakers or social scientists. In projects, students are likely to read, research, work in teams, consult experts, use a variety of technologies, write, create media, and speak publicly in the process of the learning cycle.

Distinguishing Problems From Projects

For the purposes of this book, the biggest differences between the two PBL approaches have to do with the focus, duration, and outcomes of each.

A problem-based inquiry frequently focuses on a mathematics or science problem, and study is completed in one or several class periods. Project-based learning is often intentionally interdisciplinary, and the duration of a unit of study may range from several days to multiple weeks.

In problem-based learning, the path to answers might vary, but there is a desired right answer (or answers) at the end. In project-based learning, the processes, and thereby the outcomes, are more diffuse. In a project, the learning path and work products can be as unique as the students or teams that engage in it. Many teachers who advocate for project-based learning will tell you they set a standard for minimally acceptable outcomes and are often surprised and pleased to find students' work exceeding their expectations in both creativity and quality.

To illustrate the subtle differences between the two PBLs, here is a contrasting example of each. Ask yourself, which is problem based and which is project based?

The Floor Covering Scenario I

You have been asked by your mother to suggest a covering for the floor of your room. The room is rectangular and measures 4.3 m by 3 m. There are three ways to cover the floor. You can use a carpet, a mat, or tiles, but each is of different dimensions and price. The entire project, including additional materials and labor, has to stay within a budget of $600. Explain clearly and mathematically your best choice and how you arrive at your decision. Drawing diagrams may make your explanation clearer.

The Floor Covering Scenario II

One day, Mr. Abert brought a carpet remnant to class. He'd found the scrap among a large pile of used carpeting being removed from the floors and hallways of a local office building. All the discarded flooring was in a dumpster, headed for the landfill. The project begins with students estimating how much carpet, by volume, is destined for the landfill. They go on to look at issues of—and solutions to—dumping carpet and other bulky, composite waste. Their research turns up examples of how different communities around the globe are diverting bulky waste from landfills. After reading about a project in the United Kingdom that recycles carpeting and food waste and programs in the United States that deconstruct used mattresses and construction debris, students look for opportunities in their own community. The project continues with students working with a reuse and recycle center to find ways to source, clean, donate, place, and even advertise and resell used carpeting.

The first example falls in the range of "problems" while the second is very much a project. With good design, the second example addresses the learning objectives of the first (imagine students working with clients to measure and place quantities of carpet), while taking it further—into the world of math, and into the *world*.

Inquiry in Project-Based Learning

A good project sets up conditions in which students are compelled to inquire. Inquiry is the personal path of questioning, investigating, and reasoning that takes one from not knowing to knowing. Given the right opportunities, students doing projects become accustomed to inquiring—looking for patterns, analyzing systems, scrutinizing processes, exploring relationships, and solving problems. In the next chapter, we'll explore in more detail the conditions that give rise to inquiry.

Exercise: What do you wonder about?

In this chapter, you have heard descriptions of four projects: Navigating Bureaucracy, Square of Life, Deserts in Rainy Seattle, and Floor Covering Problem II. Select one of these projects for closer consideration. (Suggestion: Pick the project that you wish you had been able to do as a student.)

We have provided you with only a summary description of each. Jot down your thoughts as you consider these questions:

- What do you like about this project?
- What do you wonder about? What might be challenging about doing this project with your students?
- What would you expect your students to know or be able to do by the end?
- If you could interview the teacher who designed the project, what else would you want to know?

WHAT'S NEXT?

Now that you have a good working definition of PBL, along with a few project examples in mind, you're ready to dive deeper into your exploration of inquiry. In the next chapter, you'll consider why humans are such curious creatures, how traditional schooling can extinguish the spirit of inquiry, and what you can do to rekindle your students' questioning nature.

2

The Inquiring Human Animal

Here's a provocative project idea: Ask young people to illuminate something that's invisible in their communities. This assignment taps issues of fairness and power that carry strong youth interest while setting the stage for critical thinking and creative expression.

For their Invisibility Project, which addressed content in both English and multimedia, teachers Margaret Noble and Lacey Segal from High Tech High Media Arts (HTHMA) in San Diego, California, gave students free rein to propose which topics they would investigate and bring to light with multimedia documentaries. Here's how the teachers described their project in *Unboxed*, an online journal published by the High Tech High Graduate School of Education (Segal & Noble, 2008):

> Seniors from High Tech High Media Arts brought the invisible to light during a multimedia exhibition exposing hidden paradigms, underground cultures, and unresolved issues. Through documentaries, photo/sound essays, and video installations, students critically explored topics such as graffiti, rave culture, youth activism, self-mutilation, and the media. Students developed their projects in HTHMA's sound lab, using technology to showcase information they gathered from expert interviews and in-depth investigations of local professional, cultural, and institutional communities.

By informing the public about a hidden topic of their choosing, students understood that they would be providing a community service. This open-ended approach yielded impressive results. Students exhibited final products at a contemporary art museum, drawing an authentic audience and well-deserved praise for their professional-quality work. Behind each successful documentary, however, was an equally compelling back story. Students traveled their own paths to arrive at the often difficult subjects they explored, such as self-harm, media bias, and teen homelessness. One student offers a telling example. At first, he struggled to find a topic that he cared about enough to investigate. It wasn't until one of the teachers suggested he explore the subject of graffiti that his curiosity kicked in. "Is graffiti art or vandalism?" was the question that finally drove his inquiry forward. He interviewed police officers and taggers, thought critically about gang culture, and produced several pieces of original artwork that became part of his documentary.

In project-based learning, curiosity is the engine for learning. It's what drives students to ask questions, conduct research, design investigations, and reach out to experts. Of course, more than curiosity is required for students to reach the finish line. But if a project doesn't get students caring and wondering from the outset, it's almost certain to fall flat.

Fortunately, humans are born curious. Our natural inquisitiveness helps us make sense of the world. Curiosity is as integral to our survival as the fight-or-flight response. Young children don't have to be encouraged to ask questions. It's their go-to method of discovery.

Yet by the time students reach the middle grades, their teachers may be noticing a decline in curiosity about school topics. By high school, the most-often-asked question is apt to be a version of, "Will this be on the test?" That's a fair question if students have grown accustomed to lecture- and test-based instruction. It's also a warning that curiosity can get constrained by classroom practices that call for passive learning.

In contrast, students who are accustomed to project-based learning aren't afraid to ask questions—and keep asking until they arrive at answers that make sense to them. They don't give up when they run into challenges. They don't crumble in the face of criticism. Instead, they know how to use feedback and iterative cycles of revision to improve their work.

What helps students develop these productive habits of mind? How can we plan project experiences to encourage not only curiosity but also persistence and confidence in learners?

In this chapter, we'll take a closer look at inquiry within the broader context of cognitive development. Insights from brain researchers, educational psychologists, and learning scientists have important implications for how we design and manage projects to maximize learning.

LEARNING FROM RESEARCH

The relatively young field of mind, brain, and education science is providing us with important insights into the learning enterprise. As the name implies, this is an interdisciplinary field working at the intersections of neuroscience, cognition, psychology, and social and emotional aspects of learning.

New technology tools—such as noninvasive imaging devices that allow scientists to study the brain at work—are helping neuroscientists gain a better understanding of the developing brain and how it changes in response to experience. Meanwhile, psychologists and cognitive scientists are paying close attention to related topics such as motivation, attention, the relationship between exercise and thinking, and how students develop the capacity to manage their own learning. By applying their findings to the classroom, we can guide students so that they develop the confidence and competence they need to be more successful in projects—and in life.

In *Mind, Brain, and Education Science* (2010), Tracey Tokuhama-Espinosa synthesizes more than 4,500 studies from this emerging field to offer five key concepts, shown in the left column of Table 2.1. These concepts are worth considering as we plan projects that will get minds engaged. The column on the right suggests implications for classroom practice.

Table 2.1 Applying Mind-Brain-Education Science Insights to Projects

What research tells us*	*What this means for PBL*
Human brains are as unique as faces.	The uniqueness of each learner underscores the importance of student voice and choice in the selection and design of projects.
All brains are not equal because context and ability influence learning.	In projects, students of mixed ability levels need to find room to be challenged yet also have support to be successful. Well-designed projects allow for differentiation and provide scaffolding.
The brain is changed by experience.	Exposure to varied project experiences and fluency with "thinking routines" that projects call into play help students become more capable learners. Doing projects together gives students common experiences they can build on while allowing for differentiation.
The brain is highly plastic.	The brain changes in response to cognition; neural pathways are strengthened in response to repetition while underutilized pathways are pruned away. PBL presents opportunities for students to practice and "hard wire" executive function, the cognitive processes that help us regulate our actions.
The brain connects new information to old.	*Sense* and *meaning* are two filters the brain uses to decide whether an idea will take hold. To *make sense*, new information has to fit with the brain's existing scheme for how the world works. If there's no connection with prior understanding, then the information is discarded. *Meaning* refers to perceived significance. For an idea to stick, it has to have personal relevance. Otherwise, the brain casts it off. PBL happens within an authentic context where it *makes sense*. By focusing on topics students care about, the teacher imbues the project with *meaning*.

**Tokuhama-Espinosa, 2010

Expanding on this framework, we can incorporate more insights from research to enhance students' ability to inquire, grapple with new ideas, and manage their own learning—all of which come into play in projects.

THE IMPORTANCE OF NOVELTY

You might not notice a person walking past your classroom or office door, but if a tiger strolled by, you would.

Our very survival depends on attentiveness. Being alert to changes in the environment allowed early humans to capitalize on opportunity ("I'll hunt that bird for dinner") and avoid harm ("I'll hide from that rhino"). Stimuli have changed with the times, but we modern humans continue to be attracted to novelty. It's easy to imagine tomorrow's anthropologists studying YouTube to figure out which sights and sounds grabbed our fleeting attention in the early 21st century.

When novelty is present in the learning environment, students' brains become alert and receptive. A part of the brain called the reticular activating system filters incoming stimuli, deciding which information to trust to autopilot and what deserves our full attention.

Without novelty, we tend to let our brains rest and conserve energy—for a while. Then we start looking for fresh stimulation. Psychiatrist and child trauma expert Bruce Perry explains why repetitive classroom activities, such as lecture or worksheets, inhibit the brain's craving for novelty and can interfere with learning. "Only four to eight minutes of pure factual lecture can be tolerated before the brain seeks other stimuli, either internal (e.g., daydreaming) or external ("Who is that walking down the hall?"). If the teacher is not providing that novelty, the brain will go elsewhere" (Perry, n.d.).

Projects build in opportunities to introduce novelty. Projects often start with a "grabber" or entry event of some kind. That's when teachers deliberately facilitate an introduction to capture attention and interest, getting students' attention and curiosity engaged. Across the arc of the project, new challenges and opportunities for discovery continue to present themselves, supplying students with ample reasons to stay interested once the project is underway.

DEVELOPING EXECUTIVE FUNCTION

We are born with more than 100 billion brain cells, or neurons. During our lives, we never add more. What we do add is neural "circuitry," synaptic fibers that connect neurons and conduct signals between them. The right kinds of learning experiences during these years help children activate the neural circuits needed to become proficient problem solvers and creative thinkers (Willis, 2011).

By age 10, children have more neural connections, or synapses, than at any other time of their lives. This is when the brain takes a use-it-or-lose-it approach and starts pruning away connections that are underutilized. The pruning away of weaker "branches" strengthens those that remain, and the brain further stabilizes these circuits with a sheath of insulation called myelin. Effective learning experiences help students strengthen the connections that will lead to deeper understanding and, eventually, to more complex and mature thinking.

From age 8 to 16, the prefrontal cortex of the brain—the part right behind the forehead—is undergoing rapid development. Sometimes called the CEO of the brain, the prefrontal cortex is responsible for executive function. This term refers to a set of cognitive processes that help us regulate our actions.

Executive function takes time to take hold. Any parent of an adolescent who ever asked, "What were you *thinking?*" knows the regulatory brain functions that help us avoid risk and make reasoned decisions are relatively slow to mature. Brain development is not complete until about age 25. That's when "conscious" control of executive function becomes more automatic.

Being able to set goals, manage time, check our impulses, and monitor our own actions are traits we often associate with high-functioning adults. But we don't develop them automatically. These processes are encouraged by childhood experiences that allow for exploration and decision making (and inhibited if these experiences are lacking). Free play—play that is not bound by predetermined rules—is an ideal context for developing executive function. So, too, are project experiences that allow for self-directed learning. Every time executive function is drawn upon and practiced, patterns of behavior become more established, and neural pathways in the brain actually become "hard wired."

Project-based learning gives students opportunities to practice capabilities that will serve them throughout life. Traditional learning experiences, in comparison, reinforce a more narrow set of capabilities.

We can help students develop their executive function by planning project activities that call on and reinforce certain skills and capabilities.

Exercise: Encourage Executive Skills

PBL naturally promotes the attitudes and skills that will serve students well—not just in school but also in life. The table below lists several skills that are indicators of executive function (Dawson & Guare, 2004). All come into play during projects. How might you help students grow into these good habits? Complete the right-hand column by adding your ideas. We have included a prompt ("Ask yourself . . . ") for each box to jumpstart your thinking.

(Continued)

(Continued)

Skill or Disposition	Means students can...	You can encourage in PBL by...
Flexibility	Adapt, improvise, shift approaches on demand	**Example:** Designing projects to be open ended with no single right answer **Ask yourself:** How do I show students that I welcome divergent ideas?
Organization	Use a systematic approach for reaching goals	**Example:** Providing students with tools (such as shared calendars or team logs) for managing project tasks **Ask yourself:** How do I encourage students to set goals for themselves?
Self-control	Control their impulses	**Example:** Modeling and having students practice respectful methods, or protocols, of engaging in discussions **Ask yourself:** How can we build a classroom culture that helps students develop emotional maturity?
Task initiation	Get started on a task without procrastinating	**Example:** Asking students to blog or keep journals about their daily goals and accomplishments **Ask yourself:** How can I encourage team members to set short-term goals?
Time management	Plan ahead, manage multiple demands on time	**Example:** Making interim (milestone) assignments that help students make progress toward final product **Ask yourself:** What tools (such as shared calendars, online workspaces, project logs) could I introduce to help students improve their time-management skills?
Metacognition	Reflect on their own thinking and the quality of their work	**Example:** Asking students to reflect frequently on their progress as learners **Ask yourself:** How am I varying reflection prompts or activities so they feel "fresh" to students?

MAKING MEANING MEMORABLE

As their brains develop from childhood to adolescence, students are able to shift from concrete, representational thinking to grappling with greater complexity and abstraction. The prefrontal cortex, along with being the seat of executive function, is also the part of the brain in which higher-order thinking happens. Like executive function, higher-order thinking skills get better with practice.

Unlike instruction that rewards memorization and rote learning, project-based learning asks students to arrive at their own meaning. In a typical project cycle, students learn important content and apply their understanding to create something new. This process causes students to meld their creativity with higher-order thinking skills of analysis, synthesis, and evaluation. With practice, critical thinking becomes a habit.

This is not to say that students are working at peak performance at every moment during a project. Attention waxes and wanes during a learning period.

During projects, when teams are engaged in research, investigations, and product development, students are likely to be working with some degree of independence. This is an opportunity to help students manage their learning by teaching them to take advantage of periods of peak attention.

Students can also learn to recognize when they need to take a break from hard thinking. They can figure out when they need to move to get the blood circulating and the wheels turning more efficiently. In effect, they can learn to reset the learning cycle and get back to peak attention. A project-based classroom should be organized to allow for these resets to happen naturally.

Good teachers assess and connect to students' prior experience as they introduce new ideas. *Meaning* refers to the personal relevance of an idea. We assign meaning to the things that we value, find interesting, or respond to emotionally.

Imagine these two introductions to a project. Which do you think would have more meaning for eighth-graders?

> In the years 1860 and 1861, the Pony Express ran mail by horse and rider between St. Louis and San Francisco. At its peak, the Pony Express employed 80 young riders who were paid $25 a week.

> In the years 1860 and 1861, the Pony Express ran mail by horse and rider between St. Louis and San Francisco. Ads in newspapers at either end of the line read: "Wanted. Young, Skinny, Wiry fellows above 13 but not over 18. Must be expert riders willing to risk death daily. Orphans preferred. Wages $25 per week."

The second introduction has meaning because it is *relatable*. The ad asks for applicants not too different in age from eighth graders. It is meaningful, too, because the riskiness of the job and preference for riders who have no parents to worry about them elicits an *emotional response*.

Project-based learning helps students not only make meaning but also make meaning that lasts. Applying what they know causes students to consolidate their understanding, making learning more memorable.

Reflection and feedback, both of which are built into the project cycle, also help to make learning "stick" in long-term memory.

Learning doesn't end when the school day is over. During sleep, the brain consolidates what it has learned, strengthening the connections between neurons that form when we absorb new knowledge. Telling students to "sleep on it" after a day of deep learning improves their ability to grasp and retain new ideas.

STRESS VS. STRUGGLE

In some classrooms, rigor is measured in pages read or problems assigned. Rigor in projects has to do with putting kids right at the edge of what they know so they have to reach to grasp new ideas. Well-crafted projects cause students to struggle just enough to be challenging without triggering the stress that can get in the way of learning.

When the brain senses danger or threat, it triggers the body to release the stress hormone cortisol. In the short term, cortisol revs up the body's metabolism, preparing us for fight or flight. Long-term exposure to cortisol, however, can hamper memory and impair learning.

Brain scans show that under stressful conditions, information is blocked from entering the brain's areas of higher cognitive memory consolidation and storage. "The learning process grinds to a halt," explains Judy Willis, who is both neurologist and educator (Willis, 2007). If a student feels threatened in class ("I might fail! And look stupid!"), literal fight or flight is not possible. Instead, "flight" can be achieved by shutting down, disrupting, or shifting attention to other things.

Compare what happens in a stressful learning environment to one in which students find learning pleasurable and related to their interests. In response to pleasurable associations, the brain releases dopamine. This neurotransmitter stimulates the memory centers and increases attention (Willis, 2007).

When stressors are minimized, students feel safe enough to tackle challenges that will stretch their thinking. "Children need to feel safe enough in school to push the limits of what they know, to venture into the unknown, to take the risk of making a mistake or being wrong. Albert Einstein said, 'Anyone who has never made a mistake has never tried anything new'" (Diamond, 2010).

PLAN FOR LIBERATING CONSTRAINTS

How can teachers strike a balance between struggle and stress? Well-designed projects are designed for "optimal ambiguity." They require learners to struggle—a bit—as they consider what they already know and plan the tasks ahead. Teachers can seek the right balance by attending to what experts call "liberating constraints" (Davis, Sumara, & Luce-Kapler, 2007).

Liberating constraints are structures of a learning experience that

- provide **enough organization** to orient students toward the work, and at the same time
- permit **enough openness** to accommodate a variety of abilities, interests, and creative approaches.

The authors of *Engaging Minds,* who conceptualized the notion of liberating constraints, provide an example that helps us understand. A soccer game is structured within a narrow set of rules. However, within those rules, or constraints, great nuance and creativity are possible. Without rules, soccer would become a free-for-all, and it would be difficult to appreciate any brilliance that might be on display. When rules are relaxed, even a little bit (by poor officiating, for instance), it becomes evident how necessary and "liberating" those constraints are.

PLAYFUL LEARNING: SIM CITY PROJECT

Where is the sweet spot for learning that's both playful and focused on serious goals? One teacher found it in the virtual environment of Sim City, the popular simulation game about urban planning.

When Julie Robison introduced her seventh-grade science students to the Sim City Project, she was deliberate about giving them class time "to just play around with the game." For the first few days of the project, students could freely explore the virtual environment, figuring out game rules and shortcuts on their own. "While they were fooling around, I looked for problem solving," Robison explains. "When I'd see a student figuring out something, I'd say, what were you looking for? How did you do it? Then I'd have them tell me about it, and then tell the class. About every five minutes during the 50-minute class period, I'd break in and say, let's listen to so-and-so tell us what he or she learned. That also meant they were learning from each other."

Only after students had time to learn in that informal way did Robison introduce the project expectations. Their assignment: build a virtual city and be able to explain growth patterns supported by data. Students had to provide evidence by taking screenshots of their city at key dates in the simulation. Graphs that the game generates provided useful formative assessment tools, as students learned to use them for feedback about their planning decisions. They also had to write a narrative explaining what they had learned about urban design principles.

"This project got them into systems thinking," Robison explains, and also got students more curious about the world around them. As they learned about urban design in the game world, they began asking questions that showed they were more closely observing the built environment of their own city. Why were bridges built where they were? Why are high-rises considered luxury housing in some cities but low-income housing in others? Experts in city planning helped students understand why land use decisions had been made in the past.

Robison knew the project had led to memorable learning when she was on an unrelated field trip with the same students. Looking out the bus window, one boy noticed a farm he had probably seen dozens of times before. Now he saw it with fresh eyes. "Look!" he said, "an agricultural zone, and it's located right next to a major transportation corridor."

→Project Signpost 3: Ignite Curiosity

You may already make a habit of launching projects with a "grabber" or entry event that captures student attention and ignites curiosity. That's good—but be careful not to fall into an entry event rut. Vary the style of your entry events from one project to the next to keep things interesting. Good entry events tend to be brief but memorable. In their novelty, these events act as a catalyst for action. They can be entertaining, but they're only worth doing if they directly relate to the project content. Consider how you might start with an event that's dramatic (role plays or scenarios), mysterious (not-easily-explained events or demonstrations), or experiential (students go on a field trip, or an "important person" comes to call on them for help in a project scenario). Successful events will get kids asking questions, setting the inquiry process into motion. We'll spend more time in Chapter 4 on how to plan effective entry events.

BRAIN-BASED PROJECT STRATEGIES

You don't have to be in a research setting to bring insights from mind, brain, and education science into PBL. Look for opportunities to incorporate these suggestions into everyday classroom activities—and pay attention to how students respond. Build your toolkit with techniques that make a noticeable difference when it comes to grabbing students' attention, nurturing creativity, and making learning memorable throughout a project.

Cultivate Curiosity. Use novelty deliberately. Give the project an attention-getting title and plan a creative "grabber" or entry event to launch the project. Capture students' questions, post them in a visible spot, and refer to this need-to-know list throughout the project. Once the project is underway, vary daily routines. Mix up team assignments from one project to the next, too, so that students work with new partners.

Shift From Wait Time to Think Time. Our brains process information at different speeds. On average, teachers ask questions and wait less than 2 seconds before calling for an answer (Stahl, 1994). Stretching out wait time by just few seconds allows more students to be ready to reply, and the quality of responses also improves. Wait time is usually associated with the teacher-centered act of instructing and typically focuses on whole-class discussions. A variation, *think time,* is more broadly applicable in student-centered projects. Think time gives students opportunities to gather their thoughts, perhaps by jotting down notes or making sketches to capture their ideas, before discussing them. Encourage think time during mini-lessons and when peers are working collaboratively. During your informal observations of project teams at work, ask questions to find out whether students are giving themselves sufficient time to think.

Encourage Better Brainstorming. Getting people to think individually about a topic before combining their ideas is more productive than starting out thinking as a group (Kohn & Smith, 2010). When students do problem identification that leads to research questions, allow time for *noodling around* and exploring ideas from many different perspectives. Create class norms for brainstorming that elicit everyone's ideas and encourage students to riff off each other's good thinking. Be careful not to make value statements about one student's ideas over another's, as that can shut down the generative processes you want to cultivate. Instead of saying, "That's the best idea I've heard," say, "Your thinking's gone in a new direction. What do others think about Andre's idea?" In this way you foster listening and encourage more good thinking.

Sleep on It. As you head into a project, introduce it, maybe do a "grabber" or entry event, but don't start the work the moment after. Encourage kids to talk about the project at home and literally sleep on it for overnight processing that makes them more ready to start.

Exercise: Take an Interest Inventory

As we've heard throughout this chapter, new learning sticks best when it makes sense and has meaning. To make sense, a concept has to connect to one's current understanding. To have meaning, a concept or investigation needs to matter on a personal and emotional level.

To make projects really *go*, take time to find out what matters most to your students. Conduct an interest inventory, such as EDC's Fun Works (http://thefunworks.edc.org), to find out about their out-of-school interests and hobbies. For example, ask students to select their top three choices from a list of options such as these:

- Visit a pet store
- Paint a mural
- Help plan a sports tournament
- Survey your classmates to see what they do after school
- Run for student council
- Try out for the school musical
- Dissect a frog and identify different organs
- Play baseball, soccer, football, or just about any sport
- Make up new words to one of your favorite songs
- Bake a cake and decorate it for your best friend's birthday
- Simulate an imaginary flight through space on your computer

(Continued)

(Continued)

Take the results into account as you consider project ideas. Compile students' individual responses to develop a class profile that reflects which activities students would most enjoy. Refer to your interest inventory when making team assignments too to make sure each team has a good mix of interests represented.

As a next step, have your students craft their own interest inventory. Their individual contributions to the survey might tell you as much as the results!

WHAT'S NEXT?

Now that you've explored some of the internal factors that drive curiosity, let's turn your focus to the external environment for learning. How can you customize the learning environment to encourage inquiry? Let's find out in the next chapter.

3

Making the World Safe for Thinking

Imagine heralding the start of a new project by flying a special flag outside your school. That's what happens at Birkdale Intermediate School in Auckland, New Zealand, where learning happens through immersive projects called Quests.

"A new flag goes up at the start of each Quest and stays up through the project," Principal Richard Coote explained to us in a Skype interview. "It announces the project and prompts parents to get involved. Instead of just asking, 'How was your day?' they can say to their child, 'Tell me about Lest We Forget.'" (Lest We Forget is a social studies project in which children study history and causal relationships through the topic of war.)

With gestures large and small, this school conveys the message that projects matter. Even before the flags start flying, "coming soon" posters appear in the school hallways to create an air of mystery and build anticipation about upcoming projects. Project titles are carefully selected to be both "engaging and simple," Coote adds. You don't need to know many details to be intrigued by a project titled The Hunt.

These tactics are part of a grand plan to get students to buy in quickly. "The key is engagement early on," Coote adds. "We know that if a project is flat at the outset, it's going to be six weeks of dragging them along."

Coote speaks from experience. Birkdale Intermediate, a public school serving about 450 students in Grades 7 and 8, has invested a decade in fine-tuning its PBL strategies. The overarching goal—indeed, the reason Birkdale shifted to project-based learning in the first place—is to develop independent learners who can think deeply. To achieve this ambitious goal, the school pays close attention to the many factors that support student success across the arc of a project.

In PBL, we ask students to think and operate in new and perhaps unfamiliar ways. Sometimes thinkers get stuck, and that has to be OK; a breakdown often leads to a breakthrough. Sometimes arguments arise, but this isn't necessarily a bad thing. Arguments can shape new understanding and build tolerance for different points of view. Ill-formed ideas and do-overs are a necessary part of projects, if students are going to take intellectual risks, revise their work, and eventually arrive at well-formed ideas and high-quality representations of their learning. The "messiness" of projects is often where the rich thinking happens.

At schools like Birkdale that embrace PBL, the school culture supports students (and teachers) as they dive into the hard work of learning through projects. The right climate and supporting mechanisms allow students to "feel the burn" of hard thinking without burning out their enthusiasm for learning.

In this chapter, we'll consider how to fine-tune the conditions around learning so that students can do their best thinking. Paying attention to physical spaces, being deliberate about teaching thinking skills, and setting high expectations all contribute to a productive environment for learning through projects.

PHYSICAL SPACES FOR THINKERS

Take a moment and imagine a creative work environment. Don't worry about the kind of work going on. Just focus on the space. Close your eyes for a moment and picture it. What is that space like? What does it sound like? How are people interacting? Is there movement? Is there evidence of work in progress? Is it tidy, or busy-messy? Can you imagine working there? What would that be like? If you are moved to do so, draw a quick sketch of your ideal creative work environment. Include every amenity that would contribute to your best thinking.

Was your mental picture anything like either of the workspaces shown in Figures 3.1 and 3.2? People in both environments appear to be engaged and productive, using flexible, light-filled workspaces that invite collaboration. It's likely that they are accomplishing significant work, too. The image at the left is of the Googleplex in Mountain View, California. The one at the right was taken at High Tech High, part of a network of 11 public charter schools in San Diego, California. Like many schools emphasizing project-based learning, High Tech High has designed workspaces specifically to foster creativity and innovation, allow for productive collaboration, and showcase student work in curated exhibits.

Think back to your mental image of a creative workplace. Was the place you imagined a school? If the answer was "no," why not? School *is* a work place for 55 million people in the United States where 51.5 million student "workers" and 3.5 million teachers are charged with shaping the future (Bureau of Labor Statistics, 2012a). That's a big job. That's work!

Companies like Google and schools like High Tech High value creativity and innovation and intentionally establish the conditions—both work spaces

Figures 3.1 and 3.2   Two 21st-Century Work Environments

Source: Photo by Jurvetson on Flickr.   *Source:* Reprinted Courtesy of High Tech High.

and opportunities—that foster the kind of thinking they are after. We might not be able to magically transform our schools and classrooms, but we can improve the setting so that it is more supportive of creative thought and inquiry. What might that look like? The emerging school design movement offers some insight.

The last time the United States experienced a school-building boom was from 1950 to 1969, when schools went up fast to accommodate the Baby Boom generation in look-alike classrooms housed in factory-style buildings. Nearly half the nation's schools were constructed during this era, and many are now overdue for remodeling or replacement. For school designers and communities alike, this offers an enormous opportunity to reconsider the form and function of schools.

Architects who are leading the new school design movement are giving careful consideration to how learning spaces encourage the deep thinking, creativity, and collaboration that we hope to develop in 21st-century learners. Their ideas may seem out of reach if you're not in a community that's investing in cutting-edge school facilities. But look closely at how architects are thinking about learning spaces and you may find ideas you can borrow for your own classroom or school community.

Trung Le, principal education designer at Cannon Design, spent 2 years leading an interdisciplinary team that looked at school design in several countries, including the United States. Their research, summarized in an idea book called *The Third Teacher: 79 Ways You Can Use Design to Transform Teaching & Learning,* includes such practical suggestion as these gems (OWP/P Cannon Design, VS Furniture, Bruce Mau Design, 2010):

- **Display learning.** Posting student work, both current and past, on the wall tracks progress in a visible way.
- **Emulate museums.** An environment rich in evocative objects—whether it's a classroom or a museum—triggers active learning by letting students pick what to engage with.

- **Make peace with fidgeting.** Think of it as brain development, which it is. Then think of how to make room for movement and physical activity in the classroom.
- **Make classrooms agile.** A learning space that can be reconfigured on a dime will accommodate different kinds of learners and teachers and allow for different learning activities.

Award-winning school architecture firm Fielding Nair has identified 18 "modalities" through which students learn and 25 space designs that support them. Every new school they plan has a mix of indoor and out-door spaces, including quiet, reflective areas; messy, lab-like spaces; and social "watering holes" that invite informal conversation. They take into account the human need for movement, relaxation, visual stimulation, dif-ferent kinds of lighting, and even colors and patterns that are conducive to good thinking.

Steven Turckes, who leads architecture firm Perkins+Will's global K–12 practice, suggests that schools would be wise to emulate successful com-panies, such as Google or the global design firm IDEO, by deliberately setting the stage for playfulness, creativity, and interdisciplinary thinking. Turckes also mentions High Tech High, which we discussed earlier, as an example of a school configured to get students out of subject-area silos. Imagine what could happen, he asks, "if the advanced physics student and the photography student had meaningful collisions in the average American high school. What if they did by design—if their classwork wove together diverse content and skills intentionally and elegantly? . . . Schools could be the breeding ground for a new millennium of Renaissance young men and women where creating something trumps memorizing it" (Turckes, 2011).

CREATIVE SOLUTIONS

We heard earlier about Birkdale Intermediate School and its long tradition of teaching through projects. The school has intentionally developed a climate and curriculum to encourage deep thinking, which is reflected by the physi-cal environment. Because the school values collaboration, it has built "nests" where small teams can work. Like glass-walled study rooms in a university library, nests are soundproofed spaces tucked between classrooms with windows that allow teachers to keep track of what's happening. Coote describes these as "semi-supervised spaces," where up to a dozen students at a time can enjoy a degree of independence. Working in the nest, students might brainstorm solutions to a problem, rehearse for a public presentation, construct a model, or have a script meeting to plan what they will say. They can engage fully in teamwork without disrupting their classmates.

Similarly, the Birkdale library is specially outfitted to reinforce project work. Displayed here are museum-quality exhibits that relate to each project. In a Quest called The Real Pocahontas?, students compare mod-ern representations of Pocahontas with historical accounts to arrive at some truths about her life. A library exhibit of blue Venetian glass trade beads circa 1700, a silver shilling from 1601, a bone powder horn, and other authentic artifacts—along with Disney snow globes and figurines—spark imagination and link project studies to the past. Developing the exhibits has involved searching eBay and antiques stores for artifacts, but it's been well worth the effort because of the increased student engagement, according to Coote.

Many teachers show similar creativity in how they expand the functionality of the classroom box. For example, English teacher Susan Lucille Davis has a space outside her office that's dubbed the Teaching and Learning Leadership Center. As she explains in a blog post, the right space offers an invitation to collaborate (Davis, 2012):

> In it we have collected books, games, a tired white board, a coffee pot and refrigerator, and a long conference table surrounded by a hodgepodge of mismatched chairs. Sometimes the students who come early like to gather there (exactly what we hoped when some of my colleagues and I put this space together).

Working with limited budgets that don't allow for wholesale remodeling, many schools are investing in no-frills makeovers that better accommodate the needs of project-based learning and teaching. For example, we've seen schools that have painted interior walls with whiteboard paint, creating giant canvases for capturing and sharing ideas. To encourage students to make their thinking visible, teachers might encourage students to write on their desks or the floor with dry-erase markers or provide them with mini-whiteboards cut from melamine shower board to use while tackling problems that may require multiple attempts to solve.

DELIBERATE FOCUS ON THINKING

If a project has been successful, students should be able to discuss or demonstrate the important content they have learned. Culminating events are hallmarks of project-based schools. These are the important, often celebratory occasions when students share what they know or can do as a result of their active learning experience. After all, deep understanding of academic content is one of the key benefits of PBL.

Equally important—but not always so overtly displayed—are the thinking skills that are engaged and strengthened by effective projects.

At Birkdale Intermediate, the PBL school we've highlighted throughout this chapter, thinking skills are a significant part of every Quest. That's no accident. Early in its transformation to a project-based school, Birkdale staff began to focus deliberately on how to teach thinking skills. Their publication, *Developing a Thinking Curriculum*, explains why: "Simply placing our students in problem-solving situations is not enough for these [thinking skills] to develop. Skillful critical thinking has to be explicitly taught" (Coote, n.d., p. 6).

To inform its approach, Birkdale has drawn on the research of experts who focus on thinking skills, including researchers Arthur Costa, Howard Gardner, and David Perkins from Harvard's Project Zero, and Adam Lefstein and Yoram Harpaz from Israel, who have developed the concept of "fertile questions."

The work of Robert Swartz, director of the National Center for Teaching Thinking in Massachusetts, has been especially influential at the New Zealand school. Each Quest highlights at least one of the thinking strategies that Swartz recommends, such as being able to compare and contrast, make a well-founded judgment, or explain the relationship between cause and effect. Teachers use graphic organizers and thinking maps to explicitly teach and reinforce these skills.

The Birkdale staff came to embrace thinking skills through their own action research. "We recognized, early on, that our curriculum lacked rigorous thinking," Coote recounts. "Students might suggest questions, but they tended to be lower-level questions that lacked intellectual rigor. It was as if we were trying to lead them to thinking by osmosis—if only we could get them inquiring, we expected their thinking to get better." Coote says Swartz challenged them to consider, "What could you do with students that wouldn't produce the same old thinking?"

Ever since, they have embedded thinking skills into Quests, in tandem with students' deep dive into content. Working as content curators, teachers provide multimedia collections of primary source materials to inform students' inquiry. The immersion into rich content and deep thinking happens simultaneously. As Coote points out, "You can't underestimate the content. Knowledge is what we use to think with. The (thinking) process is what students will take into the world. So you have to do both at once—content and process."

THINKING THAT BUILDS KNOWLEDGE

Being able to generate new ideas is an increasingly valued skill in today's knowledge-based, innovation-driven economy. One of the key challenges facing societies around the globe is figuring out how to develop citizens who not only possess up-to-date knowledge but also are able to participate in the creation of new ideas as a normal part of their lives (Scardamalia & Bereiter, 2003).

By looking closely at how people build knowledge, educators Carl Bereiter and Marlene Scardamalia (2003) have concluded that curious children and expert adults go through much the same process:

The *process* of knowledge building is essentially the same across the trajectory running from early childhood to the most advanced levels of theorizing, invention, and design, and across the spectrum of knowledge-creating organizations, within and beyond school. If learners are engaged in processes only suitable for school, then they are not engaged in knowledge building. (Bereiter & Scardamalia, 2003, p. 1371)

Knowledge building involves learners in actively gathering information, making observations, formulating questions, and then creating new ideas or solutions to answer their own inquiries. Critical thinking is embedded throughout the process.

For example, an engineering class began a recent project by taking a walking tour of a neighborhood that had been hit hard by a tornado (an example of an engaging, relevant, and novel entry event). Students observed the damage through the lens of engineering, raising need-to-know questions about why some buildings survived while others were devastated by the force of nature (a real-world use of comparing and contrasting). They also interviewed survivors of the storm, establishing an emotional connection to the project. Then they worked in teams to develop new designs that would answer their own inquiries about everything from building codes to the social aspects of how people interact with their community (Ebbetts, 2012). In constructing new ideas, student teams were going through the same thinking processes that experts would bring to a similar challenge.

PUTTING THE PIECES TOGETHER

School architects work with their clients—administrators, educators, students, parents, and community members—to design spaces that support new ideas of schooling. The assumption that teachers will deliver instruction from the front of the room and all students will engage in the same tasks at the same time is no longer accurate, which means traditional "cells and bells" (classrooms and schedules) must give way to more flexible structures.

During project-based learning, independent study, small-group work, seminars, and hands-on learning might be going on all at once. Coming up with ways to accommodate the many activities of PBL may require inventive thinking.

One example: At Science Leadership Academy in Philadelphia, students need to regroup frequently for project work, and that means moving chairs that were designed to stay put. Chairs with wheels are out of the budget, so teachers put split tennis balls on the feet of chairs. Students can rearrange seating quickly and quietly.

Think about the ways you want your PBL class to function to encourage the kinds of thinking we have explored in this chapter. Small adjustments in the learning environment will better accommodate the various tools and patterns of interaction that come into play during projects. Let's look more closely at a few patterns you can expect during projects, along with affordable solutions to accommodate them.

Independent work. A PBL classroom is busy. Sometimes students need "cave" space, a place quiet and free from distraction.

- Create three-panel cardboard "carrels" to separate desk or tabletop spaces for quiet work.

Partner and small-group work. Collaboration is the norm in the PBL classroom.

- Furnish with tables or arrange desks into groupings, or "pods."
- Make room dividers from standing chalkboards or whiteboards. Some teachers hang melamine shower panels that not only divide the space but serve as inexpensive whiteboards, too.
- Open the door for learning. Arrange with other teachers to allow self-directed teams to work in unoccupied spaces in their classrooms. See the library, hallways, entryways, courtyards, and even the office as learning spaces. One principal we know lets students work in his office. (He's a rover who is often in classrooms and hallways.) Set expectations with everyone involved for what happens in these out-of-classroom settings, including how you will monitor student conduct. Gradually release the reins as students demonstrate good self-management in more independent situations.
- If you have the means, redesign otherwise public spaces into learning studios. Birkdale Intermediate School has built two, and staff and students like them so much they are adding two more. Named for native birds, the "Kiwi" and "Tui" "nests" are 4 meters by 6 meters, accommodate up to 12 students, and have glass walls from the waist up for easy supervision.

Check-ins and seminars-for-some. During projects, teachers check in with teams and offer seminar-style lessons on tightly focused topics (for example: how to cite sources for a research project, prepare for an interview with an expert, or make a podcast). One school calls these mini-lessons "coffee talks." Optional for all but mandatory for some (based on the teacher's formative assessment), coffee talks are informal and friendly. If your classroom can accommodate soft benches or couches, this arrangement is perfect for mini-lessons and small-group discussions.

Reimagine who the stuff belongs to. We have seen classrooms in which resources are only used by the teacher or under the teacher's direction. Smart boards and document cameras are great for making thinking visible. Are your students using these tools for brainstorming, diagramming, and other kinds of group thinking?

Conversational classroom. Being "front and center" lends authority but can hamper interaction. When you stand at the front of the class, student interaction will tend to flow through you. Change things up. Put chairs in a circle, join the group, let a student lead, and encourage classmates to converse with each another, not just with you.

Student presentations. Funny how we recommend that teachers lecture less, yet students' expressions of learning in projects are frequently one-way presentations—basically, lectures. Encourage your students to move out of the front of the classroom, too, and engage their audience in participatory activities like team challenges, game-style events, gallery walks, or hands-on engagement with materials.

Tinker station. Encourage hands-on, minds-on creative thinking by providing tools for tinkering. Stock a "maker" station with everything from Legos to kits with wires, switches, and batteries, to a sewing machine. Add a library of *Maker, Craft,* and *Popular Mechanics* magazines to get creative juices flowing.

Skype on. Whenever his class works on a collaborative project with another school, a veteran PBL elementary teacher named Terry Smith keeps a Skype chat line open on a dedicated computer. Even when they are not conversing, students working at a distance stay tethered through the chat function and can hop on calls as needed with a "ping."

Video booth. Turn an empty refrigerator box into a three-sided video booth to capture student reflections. In one class, students created posters on the interior walls that evoke the themes of each project. You might set up lighting and a video camera on a tripod, or just arrange for video capture through a webcam.

Color. If you have the option of changing colors in your classroom and school, investigate the role of color on minds and bodies. Colors on the warm side of the scale (reds, oranges, and yellows) tend to be stimulating, while cool hues (blues, violets, greens) are soothing and can even slow the heart rate.

Furniture. As with color, furniture affects body and mind. Kids have a natural inclination to move, and ergonomic furniture designs accommodate rather than suppress movement. Hokki-brand ergonomic stools have a rounded bottom so kids can move a bit while seated. Bilibos are shell-shaped seats that students can curl into, rock in, or turn over and sit on. Beanbag chairs invite students to settle in for reading or quiet work. Students at TESLA (the Technology Engineering Science Leadership Academy) in Florida carry Bilibos and beanbag chairs to favorite learning spaces. Finding a student working under the reception desk is not uncommon at TESLA.

BYOD. "Bring your own device" is a growing technology trend in schools. Set expectations for use and brainstorm with students the myriad ways their personal devices can aid learning. One example: The teacher sets up an SMS poll using PollEverywhere (http://www.polleverywhere.com/) to assess teams' readiness to move from one stage to the next on a project. Students take the poll using the texting function on their mobile phones.

Exercise: Your PBL Wish List

PBL teachers model creative thinking when they find workarounds or inexpensive fixes to make their classrooms more conducive to project work. (They also model collaboration if they enlist parent volunteers and other community members to help!) Now it's your turn to put your creativity to work. We've started the following list with a few examples of how you might improve on your classroom environment to invite good thinking. What else belongs on your PBL wish list? How might you make it happen? Follow the prompts to complete the right-hand column.

(Continued)

(Continued)

PBL Activity	Make it happen by...
Storytelling	Creating a corner of your classroom that invites campfire-style gatherings *What inexpensive materials could you use to designate this space?*
Field research	Recruiting parent volunteers to help with transportation, supervision of project teams; using tools like Skype to connect students with remote experts *What processes (such as having permission slips on file or ongoing connections with local experts) would help you eliminate barriers to field research?*
Sharing work with authentic audiences	Having a guest book for visitors to sign, curating exhibits with "artist" statements, having students act as docents to greet and guide visitors *How do you use digital publishing to reach a larger audience for student work?*
Down time (allowing students to recharge their "thinking batteries" after periods of focused work)	Giving students more flexibility over how they use class time *How might you incorporate short periods of physical activity during class time?*
"Mash-ups" among students that allow for informal exchange of ideas	Mixing up team assignments from one project to the next *How transparent is your process for making team assignments?*
Scenario-based projects or simulations that put students into immersive environments	Incorporating gaming and other immersive environments (both online and nondigital) into projects *Who could teach you more about immersive environments?*
Building prototypes and models	Providing students with raw materials to make models and prototypes, making their thinking visible *Where could you create a shared "maker space" or tinkering studio within your school building?*
More PBL activities?	*How might you make it happen?*

SETTING HIGH EXPECTATIONS

Schools that emphasize project-based learning as a core instructional strategy tend to frame their approach around specific values and practices. Consider just a few examples:

- New Tech Network includes more than 100 schools across the United States that emphasize project-based learning, smart use of technology, and school culture that promotes trust, respect, and responsibility.
- High Tech High, the public charter school network in California described earlier, embraces four key design principles to prepare students for the challenges of adulthood: personalization, adult world connection, common intellectual mission, and teacher as designer.
- Science Leadership Academy, a public high school in Philadelphia, has built its successful PBL program on five core values that are emphasized in every class: inquiry, research, collaboration, presentation, and reflection.

It takes time and deliberate effort for these values and practices to be woven into school culture.

You may be teaching in a school in which everyone learns through projects or one in which your classroom is an island of PBL in a sea of traditional teaching. Regardless, it's worth investing time to set high expectations and establish norms with your students. Together, you can build a positive climate for learning through projects.

→Project Signpost 4: Build Norms for PBL

Building a positive culture for teaching and learning is an ongoing process. Engage students in discussing how they will work together during projects. Make their suggestions visible with posters or other displays. Refer to these artifacts often. Continuously reinforce norms for

- **Collaboration:** Define in student language how team members should treat one another. Use team contracts or agreements, project logs, and other project management tools to ensure that students "own" their responsibility to the team. Model and encourage productive peer feedback.
- **Work ethic:** Encourage students to set goals for projects. Define what quality looks like in student-friendly language. Help students learn time-management skills by introducing timelines, setting project milestones, and providing other scaffolds to help them become more responsible for their own learning.
- **Parent and community support:** Invite parents and other community members to support project work by sharing expertise, donating resources for classroom makeovers, and providing authentic audiences for student presentations.

George Mayo, a middle-school teacher whom we will hear more from in Chapter 7, says setting the right conditions for PBL early in the school year enables him and his students to accomplish more ambitious projects as the year unfolds. He deliberately establishes class norms by having students make a poster that defines how they will work together. The sign stays up all year as an ongoing reminder that, he says, "When we're in this space, we're all here to support and encourage one another." That supportive, respectful culture is essential for students to feel comfortable sharing the personal reflections that are often the jumping-off point for language arts projects. "You can't do project-based learning," he adds, "without the right environment."

Mayo's classroom is a busy place, with students producing podcasts, documentary films, and high-quality writing projects. "It gets crazy some days," he admits. But even on the busiest days, he tries to stick with established routines. Each day begins with a learning objective that focuses the class period and ends with at least a few minutes of quiet reflection. Those clear routines "provide organization and structure, so kids know what to expect when they come in. When we start to do large projects," he adds, "that structure helps kids feel secure." He also makes a point of leading by example. "As the teacher, you set the tone with your disposition each day. I try to act positive and excited about the project. If you can do that, I've found that students will follow your lead."

WHAT'S NEXT?

Now that you have considered the physical environment and norms for PBL, you're ready to look more closely at how questions themselves help set the stage for deep inquiry. The next chapter focuses on questioning techniques and "thinking routines" that are applicable across grade levels and subject areas.

4

The Thinking-Out-Loud-and-in-View Classroom

"I am not a teacher, but an awakener."

—Robert Frost

In a culturally diverse urban school in Northern California, fourth-graders interviewed family members for a podcasting project called Stories from the Heart. It took practice and preparation for students to gently prod their elders with just the right questions that would unlock memories: How did you play before you had television or video games? Where did Grandmother's nickname come from? What was it like to come to America as a child?

To model good interviewing and listening techniques, teacher Teresa Cheung drew on her own experiences. In a recording for the national StoryCorps project, she prompted her father, then 82, to talk about the lessons he learned while attending a Confucian school in China. In a touching moment near the end of the interview, she thanks him for passing along his strong values to his seven children (Conley, 2008).

Teachers are in an excellent position to be role models for inquiry. By making the classroom a place that invites good questions from adults and students alike, you help students understand that curiosity is not only welcome, it's expected.

To model and encourage curiosity, ask lots of questions and encourage students to do the same—when they are engaged in projects as well as at other times. For example, in informal conversations with students:

- Ask low-risk questions, ones that have no "right" answer but instead invite opinion and creative answers. "Would you rather be invisible or be able to read minds?"
- Make a space for riddles, conundrums, and enigmas. "Why is milk sold in rectangular containers while soda is sold in cylindrical ones?"
- Post unanswered or unanswerable questions. Invite kids to ponder the "grand challenges" identified in engineering, global health, environmental science, computing, and human rights. "How could the world's fresh water supply be shared equitably?" "What is dark matter?" Encourage students to volunteer their own challenges.
- Discuss daily news. Ask: "How did this event come to happen? What might happen next? Is there more to this story? Is it part of a pattern?" Many stories develop over time. Follow updates to learn what happens and whether projections hold, and whether media sources are reliable.
- Read opinion pieces and letters to the editor; invite debate. "Are security cameras an invasion of privacy?"
- Get mouths and minds moving with "buzz talks." Set pairs "buzzing," or talking, on a topic for 2 or 3 minutes. "Buzzing" prior to whole-class discussion will lead to greater participation.
- Encourage students to imagine ways to test hypotheses. "Would a penny dropped from the Empire State Building injure a person on the sidewalk below? How could we find out without hurting anybody?"

Mike Gwaltney, a history teacher in Portland, Oregon, anchors class projects in his students' interests. He refers to his method of planning as "teaching backwards." He shows interest in his students' thinking by asking, "What concerns you today? What interests you?" Then he guides discussion toward, "How does that show up in history?" By delving into students' interests as he plans, Gwaltney is assured of their curiosity about utopias, battles, economic issues, slavery, and other potential project topics.

As his class began a study of Native American history, Gwaltney asked students to reflect. "I wanted to know about their experiences and understanding of Native Americans in Portland and in the Pacific Northwest," Gwaltney says. "After some conversation, I gave them a preliminary assignment to do just 30 minutes of research. I threw out a bunch of open-ended questions and encouraged them to get online, talk to their parents, just generally think on the topic. I really want to build some interest on their part. They're going to have to do inquiry and they're going to design their own driving question, so I ask, 'What do you think you want to know?' and work from there."

Gwaltney poses an overarching question to help students shape their research questions. In this instance, he asked, "How does the story of (your individual interest) help us understand the larger experience of Native Americans in American history as a whole?"

Gwaltney helps students frame their work using disciplinary approaches of historians: What happened? Why did it happen? What is the significance of what happened—at the time, later, and now? He encourages small groups to come up with lists of driving questions and meets with students to help them shape a researchable question and their plan for investigating it. "I rely on my own training as a historian," Gwaltney says. "It's coaching intensive. I'm constantly sitting with kids, working with them on focusing, writing new questions, focusing in a new way."

A COMPELLING QUESTION AND ENTRY EVENT SET THE STAGE FOR INVESTIGATION

In planning for PBL, teachers often design projects around a driving question that captures students' imagination and compels them to investigate. Driving questions act as a framework within which students craft more questions and conduct investigations. Answering these subordinate questions naturally leads students to learn important content, think critically about what they are finding out, and master new skills. By the time they answer that original driving question, students should have met the important learning goals that the teacher has built into the project from the start.

Remember the Quests at Birkdale Intermediate in New Zealand? Each launches from a question that has passed a "fertility test" (Harpaz & Lefstein, 2000). Consider how these characteristics of "fertile" questions can serve as filters for designing and refining questions that drive rich learning activity:

- Open: Have several different or competing answers.
  - For example: *Has the importance of the individual changed over time?*
  - Or: *Are we more a part of nature or apart from nature?*

- Undermining: Make learners question their basic assumption.
  - For example: *Just because we can, should we?*
  - Or: *Does something we throw away ever really go "away"?*

- Rich: Cannot be answered without careful and in-depth research; usually, questions can be broken into (or followed up with) subsidiary questions.
  - For example: *How does the debate over genetic engineering affect our future?*
  - Or: *In what ways are stories a reflection of the time in which they were written?*

- Connected: Relevant to the learners.
  - For example: *How would your view of water change if our taps failed?*
  - Or: *How can I turn a hobby (or talent) into a business?*

- Practical: Can be researched given the available resources.
  - For example: *What does our in-depth study of the pond by our school teach us about oceans?*
  - Or: *How does the availability of local food shape our diet and culture?*

Along the same lines, the Buck Institute for Education (BIE) encourages teachers to craft driving questions that are provocative or challenging, open ended, and/or complex and linked to the core of what they want students to learn (Larmer, 2009).

To increase student engagement, BIE suggests looking for opportunities to relate the driving question to students' own lives or communities. For example, you might revise the broad question "What is a hero?" to ask, "Who were the unsung heroes of the Civil Rights Movement in our community?" Building in a "charge" for student action is another strategy to boost engagement. Revise the previous question again, for instance, to ask, "How can we honor our community's unsung heroes from the Civil Rights Movement?"

Exercise: Make Good Questions Even Better

Driving questions get better with practice. Improve on the following questions by revising them to emphasize one or more of the characteristics described in the previous section. How might you revise them to be more open? Undermining? Rich? Connected? Practical?

- Can betrayal be forgiven?
- Can anyone beat the odds?
- Is the spark of revolution always the same?
- What should we wear?
- How can we balance personal freedoms and the public good?
- Which is preferable, to be a house pet or a wild animal?
- How do classic archetypes appear in today's art and media?
- What is love?
- What is the connection between mythologies and modern-day evil?

→Project Signpost 5: Invite Feedback

Before you launch into a project with your driving question, take time to test-drive the question with colleagues or students. Do they find the question compelling enough to sustain their interest? How might they revise it to make it more relevant, authentic, localized, or actionable? Can they see how answering this question would lead them to learn important content or master 21st-century skills? Pick one of the driving questions you revised in the previous exercise and test-drive it with colleagues or students. What does their reaction tell you?

Along with a good driving question, an effective entry event sets the stage for a project launch. The entry event (which we discussed briefly in Chapter 2) will be the first exposure your students have to a project. It might unfold with a mysterious letter, jarring news, provocative video, or other unusual event. It should be *novel* (to make students alert) and have *emotional resonance* (to make them care).

Consider the following examples and imagine how your students might respond:

- A process server slaps student "witnesses" with subpoenas, compelling them to testify in an upcoming trial.
- Short documentary videos from Kiva (a microfinance site that focuses on helping developing world entrepreneurs) or Not in Our Town (an online community speaking out against discrimination) spur kids to action in their community.
- A friendly dog on loan from the humane society comes to school and delivers a letter asking students to launch a pet adoption campaign.
- A 10-minute documentary about child slavery on cocoa plantations kicks off an investigation into global commerce and fair trade.
- A teacher Skypes in her brother-in-law, who is serving in Afghanistan, at the start of a comparative study of conflict.
- A box of rosy apples is delivered to class. As they munch, students consider the question "Why these apples?," which starts an investigation into agriculture, economics, supply chains, and transportation.

Crafting the driving question and entry event is part art and part science. Proponents of PBL can debate what makes the "best" questions and entry events, but all agree that they must be *generative,* sparking inquisitiveness and a need to know. The driving question and entry event should hang together, as these do:

Entry event: An engineering class is visited by a group of marauding Vikings who demand that the engineers design a trebuchet for an upcoming siege on Paris.

Driving question: How does the design of a trebuchet influence its accuracy?

By planning a good driving question and entry event, you've set the stage for inquiry—but don't stop there. Follow up on the project launch with a whole-class discussion that elicits the questions students are now wondering about. Facilitate the conversation so that you spend little time on procedural questions (i.e., When is this due?) and get into the meatier questions that relate to content or strategies for research. Be sure to capture everyone's questions and keep a visible record of what students need to know right now. This list of questions will guide the next steps as students dig into research and problem solving.

Don't overlook the thinking strategies we've explored in previous chapters. For instance, before debriefing the entry event with students, you might ask students to "sleep on it" before getting them to unpack their need-to-know questions. After the Viking scenario described above, imagine students going home and talking with their families about this event. It's likely the whole family will want updates as the project unfolds. A strong entry event can generate new directions for inquiry and strengthen the home–school connection.

FROM A TEACHER'S DRIVING QUESTION TO STUDENT-DRIVEN INVESTIGATIONS

Presenting an entry event and posing a compelling driving question leads students right to the brink of investigation. At this stage, students will be raring to go with lots of ideas about what to do next. But there is another step to consider before handing off the project to eager investigators. Help students shape a good research question—one that will lead to meaningful investigation, and, when answered, will go a way toward answering the overarching question.

Picture eighth-grade life science students responding to this driving question: *Does competition make us better?*

Their teacher sets them off in small groups to brainstorm the many ways they might approach the question.

Which of these avenues of inquiry would be reasonable?

- Students with an interest in sports want to examine the question from the perspective of psychology, health, and physiology.
- Budding biologists want to consider the same question from the standpoint of evolution and ecology.
- Commerce and advertising interest another group.
- Others are interested in studying competition for scarce natural resources.
- Some students view war as competition and want to study that.

You might say any or all of these are significant lines of inquiry, right? And there are doubtless still more ways to interpret the question. But the class is eighth-grade life science, and while their teacher expects students to study the question using several different lenses, not all of these avenues of inquiry fit the curriculum of life science. (Two lines of inquiry in particular might better fit projects in other classes.)

At this point, the teacher could guide the project toward learning goals by helping students craft investigative questions related to the three biggest and most appropriate topics that emerged from their discussions. Here's what might happen next.

Students with an interest in sports want to examine the question from the perspective of psychology, health, and physiology, asking

- *Is blood doping cheating?*
- *Does becoming a premier athlete mean you'll be a busted wreck the rest of your life?*
- *Who is the all-around most perfect athlete?*

Budding biologists want to consider the same question from the standpoint of evolution and ecology:

- *Could a giraffe have become a giraffe anywhere but in Africa?*
- *Why do animals like starlings do well practically everywhere, while other animals, like pandas, need very specialized environments?*
- *Why do canary grass, blackberry, and kudzu crowd out native plants? Why are barred owls out-competing northern spotted owls?*
- *Are genetically modified crops doing us any favors?*

Others are interested in studying competition for scarce natural resources:

- *What can we do to prevent global water wars?*
- *How can we reduce our school's carbon footprint?*
- *How can we help a local business create new jobs by going green?*

The teacher now has a rationale for making team assignments based on student interests in these three topics, each of which connects to important content in life science. Students are ready to dive deeply into their team investigations. The inquiry project is fully launched.

> *"The shrewd guess, the fertile hypothesis, the courageous leap to a tentative conclusion—these are the most valuable coins of the thinker at work."*
>
> —Jerome Bruner

HELP STUDENTS BUILD A THINKING TOOLKIT

Experienced teachers draw from a toolkit of practices that help their classes run smoothly and productively. Smooth operations ensure that maximum class time is focused on learning. Structure and predictability help students feel secure and ready to learn. Routine practices might include homework procedures, norms around behavior, rules for bathroom breaks, and the ways students operate in groups.

Another set of tools is called for in PBL—tools that help students become confident, productive thinkers and project doers. As they take charge of their own learning, students need help to become more autonomous in their thinking and learning. Even traditionally high-achieving learners aren't necessarily good at PBL on their first try. Why not?

- They are used to being told what to do, so having to decide what a task requires is unfamiliar.
- They are used to assignments that have a clear (and likely short-term) start and finish, so time management during extended projects is a new challenge.

- They are used to right answers, so open-ended questions and false starts can feel like failure.
- They are used to working for adult approval, so developing personal standards for quality is new.

In setting students to work in projects, you need to rely on more than good luck. Be deliberate in teaching students to think their way through PBL.

Veteran primary teacher Kathy Cassidy, for example, recognized that her young learners have a little trouble distinguishing research questions from their own stories. "I can't tell you how many times a child has wanted to 'ask a question' but has told me about something that happened at home the night before instead," she wrote in a thoughtful blog post, "PBL in Primary: Who Asks the Questions?" (Cassidy, 2012). To prepare students for a class visit from a police officer, she guided them through a process of drafting questions that would advance their investigation. She explained:

> Because of the predisposition of a six-year-old to want to tell the constable every incident from their family's history that might touch on law enforcement, we prepared the questions on cards ahead of time. We talked about what made a good question, the words that questions started with, and so forth. Then, as the students verbalized their wonderings, I gave them a card to write their question on. Those who are still having difficulty with letter/sound association drew a picture and I wrote their question out for them.

> For some students, thinking of something they wanted to ask was difficult. Sometimes the questions were really stories and needed to be rethought. Sometimes I knew that the student already knew the answer to their question, so I helped them to reframe it to ask something else that they might be interested in knowing.

When the officer came to visit her class, Cassidy prepared him by asking him to focus on students' questions rather than using a prepared script. Here's how the visitor—Constable Mohle—responded:

> Constable Mohle answered every question patiently and with serious intent. It was a validation for all of the students that the things they wanted to know were important. For me, this was a far more satisfying way to have a guest in the classroom. First, the students were more involved and not just passive listeners. Second, they learned that what they wonder matters to those from outside our classroom as well as those within it. And third, they practiced asking questions—an important skill.

> If I ask the questions, I am in charge of the learning. If the police officer asks them, he is. If the students ask the questions they are in charge of their own learning. They did and they were. (Cassidy, 2012)

At any age, the trick to doing your best thinking is to have lots of ways to think, and knowing how to think in the ways that best suit the situation. Think about a time when you had trouble making a choice. Perhaps you wrote down the pros and cons of each option and then gave each a hard look. This sort of analytical (compare-and-contrast) thinking aids decision making.

When you use a variety of thinking strategies regularly and flexibly, they become second nature. Whether your students are trying to make connections, bring a fuzzy thought into clear view, or build explanations, they will be more successful if they have a variety of strategies to draw from to tackle each challenge.

Here is an assortment of thinking routines, study strategies, and conceptual organizers students will find helpful when faced with common challenges during projects. Plan on modeling how and when to use them.

Developing a Research-Worthy Question

Brainstorm a list of at least 10 (more is better!) questions about the challenge. Teach students to use these sentence-starters:

Why . . . ?

How would things be different if . . . ?

What are the reasons . . . ?

Suppose that . . . ?

What if we knew . . . ?

What is the purpose of . . . ?

What would change if . . . ?

Distinguishing What You Know From What You Don't Know

Create a circle of knowledge. Make a circle on a large piece of paper and put everything you know about the topic, issue, or problem in the middle and everything you don't know outside the circle. Of the "known" ideas, put those you are most certain of in the center and the ones you are less certain of further toward the edge. It is OK for ideas to straddle the line between known and unknown. This might be the "sweet spot" for an investigation.

Understanding a Key Idea

Write a newspaper headline that captures the essence of the topic. Draft several of these until you are satisfied that one summarizes what you know.

Example: A student is investigating the health management options of people with Type 2 diabetes. Her headline reads: *Medication Without Lifestyle Changes Has Limited Impact on Health of Diabetics.*

Understanding How Something Happened or Came To Be

Create a causal map to illustrate how factors influence an outcome (illustrating cause-and-effect thinking in systems). Put the central concern (car accidents, poverty, war) at the center of the map. Investigate influencing, or causal, factors and represent them as nodes on the map that connect with arrows to the center. Primary factors that have a direct impact connect directly to the center. Show secondary factors (those that influence other factors), too.

Example: *Car accidents* is the topic at the center, with distracted drivers, bad road conditions, speeding, car malfunction, and other factors showing as contributing to car accidents. Most factors are influenced by secondary factors. Factors contributing to distracted driving might include cell phone use, crying babies as passengers, eating while driving, or seeing another accident!

When Stuck

Try a variety of ways to get unstuck.

- Write a letter to a friend explaining that you are stuck. Describe in detail what it is you are trying to accomplish.
- Take a break. Walk around and get blood circulating. Recharge your "thinking batteries."
- Get a change of scenery; move to a new spot to work.

Instead of Waiting for Help

Sometimes students ask for adult help right away. Help them build stamina for thinking through a challenge on their own. Establish an expectation that they try several tactics before seeking help. One approach is *Do Three—Ask Me.*

Try to think through your challenge before asking for adult help. "Do Three" means you: (1) review the task, (2) try something, and (3) talk to a classmate before you "ask me." When you "ask me," be ready to explain what you have already tried.

When Feeling Overwhelmed

Break the task into smaller parts. Start working on the part that is most approachable.

Getting Thoughts Flowing

"Buzz" your way into the work. Get a classmate to listen as you talk for 2 or 3 minutes about your project. Imagine you are describing the project to someone for the first time—start at the beginning and bring your listener up to the point at which you are working now.

Solving a Problem Creatively

Almost every new solution is an adaptation of another. The letters in SCAMPER represent different ways to shift from an existing idea or solution to develop something new.

S = Substitute

C = Combine

A = Adapt

M = Modify

P = Put to other uses

E = Eliminate or minimize

R = Rearrange or Reverse

Giving Feedback

Give classmates constructive feedback with a CLAM Sandwich. Listen to the speaker, then ask C = *Clarifying* questions; describe what you L = *Like;* offer A = *Advice;* and M = *Meet* in the middle (discuss).

→Project Signpost 6: Think More Strategically

If a visitor were to walk into your classroom, could he or she tell what kind of thinking your students are engaged in? Would your students be able to explain their own thinking strategies? Help students think more strategically by introducing them to thinking tools that fit specific project needs. Develop their vocabulary for talking about thinking. If you're not sure which tools to use when, browse the collection of guides and graphic organizers available from the National Center for Teaching Thinking (www.nctt.net), including tools to help thinkers:

- Compare and contrast.
- Predict.
- Make a well-founded judgment or informed decision.
- Understand causal relationships (cause and effect).
- Determine how parts relate to the whole (systems).
- Identify patterns or trends.
- Examine perspectives and alternate points of view.
- Extrapolate to create something new.
- Evaluate reliability of sources.

TEACH FOR THINKING—AKA BECOME THE "MEDDLER IN THE MIDDLE"

Chances are, you're already using many of the strategies we just discussed to help students become better thinkers. Becoming a PBL teacher doesn't mean starting from scratch or ignoring the insights you have gained over the years. However, some traditional classroom patterns and practices won't suit the project context. Let's compare and contrast a few:

Traditional Classroom	*PBL Setting*
Teacher presents lessons in digestible "chunks"	Teacher helps students navigate through the various stages of the project cycle
Teacher does most of the talking	Teacher does more listening
If students struggle with content, teacher responds by reteaching	If students struggle with content or project management, teacher encourages, asks questions, and models persistence, troubleshooting, and creative problem solving
Teacher gives grades that emphasize final product or end-of-unit exam	Teacher uses formative assessment to intervene in the processes that lead to high-quality final products

This means you will need to be ready to think and operate in new ways during projects, just as your students will do. As New Zealand Principal Richard Coote suggests, a teacher becomes the *meddler in the middle* during PBL.

Try these methods for effective "meddling" in order to expose and support good thinking. Many are PBL adaptations of the thinking routines developed by Project Zero at Harvard.

Focusing

Ask: What is going on here? What are you trying to accomplish? What is important to understand?

Extending

Say: Yes, and what else?

Ask: How does this help us understand the bigger picture? Have you considered . . . ? What would happen if . . . ?

Justifying

Ask: How can you be certain that . . . ? What evidence backs up your statement that . . . ?

Provoking

Ask: Why do you think so? Why does that matter? What would ___ say?

Observing

Set an expectation that activity doesn't stop because you appeared on the scene.

Say: Go ahead—I'm just interested in watching and listening.

Monitoring

Ask: Show me what you're doing. Where are you in the process? What happened right before I arrived? What do you plan to do next?

Evaluating

Say: Show me how you arrived at that conclusion.

Ask: Why do you think so?

GET OFF TO A GOOD START

If your students are new to PBL, it's wise to introduce them to this way of teaching and learning with a meaningful "starter" project. Even a low-stakes project can explicitly teach the expectations, language, and processes of PBL. Continue to build on students' shared experiences to create a positive classroom culture for ongoing learning through PBL.

Diana Cornejo-Sanchez, a ninth-grade humanities teacher at High Tech High Media Arts (HTH), gets acquainted with her incoming freshmen—and gets them acquainted with PBL—in a fall-semester project called A Hero in My Eyes. Students explore issues of identity and literary themes by answering the driving question, "What is a hero in today's society?" For their culminating exhibition, they produce black-and-white portraits that capture a heroic moment and write accompanying narratives that tell the stories of the heroes who have influenced their young lives.

Getting to that final exhibit requires artful facilitation by the teacher, learning a new set of skills by the students, and, as Cornejo-Sanchez says, "a lot of scaffolding."

Students come to HTH from across the San Diego area. "They might have spent middle school in a private school, charter school, or traditional public school. I act as if nobody knows anything about PBL when they first come here," the teacher explains.

It's important for her students to build a strong foundation of the project skills they will use throughout their 4 years at HTH. By the time they are seniors, they will be designing their own inquiry projects. But as freshmen, they start with the basics. For their first project, the teacher makes most of the decisions about project design.

Cornejo-Sanchez explains: "When I introduce the project, I give students a detailed description sheet. It explains why we're doing it, what it will involve, the community resources they may want to take advantage of, the skills they will need. And there's a very detailed timeline that helps them with time management. I include everything we're going to do so they can see the steps: interviewing, drafting, giving feedback, working on photography, learning from expert visitors." In later projects, students will need less direction as they gradually take on more responsibility for their own learning. But for their first PBL experience, she says, "It's all there, day by day."

Because Cornejo-Sanchez wants to learn about the strengths and interests of each student at the start of the year, she has them produce individual products. Students also team up on aspects of the project, however, which gives them opportunities to build collaboration skills.

Students learn to work collaboratively through a series of planned activities, such as interviewing a partner and providing critical feedback to inform revision. Here, too, the teacher is deliberate about teaching collaboration skills.

"We might spend two or three days talking about why you critique each other's work, why it's scary, the kind of feedback you would like to receive." She models the process by sharing with students feedback she received on her writing from a college professor.

Field trips and guest speakers are routinely incorporated into projects at HTH. Once again, Cornejo-Sanchez deliberately guides students to take advantage of these resources. A Hero in My Eyes, for instance, involves producing a photo portrait that captures a heroic moment. There's no photography teacher on campus, so Cornejo-Sanchez takes students to a local museum of photography and invites a local photographer to come work with students. Through her facilitation, they are learning how to access resources. That's a skill they will continue to draw on throughout high school. She adds, "Our students learn how to ask experts for specific help. That's part of our school culture."

For their culminating event, students present their work in a gallery setting. Standing next to their exhibits, students talk with parents and other community members about what defines a hero to them (using presentation skills they have practiced in class with their peers). Once again, this is a "right-sized" event that gets them ready for the larger audiences they will share their work with later in the year.

By the end of the year, these ninth-graders have developed the confidence and competence to perform before an audience of 200 as part of a spoken-word project. It's no accident that the ambitious final project is also about identity. "It brings the year to a full closure," Cornejo-Sanchez says, "and it takes us all year to build up to it."

Exercise: Evaluate Starter Projects

A good starter project accomplishes several important goals:

- It breaks the ice, getting students and teacher better acquainted.
- It teaches the language and process of doing projects, with scaffolds built in to introduce students to timelines, peer review, and other deliberate strategies to support success.
- It emphasizes and deliberately teaches collaboration skills.
- It may set low-stakes content-learning goals, allowing students to learn from mistakes and get comfortable with new ways of working.
- It sets the stage for reflection and builds positive classroom culture for doing PBL.
- It generates success that you can continue to build on.

If you have used starter projects with your students in the past, think about how well the projects have met these goals. How might you improve your starter ideas?

If you are new to PBL, investigate examples of short-term projects that you might want to borrow or adapt to introduce students to the project approach:

- A Hero in My Eyes is a good example for the high school level (read more and see student work samples at http://www.hightechhigh .org/unboxed/issue3/cards/3.php).
- Middle-school science teacher Sue Boudreau blogs about introducing students to PBL at the *Take Action Science Projects Blog* (http:// takeactionscience.wordpress.com/2012/04/04/yeah-yeah-yeah- but-how-do-you-get-started-with-pbl/).
- Elementary teachers might want to consider joining the Monster Project (http://www.smithclass.org/proj/Monsters/), a well- structured project that emphasizes collaborative problem solving with a fun challenge.

WHAT'S NEXT?

Before moving into subject-specific project discussions in Part II, we conclude the first half of the book with an overview of project design principles. If you are brand new to PBL, you may want to explore additional resources for more detailed planning advice. If you are a PBL veteran, Chapter 5 offers a reminder of the key considerations to keep in mind for effective project design.

Designing Rich Learning Experiences

When students engage in quality projects, they develop knowledge, skills, and dispositions that serve them in the moment and in the long term. Unfortunately, not all projects live up to their potential. Sometimes the problem lies in the design process. It's easy to jump directly into planning the activities students will engage in without addressing important elements that will affect the overall quality of the project. With more intentional planning, we can design projects that get at universal themes that have explicit value to our students and to others. We can design projects to be *rigorous,* so students' actions mirror the efforts of accomplished adults. They will feel the burn as they learn and build up their fitness for learning challenges to come.

Since the "backward design" approach was outlined by Grant Wiggins and Jay McTighe in *Understanding by Design* (2005; first published in 1998), a lot of good thinking has gone into the processes for project planning. Because comprehensive planning advice can be found elsewhere (including our previous book, *Reinventing Project-Based Learning,* and resources from the Buck Institute for Education), our treatment here is intentionally brief, focusing on details that warrant particular attention to improve the inquiry experience.

See the Appendixes for more project planning resources. We also encourage you to tap networks of PBL enthusiasts for advice as you plan—see networking suggestions in Chapter 11.

There are several ways to start designing projects. One is to select among learning objectives described in the curriculum and textbooks that guide your teaching and to plan learning experiences based on these. Another is to "back in" to the standards, starting with a compelling idea and then mapping it to objectives to ensure there is a fit with what students are expected to learn. The second method can be more generative, as any overarching and enduring concept is likely to support underlying objectives in the core subject matter and in associated disciplines, too. Either way you begin, the first step is to identify a project-worthy idea.

PROJECT DESIGN IN SIX STEPS

We have condensed the project design process into six steps. After outlining the steps briefly below, we offer examples that show how one might use these steps to develop a germ of an idea into a project plan that emphasizes inquiry. Read the steps and examples all the way through before digging in to your own plan.

Step 1—Identify Project-Worthy Concepts

Ask yourself: What important and enduring concepts are fundamental to the subjects I teach? Identify four or five BIG concepts for each subject.

Step 2—Explore Their Significance and Relevance

Now, think: Why do these topics or concepts *matter?* What should students remember about this topic in 5 years? For a lifetime? Think beyond school and ask: In what ways are they important and enduring? What is their relevance in different people's lives? In different parts of the world? Explore each concept, rejecting and adding ideas until you arrive at a short list of meaningful topics.

Step 3—Find Real-Life Contexts

Look back to three or four concepts you explored and think about real-life contexts. Who engages in these topics? Who are the people for whom these topics are central to their work? See if you can list five to seven professions for each concept.

With that done, now think: What are the interdisciplinary connections? In what ways might the topic extend beyond my subject matter? For example, if your subject specialty was math and you imagined an entrepreneur taking a product to market, the central work might involve investment, expense, and profit analyses. The project might also involve supply chains and transportation (geography), writing a prospectus for a venture capitalist (language arts), and designing a marketing campaign (language arts, graphic design, technology).

Step 4—Engage Critical Thinking

As you begin to imagine these topics in the context of a project, ask yourself, what might you ask of students? How might you push past rote learning into investigation, analysis, and synthesis? Consider how you can engage critical thinking in a project by asking students to

- Compare and contrast
- Predict
- Make a well-founded judgment or informed decision
- Understand causal relationships (cause and effect)
- Determine how parts relate to the whole (systems)
- Identify patterns or trends
- Examine perspectives and alternate points of view
- Extrapolate to create something new
- Evaluate reliability of sources

Step 5—Write a Project Sketch

Now, step back and write a project sketch—or two or three. For each, give an overview of the project. Describe the scenario and the activities students are likely to engage in. Anyone reading it should be able to tell what students will learn by doing the project. The process of writing will help you refine your ideas. There are dozens of project sketches in this book (and all are included in the Project Library in Appendix A). Use them as a guide.

Step 6—Plan the Setup

Three small but useful elements are left, and together with the project sketch, they provide a framework for the project. Write a title, entry event, and driving question for your project.

Project title. A good title goes a long way toward anchoring the project in the minds of your school community. A short and memorable title is best.

Teachers at Birkdale School in New Zealand take their projects seriously. They not only provide them with proper names but also fly a special flag in the school's entry when a new project begins. You might not need to go this far, but a good title conveys a sense of importance and helps make a project memorable. Let these project titles inspire you.

- Lest We Forget—A project involving war memorials in New Zealand
- Mingling at the Renaissance Ball—A social studies investigation that culminates in a celebration of human achievement
- Lessons from the Gulf—A collection of collaborative projects by schools concerned about U.S. Gulf Coast devastation
- AD 1095 and All That—Time-traveling students intervene to stop religious wars in medieval Europe.

- Risk and Reward—Students acting as financial counselors present stock information to clients and advise on investments.
- Stay or Leave?—Students examine economic factors that influence people's decisions about where they live.
- YouVille—Students explore past civilizations to design their own utopias.

Entry event. Plan to start off the project with a "grabber," a mysterious letter, jarring "news," a provocative video, or other attention-getting event. As we discussed in Chapter 4, make sure it is *novel* (to make students alert) and has *emotional significance* (to make them care). Read these examples and imagine how your students might respond. Then plan an entry event for your project.

- A newspaper article describes hazards associated with a clinic's use of poorly refurbished X-ray machines.
- Distraught warrior king Gilgamesh appears in class and appeals to his "subjects" to help him learn why an enemy's technological prowess in battle outstrips his own.
- A process server slaps student "witnesses" with subpoenas, compelling them to testify in an upcoming trial.
- A letter from an elder describes her desire to capture stories before she and other storytellers are no more.
- A television news story on "designer" babies kicks off an investigation about the ethical implications of genetic manipulation.
- A forest owlet from a wildlife rescue center visits school bringing Owl Mail and asks students to investigate hazards to its survival.

Driving question. Kick off your project with a research question students will feel compelled to investigate. Imagine a driving question that leads to more questions, which, in their answering, contribute to greater understanding. Good questions grab student interest (they are provocative, intriguing, or urgent), are open ended (you can't Google your way to an answer), and connect to key learning goals.

Consider how to write a good question based on these "remodeled" examples (Larmer, 2009):

- *What are archetypes in literature?* → To increase relevance, you might ask → *How do archetypes inform our culture today?*
- *What causes tornadoes?* → To add context, you might ask → *How can we prepare for a natural disaster in our region?*
- *What are the requirements to sustain life?* → To add interest, you might ask → *How can we design a biome that is self-sustaining?*
- *How can we purify water?* → To increase challenge, you might ask → *How can we advise a village in the developing world to choose an inexpensive water purification system?*

ONE LAST STEP

Workshop your project idea, especially at steps 5 and 6. Colleagues, students, parents, and subject matter experts will ask questions that will clarify your thinking and contribute ideas you might not have considered.

PROJECT DESIGN IN CONTEXT

Table 5.1 below illustrates the thinking that went into designing several projects. Reading from left to right, you can see the progression: from subject and big ideas to real-world connections and, finally, to a project sketch. The sketch is well formed enough to share with colleagues for critical feedback but not so tightly planned that you hesitate to change it. Once you are satisfied with your sketch, you are ready to proceed with a more detailed plan (including a project calendar, deliverables, and assessment plan) that will help you consider all the essential ingredients for a successful project.

For additional resources to help you with in-depth project planning, see Appendix D (p. 183).

WHAT'S NEXT?

This chapter concludes Part I. In Part II, we will dive deeper into subject areas for inquiry projects. If you teach a specific content area, we encourage you to also read the chapters that focus on other disciplines and look for interdisciplinary project opportunities. Chapter 6 sets the stage with an exploration of interdisciplinary thinking.

Table 5.1 Thinking That Went Into Designing Several Projects

Subject	Key Concepts	Significance and Relevance: Why are these subjects important to teach? Who do they affect?	Out of school, who engages in these topics? How might students engage in these topics in an interdisciplinary and real-life way?	Engage Critical Thinking	Project Sketch	Great Project Title / Entry Event / Driving Question
Language Arts	Point of view, literary devices, reporting, opinion, archetypes, argument and *persuasion*, creative expression, vocabulary	Persuasion influences the minds and actions of others. Being persuasive is a life skill and so is knowing when one is being subjected to persuasion.	Among others, politicians, advertisers, and charities use persuasion to influence people. Students can debate the validity of a scientific argument, sway voters in a mock election, stage a historical debate, publish a political cartoon, write an editorial, promote a cause, take an IPO public, *appeal for charitable donations*, persuade a jury, launch an advertising campaign, or put a candidate up for office. Interdisciplinary ties: Many scenarios in which persuasion is applied are civic in nature. Social studies is a natural interdisciplinary tie.	Choosing a charity to fund requires critical thinking to make an informed judgment. Crafting a persuasive argument is necessary to convince others to give. Students apply supported reasoning to draft operational definitions of both "need" and "doing good" to select among causes and charities that address those causes. They evaluate persuasive talks and identify important	Student advisors help philanthropists select local charities to support. They identify problems in their community and do a gap analysis to determine the nature and severity of the problems in relation to efforts to resolve them. They plan a night of persuasive "lightning" talks to garner support for charitable causes. They advertise the event using Twitter and Facebook, set up FirstGiving accounts (www.firstgiving.com) to collect donations, and on show night watch as donations roll in. *In this project, students turn to social media to learn how to*	Title: *Make Me Care* Entry Event: Students learn how much money goes to charitable causes in their community each year. They draw pie charts showing how they imagine the money is apportioned to local causes, then compare this to the actual distribution. Driving Question: How can we spend money to do the most good?

Subject	Key Concepts	Significance and Relevance: Why are these subjects important to teach? Who do they affect?	Out of school, who engages in these topics? How might students engage in these topics in an interdisciplinary and real-life way?	Engage Critical Thinking	Project Sketch	Great Project Title Entry Event Driving Question
				features they can apply in their own presentations.	be persuasive, get help from experts, and promote a cause.	
Social Studies	Change, causal relationships, cultural understanding, systems, production of goods, movement of people, power, government, laws and other social contracts	Life on earth is a complex web of interconnected natural and human-made systems. Any assortment of things that have some influence on one another can be thought of as a system. Understanding how elements in a system interact helps us grapple with complexity.	Among others, historians, economists, legislators, city planners, and manufacturers deal with systems. Understanding power dynamics in war, patterns of human migration, how to prepare for natural disasters, bringing a product to market, and designing a waste-management plan or a transportation system all require systems thinking. Interdisciplinary ties: Project work could involve visual representations of systems.	Understanding complex interactions is fundamental to problem solving and innovation. Any systems-oriented project would benefit from diverse perspectives. Technology can be instrumental in representing—and making sense of—dynamic systems.	1. A second-grade class designs its own airport. Their challenge is to get all the parts working together so "passengers" make their way through ticketing, security and boarding and get to their seats in time for a scheduled "flight." 2. Ninth-grade English students examine how events unfold to	1. Title: *Come Fly with Us* Entry Event: A pilot visits school, gives every "junior pilot" wings, and invites them to design their own airport. Driving Question: How do airports work? 2. Title: *The Dane's Destiny* Entry Event: Kids draw diagrams that show how plot

(Continued)

Table 5.1 (Continued)

Subject	Key Concepts	Significance and Relevance: Why are these subjects important to teach? Who do they affect?	Out of school, who engages in these topics? How might students engage in these topics in an interdisciplinary and real-life way?	Engage Critical Thinking	Project Sketch	Great Project Title Entry Event Driving Question
				In "systems" projects, students might use modeling software to make sense of a system and data visualization tools to represent their understanding.	determine whether Hamlet's fate would have changed if his actions, such as his timing for killing Claudius, were different. 3. An ecology class considers factors of regulation and equilibrium by modeling population dynamics in a desert ecosystem. 4. History students examine events and conditions that contributed to the U.S. Civil War and compare these to factors	points interact in story arcs of favorite movies or books. Driving Question: Was Hamlet's fate inevitable? 3. Title: *Life in the Balance* Entry Event: Students plot data and look for relationships between coyote and desert hare populations over time. Driving Question: How does an ecosystem hang together or fall apart?

Subject	Key Concepts	Significance and Relevance: Why are these subjects important to teach? Who do they affect?	Out of school, who engages in these topics? How might students engage in these topics in an interdisciplinary and real-life way?	Engage Critical Thinking	Project Sketch	Great Project Title / Entry Event / Driving Question
					influencing contemporary civil wars.	4. Title: *Conflict Then and Now* Entry Event: Students watch a news report about the conflict that led to the formation of South Sudan. They meet a newly minted citizen of South Sudan over Skype. Driving Question: Is war inevitable?
Science	Compounds, forces, *electromagnetic waves*, speciation, interdependence, interactions of matter and energy, atmosphere and climate, geologic processes	Electromagnetic waves transfer energy, which governs natural processes and can be harnessed by humans.	Physicists' discoveries influence developments ranging from space flight to house paints that hold up to solar radiation. As they bring products to market, engineers and manufacturers create schematics (involving computer-assisted design) and product manuals	Students working in teams as consumer advocates develop product guides for manufactured goods that involve the electromagnetic spectrum.	In physical science, students are expected to understand the nature of electromagnetic waves and differences and similarities between kinds of waves as a means of transmitting	Title: *Los Rayos X* Entry Event: A news article about health damages to children and technicians in Central America that happen during X-ray scans from badly refurbished

(Continued)

Table 5.1 (Continued)

Subject	Key Concepts	Significance and Relevance: Why are these subjects important to teach? Who do they affect?	Out of school, who engages in these topics? How might students engage in these topics in an interdisciplinary and real-life way?	Engage Critical Thinking	Project Sketch	Great Project Title Entry Event Driving Question
			(technical writing). Retailers work with advertisers to create marketing campaigns (persuasive imagery and language) to sell products. Watchdog groups attend to safety and help consumers select quality products (awareness campaigns and publications). Government policy makers and waste-management experts set (and communicate) policies for the use and disposal of consumer goods that make use of electromagnetic waves.	They draw on the expertise of physicists, engineers, and consumer-protection advocates to make judgments about tradeoffs between product functions and associated risk.	energy. Students study this by examining consumer products that put electromagnetic waves to work.* Their task is to write consumer manuals that explain how products function and to advise on their safe use and disposal. *Products or devices involving electromagnetic waves include but are not limited to: X-rays, MRIs, and other imaging technologies; compact fluorescent, incandescent, and LED bulbs; ultraviolet light-protecting products like house paints and sunscreen; laser beams; digital,	second-hand equipment. Driving Question: How can we put energy from the electromagnetic spectrum to work?

Subject	Key Concepts	Significance and Relevance: Why are these subjects important to teach? Who do they affect?	Out of school, who engages in these topics? How might students engage in these topics in an interdisciplinary and real-life way?	Engage Critical Thinking	Project Sketch	Great Project Title Entry Event Driving Question
					plasma, and LCD televisions; wifi, radios, microwaves, satellite dishes, repeaters, and antennas for telecommunications; surgical gamma ray knives; infrared and radio-frequency remote controllers such as automobile key fobs, garage door openers, TV remotes, and Bluetooth devices; bombs that create an electromagnetic pulse.	
Math	Pattern, quantity, trends, size/shape/position/	Linear equations help us solve for the unknown and	Among others, architects, engineers, pharmacists, and economists use algebra and	An investments project asks students to solve	Student consultants advise a city council, the director of a	Title: *Energy Diet* Entry Event: Students turn the

Table 5.1 (Continued)

Subject	Key Concepts	Significance and Relevance: Why are these subjects important to teach? Who do they affect?	Out of school, who engages in these topics? How might students engage in these topics in an interdisciplinary and real-life way?	Engage Critical Thinking	Project Sketch	Great Project Title Entry Event Driving Question
	scale, inequality, ratios, *linear equations*, probability, logic, statistics	find patterns, trends, slope, change over time, and proportional relationships.	linear equations. Linear equations are useful in designing roller coasters, calculating drug dosages, structuring bank loans, *investing in energy-saving measures*, determining how much oxygen a space-walking astronaut or deep-sea diver needs, anticipating demographic changes, and planning railway timetables.	problems using well-founded judgment. Realistic scenarios would require research, data collection, calculations, and analysis. A lifelike situation that involves a "client" would have students writing expository text with technical vocabulary, producing graphical representations, and speaking authoritatively.	retirement home, a business owner, or other ratepayers on ways to invest in improvements (i.e., solar panels, insulation, regulation sensors) that will save them energy and money. On the way to proposing a plan of action, each team conducts an energy audit, evaluates options for saving energy, and calculates investment costs, loans, and payback based on the client's budget. They seek advice from a nonprofit that helps utility customers save energy and run their proposals by experts here before sharing them with clients.	school's energy bill into fun equivalencies, such as number of: miles of car travel, laptops powered, gallons of soft ice cream dispensed. Driving Question: Can we spend money to save money?

SECTION II

Taking a Page From the Experts

6

Thinking Across Disciplines

In 2000, Charles Best was a 25-year-old social studies teacher at a public alternative school in the Bronx. Like many of his colleagues, he was frustrated by the lack of funds to buy basic classroom supplies. Materials for special projects? Forget about it. But Best had a hunch. If ordinary citizens knew that teachers needed additional books or art supplies, wouldn't they be willing to pitch in? To test his idea for citizen philanthropy, he built a website on which teachers could post modest requests for materials. That was the birth of Donors Choose. By 2012, the award-winning nonprofit had raised more than $100 million for schools across the United States.

The basic idea of Donors Choose remains elegantly simple, but it takes a well-oiled team to make this social enterprise so effective. Behind the scenes, there are Web programmers and social media experts who use various tools and platforms to connect donors and teachers. Data analysts crunch the numbers to show impact, while accountants track the dollars so that donors have confidence about where their money's going. Marketing experts turn celebrity endorsements (such as repeat shout-outs from comedian Stephen Colbert) into opportunities to expand this successful brand.

Look closely at almost any real-world activity—developing a new consumer product, running a political campaign, investigating a crime, managing a small business—and you'll find an interdisciplinary team contributing discrete sets of skills and knowledge to the effort. In today's complex world, this is how important work gets accomplished.

As we've discussed in previous chapters, project-based learning prepares students for the world that awaits them by giving them opportunities to work with peers on authentic problems. Good solutions often result from people with different kinds of expertise contributing their best thinking—and building on each other's ideas. Learning to collaborate with team members is one important outcome of projects. Just as important is the chance to walk in the shoes of expert problem solvers.

This chapter sets the stage for the second half of the book, in which we will explore project-based learning in four core academic disciplines. It might be tempting to think of these fields—language arts, mathematics, science, and social studies—as separate areas of a library, each containing its own collection of content that students need to master. But that would be short sighted. Along with important content, each discipline also offers a distinct set of lenses for viewing the world, investigating questions, and evaluating evidence. As students become more deeply steeped in the disciplines, they learn both rich content and expert ways of thinking.

When students are confronted with real-world problems, they may need more than one set of disciplinary lenses to "see" a complex issue or design a solution. Constructing an answer may require them to integrate ideas or approaches from diverse perspectives.

Before we dive deeply into discussing inquiry strategies for projects in language arts, mathematics, science, and social studies, let's take time to consider the nature of interdisciplinary thinking and the role it plays in expert problem solving.

PREPARING TO TACKLE COMPLEX PROBLEMS

Most intellectual life outside of school makes connections across disciplines. Indeed, it's hard to think of a career field or profession that operates in isolation. Filmmakers need financial backers. Doctors must stay current with pharmaceutical research. Anthropologists help technologists understand how people interact with computers. Professional athletes often have teams of trainers, nutritionists, and psychologists to help them stay at the top of their games. Even solitary artists and writers must eventually collaborate with gallery owners, publicists, and publishers if they want to get their creative work to an audience.

People who are experts in their fields have developed a familiarity and fluency with a particular set of tools, methodologies, and types of evidence and argument used in solving problems, accomplishing tasks, and sharing results. They're part of a culture that has its own history, accomplishments, vocabulary, and perhaps special notations. The most skilled are able to work across disciplines, connecting and integrating what they know about in depth with understanding that comes from other fields. A patent lawyer, for instance, has to be able to "speak" both law and engineering. Someone who coordinates public health campaigns may need to draw on expertise in medicine, behavioral psychology, marketing, and social media.

It's primarily in school that we wall off the disciplines into content-specific silos and shift students' attention from one subject to the next with the ring of a bell. John Dewey (Dewey, 2011, p. 62) cautioned against this practice nearly a century ago when he observed, "We do not have a series of stratified earths, one of which is mathematical, another physical, another historical, and so on . . . All studies grow out of relations in the one great common world." Learning driven by the traditional bell schedule is distinctly unlike real life, something that critics continue to point out. "We simply do not function in a world where problems are discipline specific in regimented time blocks," noted Heidi Hayes Jacobs in her 1989 publication *Interdisciplinary Curriculum: Design and Implementation* (Jacobs, 1989).

The complexity of today's challenges and the connectedness that technology affords are making interdisciplinary thinking increasingly important. Veronica Boix Mansilla, principal investigator of the Interdisciplinary Studies Project at Harvard's Project Zero, describes interdisciplinarity as the hallmark of contemporary knowledge production and professional life (Boix Mansilla, 2006; Boix Mansilla & Dawes Duraising, 2007). Cross-cutting issues facing today's youth range from the ethics of stem cell research to the human role in climate change to the politics of financial reforms. Preparing young people to engage in the major issues of our times requires that we nurture their ability to produce quality interdisciplinary work (Boix Mansilla & Dawes Duraising, 2007).

PROJECTS ALLOW FOR CONNECTIONS

When projects mirror real life, they take learning out of the content silos and challenge students to make connections across disciplines. But this doesn't mean discounting or discarding subject-area content or ways of thinking that come with the disciplines. Nor does it mean tossing in a dash of math or a smidge of science to make a writing assignment interdisciplinary. Rather, students demonstrate true interdisciplinary understanding when they integrate knowledge, methods, and languages from two or more disciplines to solve problems, create products, produce explanations, or ask novel questions in ways that would not be feasible through a single disciplinary lens (Boix Mansilla & Jackson, 2011).

Informed by both research and classroom practice, Boix Mansilla and colleagues at Project Zero have identified four key features of quality interdisciplinary understanding (Boix Mansilla & Jackson, 2011, p. 13):

Interdisciplinary understanding is *purposeful:* Students examine a topic in order to explain it or tell a story about it in ways that would not be possible through a single discipline.

Understanding is *grounded in disciplines:* It employs concepts, big ideas, methods, and languages from two or more disciplines in accurate and flexible ways.

Interdisciplinary understanding is *integrative:* Disciplinary perspectives are integrated to deepen or complement understanding.

Interdisciplinary understanding is *thoughtful:* Students reflect about the nature of interdisciplinary work and the limits of their own understanding.

These qualities are worth considering at the project design stage, when teachers are determining the key learning goals they aim to achieve through a project. Is a project idea grounded in a specific content area, or does it allow for meaningful connections across disciplines?

Collaborating with colleagues from other content areas can help teachers recognize natural connections in their content standards. In *Meeting Standards Through Integrated Curriculum,* authors Susan Drake and Rebecca Burns suggest, "Teachers can chunk the standards together into meaningful clusters both within and across disciplines. Once teachers understand how standards are connected, their perception of interdisciplinary curriculum shifts dramatically." Indeed, they emphasize that "some teachers see it as the *only* way to teach and to cover the standards" (Drake & Burns, 2004).

The Common Core State Standards take a similarly holistic view of learning, with a call for integrating the English language arts and incorporating critical thinking and nonfiction reading across the curriculum.

Allowing students latitude in deciding how they will approach a project may also open the door for more interdisciplinary work, as students will naturally draw on the knowledge, skills, and interests they have developed in other studies and through life experiences.

LOOK FOR AUTHENTIC CONNECTIONS

The project planning stage is the time to look for genuine connections between disciplines. Avoid the PBL pitfall of "tacking on" a little bit of content from another subject area once you already have a project well underway.

For an example of real interdisciplinary work, consider a project designed by art teacher Jeff Robin and physics teacher Andrew Gloag. Their 12th-graders at High Tech High published a book called *Phys Newtons,* an illustrated guide to the California State Physics Standards (Robin, 2011). As preparation, each student researched one of Newton's laws (motion, gravity, energy, circular motion, or projectiles). Students then painted images to visually demonstrate the law (while also meeting standards for visual arts). Each student designed a page of the book using a combination of images and text. A page explaining Newton's Second Law, for instance, features a series of images showing a baseball player going through the motions of pitching. Accompanying text explains the relationship between force and acceleration. In an authentic performance assessment, students used their book—relying on both science and art—to teach their peers about Newton's laws.

Exercise: Picture Career Connections

Many of today's students are likely to enter career fields that overlap one or more disciplines. Take a close look at the Venn diagram in Figure 6.1. It shows overlaps between various careers and the four core content areas. You'll notice that the English language arts are represented in this model as common ground. Being able to communicate and explain your thinking is essential in every field.

Think about the current interests of your students. Which career opportunities mesh with their passions? How could a project give them a chance to explore these career fields now?

Think, too, about the careers you don't see represented here. New specialties are emerging all the time. What kinds of thinkers will be needed for future careers in computational biology, food politics, cybersecurity, or space travel? How could projects prepare students for these opportunities?

Figure 6.1   Venn diagram shows overlap between core content areas and careers. Language arts (LA) is represented as the "common ground" for each of the other three: social studies (SS), mathematics (M), and science (S).

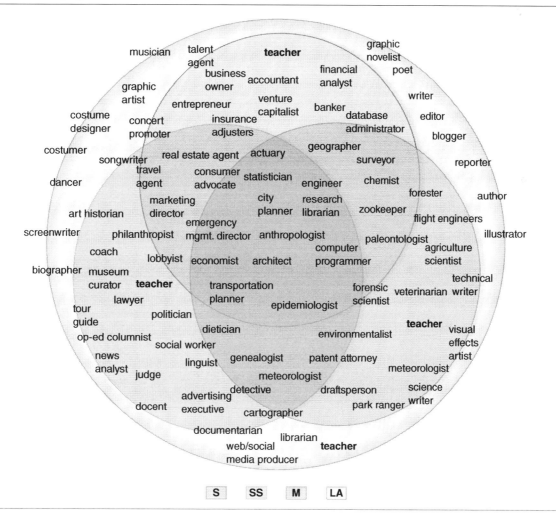

WHAT'S NEXT?

In the next four chapters, we take a close look at inquiry in each of these core content areas: language arts, social studies, science, and math. You will hear from experts working in each discipline about what inspired them to pursue their professions and how they have honed their specialized thinking skills. If you are a content-area specialist, we encourage you to read outside your discipline and look for interdisciplinary project opportunities. In Chapter 7, we start with language arts—an area that touches all disciplines.

7

Language Arts

"Life isn't always what you want it to be. Sometimes, your parents get divorced. Sometimes, you have to start over in a new city, state, or even country. Sometimes, you have to seek professional help for emotional issues."

These insights come from an eighth-grader named Zoe (Nerdy Book Club, 2012). She took part in a publishing project in which student writers shared their wisdom to help other children learn from life's challenges. *Transitions*, their beautifully illustrated book of stories, is available for sale on Amazon.com. What's the authors' strategy to help children develop better coping skills? "You have to speak their language," Zoe explains.

The *Transitions* project offers a powerful example of students using language for authentic purposes. Reading, writing, speaking, and listening skills all belong in the toolkit of a literate person in today's world. Students applied these skills, along with visual literacy, creativity, empathy, and an understanding of media arts, during this ambitious interdisciplinary project.

As the Common Core State Standards for Language Arts and other 21st-century frameworks make clear, literacy involves a complex set of competencies. Students who meet the standards know how to read carefully for understanding. They can critically assess the quality of information. They are able to engage with a variety of texts and make well-reasoned arguments. They can harness their own creativity and use digital tools to produce original work that engages audiences.

Project-based learning offers an excellent vehicle to help students reach these important goals—and not only in the English classroom. Perhaps more so than any other core content area, the foundational skills of the language arts reach across the curriculum. The deep and authentic connections between literacy and other subjects set the stage for interdisciplinary projects that emphasize thinking critically about information and using creativity when it comes to expressing ideas.

What's more, projects afford students opportunities to use language in the same ways that expert writers and thinkers do. Students like Zoe don't have to wait to become adult authors who can inform, influence, or help others through the power of words. Publishing tools, online platforms, and invitations to speak publicly are available to students now. If they hope to take advantage of these opportunities, however, students need to produce high-quality work that is audience ready. As any author will tell you, that takes deliberate practice.

Let's start this chapter with a closer look at *Transitions* to see how PBL practices support language arts goals. Next, we'll examine what inquiry means for writers and for readers across disciplines. Finally, we'll explore strategies to ensure that students expand their literacy skills across the arc of projects.

A PROCESS FOR PROJECT SUCCESS

When teacher George Mayo launched the *Transitions* project, he wasn't sure exactly what the final product would look like or which stories students would contribute. He did start with some key learning goals. Specifically, he wanted to make sure students understood the basic elements of plot and the concept of theme. He also had a process in mind to help students produce high-quality work that would incorporate visual literacy along with written storytelling skills.

To get students engaged, Mayo asked them to freewrite about difficult challenges they have experienced. This entry event ensured that students were invested in the project from day one. After all, they were drawing on their own life experiences as raw material. That meant student voice was a given.

Once students started sharing their freewrites, they noticed common themes in their classmates' stories. Students formed teams around shared challenges, such as dealing with a family illness, making new friends, or immigrating to the United States. Right from the start, teams had a mutual reason to work together and to listen to each other's ideas.

It takes a safe, respectful classroom for students to feel comfortable sharing their writing with peers, especially when topics get personal. "Before you can get students to open up in their writing, you have to make sure they feel comfortable, that they respect one another, and that they will not be put down if they honestly share ideas. If you can't create that environment," Mayo cautions in a phone interview with the authors, "you'll have a hard time getting authentic ideas from them."

Mayo started building this collaborative culture well in advance of the *Transitions* project. A poster at the front of his classroom captures—in students' words—what it means to share "Our Home Turf." Mayo had students make the poster at the start of the school year, setting the stage for an environment that supports projects. (He teaches many students for three consecutive years, so they already "own" this space.) As the teacher explains during our interview, "When we're in this room together, we're all here to support and encourage one another. It's a no-put-down zone. I want even the quietest, shyest kids to be able to speak up and feel part of the group. We start setting that tone early."

After the freewrites and formation of project teams, Mayo quickly shifted gears—and genres—so that students were focusing on broader themes. Each team's challenge was to turn their shared experiences into a metaphorical story. That meant students needed to understand the qualities of a good story. Children's literature offered them familiar and accessible examples for close reading.

Mayo provided a selection of children's books for students to examine and also invited them to bring in their favorites from home. When students began sharing dog-eared copies of the books they had loved as younger readers, they were primed for rich conversations about why certain titles have lasting appeal. Each day, they read aloud another book from the growing collection.

For more deliberate instruction in literary devices, Mayo used a book called *Two Bad Ants* for a whole-class discussion. "We picked it apart—the story structure, rising action, character traits of the ants. We analyzed it for metaphors and examined the theme," Mayo said during the interview. After this close read of a text, Mayo invited local children's book authors (a husband-and-wife team) to describe the process they go through to create a book. "We did a lot of modeling," the teacher adds.

With that foundation, teams were ready to start collaboratively writing their own stories. To engage creativity, Mayo introduced a variety of visual thinking tools to help students generate original plots. In his language arts class (which in eighth grade is called "Lights, Camera, Media Literacy!"), he makes regular use of storyboarding, plot diagramming, and other methods of capturing ideas in quick sketches. Once students had done enough visual brainstorming to get them ready to write, they shifted to Google Docs. This platform enabled teams to collaborate in real time, providing one another with just-in-time peer feedback to improve their compositions.

Students understood that illustrations would be important for appealing to younger audiences. Many of Mayo's students, however, lacked confidence in their artistic abilities. That changed when Mayo invited a professional artist, Arturo Ho, to share his expertise. As Mayo watched the artist guide students through the stages of creating illustrations, the veteran teacher had a revelation of his own. Mayo shared his reflections on *Digital Is,* an online journal of the National Writing Project (Mayo, 2012):

The art process is very similar to the writing process . . . Students first had to create their rough sketches, just like writers must first create their rough drafts. Then students slowly developed more refined illustrations based on their rough sketches. By the time the master storyboards were done, each group had a clear sense of what they wanted their illustrations to look like. They also had the confidence they needed to complete the project.

Before they moved on to their final drafts, the eighth graders took time to invite critique from a class of third graders. Just as Hollywood directors invite focus-group feedback before films are released, these authors enjoyed the benefit of honest review from younger readers. The authors relied on comments to polish their writing, improve clarity, and fine-tune their illustrations. Their attention to detail shows in the final product, which is sold on Amazon.com. "They understood that their work is going for the whole world to see," the teacher said during the interview, "and that makes a difference."

In this project, both students and teacher made an important discovery: The process of writing and revising based on feedback is similar to the way visual artists work. What's more, students had to make their words and pictures work in tandem. Neither was a stand-alone product. Art wasn't added at the end but integrated as part of the creative process. Teams had to evaluate multiple suggestions and come to consensus about the best way to convey their ideas, drawing on their expertise in two disciplines.

When you are planning interdisciplinary projects that include language arts, look for opportunities to integrate disciplines in similarly meaningful ways. The Common Core State Standards emphasize integrating English language arts into history, science, social studies, and technical subjects. When we look more closely at how the language arts and critical thinking are used in the world beyond the classroom, it's easy to see the wisdom of this approach.

THE POWER OF GOOD QUESTIONS

In the prologue to her nonfiction bestseller, *The Immortal Life of Henrietta Lacks,* author Rebecca Skloot (n.d.) tells a story about the day that launched her writing career. Skloot recalls being a 16-year-old, sitting in a biology classroom, and learning about an African American woman whose cells have been used for decades of scientific research. Millions of "HeLa" cells—used to develop the polio vaccine, for cloning, and in gene mapping—were grown from cancerous tissue taken from Henrietta Lacks in 1951, shortly before she died.

When that biology class ended, Skloot followed her teacher, Donald Defler, into his office to ask a string of questions: *Where was Henrietta Lacks from? Did she ever know how important her cells were? Did she have any children?* He had no idea, but Skloot knew there must be more to the story. Then he made a suggestion that stuck with her: If you're curious, why don't you see if you can find out anything more about her? He even offered extra credit. Over the years, as she went on to pursue college and graduate studies, Skloot kept returning to the mystery of Henrietta Lacks. *Who was this woman?*

"I couldn't shake the questions Henrietta's cells raised in my mind, and nearly a decade later when I took my first writing class, my curious obsession with Henrietta was the first thing I wrote about," Skloot explained in an interview after her book was published (Skloot, n.d.).

In hindsight, Skloot can see how her own family circumstances fed her youthful curiosity. When she was a teenager, her father fell ill with a mysterious virus that affected his brain, sapping his concentration along with his physical strength. She regularly drove him to the hospital for experimental treatments. Reflecting on that experience years later, she said, "I was experiencing the hopes that can come from science, but also the frustration and fear . . . I asked the questions I did because I was a kid wrestling with watching my own father being used as a research subject" (Skloot, n.d.).

That personal connection helps to explain Skloot's initial inquiry in high school. But it also took extreme persistence—overcoming one hurdle after another—to keep her going on the topic for a decade. She credits her staying power to the same personality traits that had caused her to struggle in school when she was younger. She failed her first year in a traditional high school, only to thrive in an alternative setting. The difference was the invitation to direct her own learning. Her parents, she said in a public presentation about her work, "allowed me to follow my curiosity because they realized it was the best way to make sure I actually did something."

As an adult, when Skloot hit roadblocks in her HeLa research or when publishers rejected her early book proposals, "the teenager in me refused to listen. That's the side of me that doesn't give up. What had been a liability when I was younger became a big asset later" (Boss, 2012).

Her dogged pursuit of answers took her from university science labs to dirt-poor tobacco farms. Skloot interviewed everyone from faith healers to family members of the late Henrietta, delving into hard questions about race, medical ethics, and social justice. As a writer intent on making science accessible to a wide audience, she set a high bar for satisfactory answers. "I really wanted to tell all sides of the story in a balanced way, so I spent extensive time researching the science and the scientists, and the evolution of bioethics, as well as Henrietta, her cells, and her family," she explained (Skloot, n.d.). She stuck with it like a detective on a case until, finally, she was ready to share the amazing story of Henrietta with the world. Skloot's story shows just how far a good question can take us.

For another example of the power of inquiry, consider a young journalist named Eli Boardman. At age 6, he started publishing a weekly newspaper about his community of Boulder, Colorado. By age 11, he had published his 200th issue. He got the idea to start his own newspaper during family walks around the neighborhood. "He said, 'We see them [neighbors] all the time, and we don't know who they are, and I want to know them better,'" Eli's mom, Karen Boardman, explained in an interview with Boulder's "other" newspaper, the *Daily Camera.* Eli summed up what he has learned through his writerly investigations with this bit of wisdom: "Every person has a story and you just have to ask" (Snider, 2012).

Sometimes, students leverage the power of inquiry to make a difference in their world. That was the case for a class of eighth graders at Amana Academy, a public charter school in Alpharetta, Georgia, that emphasizes STEM along with service learning and environmental stewardship. Students focused a recent investigation on the issue of homelessness. Specifically, they wanted to find out if they could use their understanding of science to improve temporary housing for homeless people in their community.

Teacher Cherisse Campbell partnered for the project with an Atlanta nonprofit called Mad Housers that provides temporary huts for people who are homeless. Before her students could suggest and test design improvements for the huts, they first had to understand what it's like to be homeless. The entry event for the project was a visit to a homeless camp, where students used their communication skills to interview residents. What they learned firsthand—and from follow-up research about homelessness—caused them to confront their own biases and to challenge media portrayals of homeless people. One student observed: "The media portrays that the people who are homeless are out there for a reason. That was stuck in my head until I was out there and met the people. They were normal like me and they wanted a way to come back. I think that the huts are the first step" (Felton, 2012).

Based on their interviews and observations, students gained new understanding of the shortcomings of the huts, such as trouble with heating, cooling, lighting, safety, sanitation, and so forth. Back in the classroom, students dug into research and problem solving. They used the scientific method to experiment with heat-transfer options, for instance, comparing the results for conduction, radiation, and convection. They made prototypes of suggested design improvements that incorporated sustainable resources. One team suggested making insulation out of lunch trays. Another designed a solar oven to heat bricks, which would keep a hut occupant warm at night.

Finally, students shared their proposals in a public exhibition. It was attended not only by parents but also by the director of the Mad Housers. Nick Hess said later, "What pleased me is that these students really were doing it right" (Felton, 2012). Students were able to thoroughly explain and advocate for their proposals, backing up their suggestions with scientifically reliable data.

By emphasizing inquiry in interdisciplinary projects that draw on the language arts, we set the stage for students to pose and pursue the questions that most interest them. Whether they wonder about neighborhood news or improving housing for marginalized citizens, they can hone and apply their language skills through research, interviews, observations, and writing and speaking in a variety of genres and formats. When students share the results of their inquiries with audiences—in podcasts, broadcasts, public or online forums, or print or digital publications—they gain even more opportunities to use language in authentic ways.

Here are a few examples of driving questions for projects that integrated the language arts and the real-world results of the investigations that followed:

Driving Question: How can we all cross the finish line together?

Result: Students took part in "26 Seconds," a national advertising campaign in which they challenged one another not to become statistics (every 26 seconds, a student in the U.S. drops out of high school). Students produced a video intended to appeal to a specific audience—their peers.

Driving Question: Can we help the blue fender butterfly?

Result: Students learned that a butterfly species relies on a prairie habitat that is rapidly diminishing. Their letter-writing and leafleting campaign got the community's attention, and a local park was returned to prairie.

Driving Question: How is a story like a pebble dropped in water?

Result: Elementary students interviewed family members for a podcasting project called Stories from the Heart (Cheung, 2010). By making their interviews public, the class helped listeners learn from each other's stories and recognize the importance of drawing out stories from their own families.

Driving Question: What can we do to address modern-day slavery around the world?

Result: After reading a novel about a girl who was trafficked, students launched a social media campaign to speak out against modern-day slavery. They incorporated research on human rights to add authority to what could have been a strictly emotional appeal.

Driving Question: How should we honor the heroes in our community?

Result: Students interviewed civil rights activists who were Freedom Riders during the 1960s and created a traveling museum exhibit about their contributions and sacrifices. By gathering oral histories and photographs, students created historically valuable primary source materials. They interpreted their findings with the dual goals of educating others and also honoring the contributions of important citizens.

Driving Question: How can ethics keep up with science?

Result: After reading Mary Shelley's *Frankenstein*, students investigated contemporary ethical issues of cloning, stem cell research, and bioengineering. For an online publication, they weighed pros and cons of controversial issues and supported their positions with scientific evidence and expert testimony.

In each of these examples, students are using language to help them figure out—and share—the answers to their open-ended questions.

They are writing to understand, just as experts do. As author Joan Didion (1976) reminds us: "I write entirely to find out what I'm thinking, what I'm looking at, what I see and what it means."

ENCOURAGE GOOD TALK DURING PROJECTS

Published work—which may involve learning about different formats, genres, and publishing tools—is often the culminating product of PBL in the language arts. En route to publication, however, students are engaged in a range of activities that deepen their literacy skills. Along with reading and writing, projects engage students in the equally important activities of talking and listening, thinking and rethinking. When students are in the midst of active project investigations, encourage robust discussions—between peers, among groups, and as a whole class.

If students are grappling with challenging texts as part of their research, help them deepen their understanding by encouraging what reading experts describe as "literate conversations." As Allington and Cunningham (2011) explain:

> Literate conversation is different from literacy interrogation, yet interrogation is most commonly used in classrooms. Interrogation involves asking students questions you know the answer to . . . Questions that facilitate literate conversation have no single correct answer. Ask the first question to ten different readers, and you will get ten different—and equally correct—answers. Each student response provides the opportunity for a follow-up question or comment, and the follow-up question won't typically have one correct answer either. (p. 141)

A teacher who is engaging in literacy interrogation might ask students a general question (for example: What is the main idea the author is trying to convey?). Or an interrogation might get more specific (for example: Why does Martin Luther King, Jr., say he came to Birmingham?). Questions that generate literate conversations, in comparison, sound more like this: Does this story remind you of anything else you have read? What were you thinking about as you finished reading? (Allington & Cunningham, 2011, p. 142). Instead of glossing over the surface details of a book (asking for recall of who-what-where-when details), literate questions encourage students to think more deeply about what they have read and why it matters. Such conversations feel more like a lively book club discussion than a question-and-answer session led by a teacher.

By facilitating more literate conversations, a teacher also models the kind of conversation he or she hopes students will have with one another. With less emphasis on direct instruction and more small-group discussions, projects should naturally lead to robust classroom conversation. In one study, an elementary school that combined inquiry-based science with language arts saw gains in student achievement. The longer students spent in the inquiry setting, the more they improved in core content areas. Researchers found that hands-on inquiry activities not only provided a context for learning but also allowed learners to engage in more authentic conversation (Amaral, Garrison, & Klentschy, 2002). Similarly, a study of middle school and high school language arts students found that discussion-based inquiry approaches improved students' literacy skills. Students showed gains across the board, including high-achieving and struggling students (Applebee, Langer, Nystrand, & Gamoran, 2003).

LITERACY-BUILDING ENVIRONMENT

A language arts teacher we met recently was eager to give her students opportunities for more authentic literacy experiences. She signed up for a PBL workshop we conducted for her district. By the end of our 2 days together, she seemed like an enthusiastic convert to project-based instruction. During a follow-up call a few weeks later, however, she was voicing doubts. Why? She worried about letting go of classroom strategies that had always served her students well. For instance, she encouraged a love of literature by asking students to read at least one book each term for pure enjoyment. When we asked why she was jettisoning this fine tradition, she said, "It just isn't part of the project."

Time for a course correction! We asked her to picture an accomplished person who works with language—perhaps a journalist, songwriter, or documentary filmmaker. Wouldn't this person keep a stack of books or magazines on the nightstand (or perhaps downloaded on an e-reader) and read for pleasure? Isn't this someone who would choose words with care, drawing on a vocabulary that continues to expand through personal engagement with literature, film, and other media? Reassured, the teacher reinstituted her reading-for-pleasure assignment, which she now saw as part of the larger context for helping her students become proficient readers, writers, and critical thinkers.

A good project environment doesn't eliminate proven strategies for increasing literacy. Instead, projects offer students motivating reasons to expand their language arts skills.

At Manor New Technology High School in Texas, for example, students were drawn into reading classic literature by a project that integrated science and engineering. Their challenge: improve on the weaponry used by the losing side in *The Epic of Gilgamesh* so that the vanquished might emerge as victors. To succeed, students had to understand the epic poem in detail.

In a few carefully phrased sentences, the *Common Core State Standards for English Language Arts* describe the skills and dispositions of a literate person:

> [They] readily undertake the close, attentive reading that is at the heart of understanding and enjoying complex works of literature. They habitually perform the critical reading necessary to pick carefully through the staggering amount of information available

today in print and digitally. They actively seek the wide, deep, and thoughtful engagement with high-quality literary and informational texts that builds knowledge, enlarges experience, and broadens worldviews. They reflexively demonstrate the cogent reasoning and use of evidence that is essential to both private deliberation and responsible citizenship in a democratic republic. (National Governors Association Center for Best Practices, Council of Chief State School Officers, 2010, p. 3)

What's more, the standards call for increasing rigor and critical thinking as students progress from grade to grade. By their senior year in high school, students are expected to spend 70% of their reading and writing time on nonfiction. Meeting these goals is unlikely without an emphasis on increasingly challenging yet engaging literacy experiences throughout a student's K–12 years.

The National Council of Teachers of English, in a publication that addresses the *CCSS*, emphasizes that it remains up to teachers to determine *how* to meet these learning goals:

Teachers who immerse their students in rich textual environments, require increasing amounts of reading, and help students choose ever more challenging texts will address rigor as it is defined by the *CCSS*. This means keeping students at the center, motivating them to continually develop as writers and readers, and engaging them in literacy projects that are relevant to their lives. When students feel personal connections, they are much more willing to wrestle with complex topics/texts/questions. (Wessling, 2011, p. 11)

Across the arc of a project, students are likely to encounter a variety of situations in which they will need specific, deliberate help to build their literacy skills. Some will be opportunities for whole-class instruction, while other situations will lend themselves to just-in-time work with small groups or individuals.

Here are a few scenarios that are likely to arise during projects that integrate the language arts.

CURATING CONTENT

Early in her teaching career, Sarah Brown Wessling, 2010 National Teacher of the Year, started designing reading experiences "in such a way that texts would talk to each other." This approach helps students understand that reading doesn't happen in isolation; understanding comes from making connections. As she explains:

The Stranger wasn't as powerful without excerpts of *Sophie's World*, Charlie Chaplin, or punk rock music to amplify it. Our investigation of it wasn't complete without juxtaposing Camus to Jean-Paul

Sartre's *No Exit* to offer contrast, to spark questions, to prompt curious distinctions. Before long, we were hearkening back to Salinger, Peter Kuper's graphic novel of *The Metamorphosis*, and *One Flew Over the Cuckoo's Nest*. . . . I had not only learned to teach thematically, but I had also learned how to design a recursiveness in text selection that mirrored and honored the kind of recursiveness we practiced as writers, thinkers, viewers, and readers. (Wessling, 2011, p. 23)

Through her careful and deliberate selections of texts, Wessling acts as content curator for her students' learning experience. Her choices—including graphic novels and music along with more traditional readings—set the stage for students to make connections across genres, leading to deeper understanding.

Remember Birkdale Intermediate, the New Zealand school that teaches through inquiry-based projects called Quests? The Birkdale staff is similarly deliberate about curating content for each Quest so that students have ready access to high-quality, multimedia resources during their investigations. These might include texts, maps, photos, videos, and perhaps interviews with expert sources. "Students can still go find more resources on their own," notes Birkdale Principal Richard Coote during a personal interview, but teachers are assured that students will be starting their investigations with a storehouse of rich and meaningful content.

The school's long-term goal, of course, is to produce independent learners who can find and assess information on their own and then make their own meaning. They will become their own curators who know how to search for, assess, and give credit for content; provide context; and remix material in original ways to create something new. Getting students to that level of information fluency takes time. In the meantime, Coote says, content curation by teachers provides students with necessary scaffolding "to make sure they set off in the right direction."

Teachers who are accustomed to more traditional instruction may need to rethink when and how they introduce specific readings or offer background explanations during PBL. In an ongoing research project led by researchers from the University of Washington, teachers have redesigned Advanced Placement courses to integrate project-based learning methods. Goals are to encourage deeper mastery of content and to make AP courses more accessible to diverse student populations. The PBL design emphasizes putting engagement first before introducing lectures, texts, or more traditional explanations of content (Boss et al., 2012).

What does this look like in practice? Here's how researchers described a project called Congress 111 in a redesigned AP government class. Notice that students are demonstrating a high level of competency when it comes to reading, writing, listening, and speaking:

One day of Congress 111 might feature legislative committee work, the next day a lecture or preparation for a floor debate, and the next day a mid-unit assessment of student learning. Homework consisted of reading, planning, and reviewing as well as working collaboratively at the project's website at www.legsim.org. A few students in each classroom were designated videographers and would use Flipcams to interview classmates and film committee meetings and other legislative events. Eventually, a culminating performance activity—a floor debate with an elected speaker presiding—completed the project. An adult expert (e.g., a lawyer or legislator) was invited to play a role in the culminating performance. This elevated the authenticity of the project while affording students feedback on which aspects of their performance rang true or not to the expert's knowledge and experience. (Parker, Mosborg, Bransford, Vye, Wilkerson, & Abbott, 2011, p. 541)

→Tech Spotlight

A number of technology tools help with content curation, enabling teachers or students to pull digital information from a variety of sources, comment on it, and make it shareable. For example:

- Storify (http://storify.com/) enables users to turn content published on social media (such as Twitter, Facebook, YouTube, Flickr) into annotated stories. For example, after each weekly #PBLChat on Twitter, a curator from New Tech Network produces a Storify that serves as an archive of that week's event. See examples here: http://storify.com/newtechnetwork.
- Scoop.it (www.scoop.it) is a curation tool that allows anyone to create an online magazine on any topic. Users pull content from the Web using RSS feeds or keyword searches. Here's an example of a Scoop.it focusing on PBL: http://www.scoop.it/t/project-based-learning-a-recipe-for-lifepractice.
- Pinterest (http://pinterest.com/) is a virtual bulletin board tool. Users "pin" images or other content to their interest boards. Here's an example that focuses on reading: http://pinterest.com/mydaisydoodle/reading/.

BUILDING INFORMATION LITERACY

Today's students live in a world awash in information. Information literacy means being able to gather, evaluate, and make use of that ever-expanding store of data. ISTE's National Educational Standards for Technology-Students, the NETS-S, offer a vision of a competent learner who can plan strategies to guide inquiry and locate, organize, analyze, evaluate, synthesize, and ethically use information from a variety of sources of media. These learning goals align with inquiry projects that make good use of digital tools.

During the investigation phase of a project, help students focus on how to find and evaluate information. This is an opportunity to deepen students' critical thinking by encouraging them to ask and discuss such questions as

- What do I know about the source of this information?
- How reliable or trustworthy is this source? (How can I find out?)
- Does the author or publisher have a bias or specific point of view? (How can I tell?)

(Schloss, Franz, Thakur, & Wojcicki, 2012)

As students proceed with creating and perhaps publishing original content, teach them to be mindful of proper attribution of content. Library media specialists can be excellent resources and collaborators to help students address these goals.

→Tech Spotlight

A variety of technology tools can help students navigate online research. For example

- Diigo (www.diigo.com) is a social bookmarking tool and then some. At its simplest, Diigo enables users to track links online and share resources with an online community (such as a project team or classroom group). In addition, users can add comments to text with virtual sticky notes. This enables readers to engage directly with the text, practicing critical-thinking skills and close reading.
- Instagrok (www.instagrok.com) is a search engine specifically for education. Special features include visual representations that show connections among topics. Users who create accounts can track their research in online journals.

LEARNING SCAFFOLDS FOR READING, WRITING, AND SPEAKING SKILLS

Guiding students toward high-quality project work involves supporting them throughout their learning journeys. When students are provided with appropriate scaffolding to tackle challenging reading and to develop as writers and speakers, they are able to perform at levels they couldn't reach otherwise (National Research Council, 2000).

During the research phase of a project, for instance, students may encounter unfamiliar vocabulary and challenging texts beyond their reading levels. Guide students to break complex reading into manageable chunks and deliberately teach strategies to analyze texts for reliability, bias, or faulty logic (Marzano & Heflebower, 2012). Use techniques such as paired reading or reciprocal teaching to help students support each other's understanding. Introduce Socratic seminars to help students think critically (and audibly) about what they are reading.

→Project Signpost 7: Ensure Individual Growth in Team Efforts

Students collaborating on a project team are likely to bring to it a wide range of literacy skills. Make sure all students on the team—not just the strongest readers—are thinking critically about important content and developing their skills as writers and speakers. To ensure that all learners are developing their language arts skills, your assessment plan might include individual writing assignments in addition to team products. For example, students might be expected to submit individual research papers about a particular aspect of their team project. If public speaking skills are going to be assessed, your rubric or scoring guide should set expectations for all team members to contribute to the presentation.

The writers' workshop model—with built-in cycles of peer feedback and revision—is an ideal fit for the writing that happens during projects in any subject. Remind students that engaging in writers' workshops is not just for English class; doing so will help improve results in every discipline.

Teachers will likely use a variety of formative assessment tools during projects to monitor students' progress and adjust their instruction. Mini-lessons for a project that integrates language arts might focus on an aspect of grammar or essay organization that's proving to be difficult for student writers, guided reading of difficult texts, or technology tips for editing a digital story or podcast. Some teachers encourage students to request mini-lessons when they feel the need for specific help. One corner of a classroom whiteboard, for example, might be reserved for posting such requests relating specifically to the language arts.

The interdisciplinary nature of projects may prove an advantage to students who struggle in a particular discipline. Framing a scientific concept in the context of history or art, for example, may draw in students who do not express a strong interest in science (Moje, Young, Readence, & Moore, 2000). Incorporating student voice and choice in projects is a motivator for all students, but perhaps especially so for youth at risk of disengaging from academics.

WHAT'S NEXT?

Chapter 8 focuses on inquiry in the social studies. A professional historian reflects on the thinking skills and dispositions that are essential in his field. We hope you will journey with us into this exploration of the social studies even if it's not the subject you teach. Much like language arts, social studies offers authentic opportunities for interdisciplinary projects.

8

Social Studies

Canadian history teacher Neil Stephenson sees the world as one big learning opportunity. When he came across the museum exhibit Canada in a Box: Cigar Containers that Store Our Past, he knew he'd struck it rich. Collected and curated by Dr. Sheldon Posen of the Canadian Museum of Civilization, the cigar box exhibit covers a large swath of Canadian history, with each box telling a bit of what Canadians are about, who and what they value, what they think is funny, and what it means to be Canadian. Thus, Stephenson's Cigar Box Project was born.

Stephenson's 12- and 13-year old students set to work, operating as historians do to understand Canada's colorful history. They examined the commercial art on cigar boxes, researched the people and events they portrayed, and sought to interpret the stories the panels illustrated. They met with museum curator and historian Posen to share their interpretations, ask questions, and go deeper.

Students started to wonder, as historians do, about the stories the boxes *didn't* tell. Intent on revealing a more comprehensive account of the past, students pulled on gloves and wielded magnifying glasses to study other artifacts of history. Through iterative cycles of questioning, research, and interpretation, a more nuanced story of Canada emerged, one that included human events that often escape the history books.

Now Stephenson's students were ready to present their interpretations of the past in cigar boxes of their own. They studied graphic design and learned to use a digital editing program to create illustrated panels that were historically accurate and beautiful to behold.

At first glance it would appear the theme of cigar boxes was the glue that held the project together, but at a deeper level it was the disciplinary practices of historians that shaped the investigation. With Stephenson's guidance and mentoring from their "colleague" Dr. Posen, students donned the mantle of the expert, inquiring, investigating, using the tools and methods of the discipline, holding up their conclusions for the scrutiny of others, and presenting their interpretations in meaningful ways.

Even those of us who are not history teachers can appreciate the power of the Cigar Box Project. Stephenson's students learned deeply because they inquired as experts do. They honed new skills, many of the 21st-century variety. They worked in earnest to produce high-quality and memorable work.

Many social studies teachers, like Stephenson, are retooling their learning environments and creating opportunities for students to work as economists, lawyers, city planners, folklorists, activists, philosophers, anthropologists, and philanthropists.

Subjects of the social studies lend themselves to the project approach. Because they are based in the human experience, real-world connections abound. In this chapter we examine three principles for designing quality projects. They include

- Aligning student work to the values embodied in the social studies
- Designing for personal meaning
- Working in the manner of professionals and active citizens

A SUBJECT AT RISK

Given stringent testing mandates for other subjects, social studies subjects risk being put in the back seat of the school curriculum. With lengthened periods or even double doses of reading and math, students spend less time studying the arts, science, physical education, and social studies.

A 2007 report by the Center on Education Policy describes the shift in time in instruction among subjects as school districts responded to the *No Child Left Behind* mandate.

Grades K–5. Among districts that reported increasing time for English/language arts and math (i.e., most of them), 72% indicated that their elementary schools reduced time by a total of at least 75 minutes per week for one or more other subjects. Of these, more than half (53%) cut instructional time in social studies from 239 to 164 minutes, or exactly 75 minutes.

Grades 6–12. Middle and high school programs have increased credit requirements for math and science and, in low-performing schools, increased the number of reading/language arts credits students must take. Reporting for these grade bands isn't as tidy as for K–5, but any way you look at it, for most of their school career, today's students are spending less time learning social studies.

Why is this a problem? Competence in these subjects has a benefit that goes beyond the individual. The ideals embodied in the study of culture, history, economics, government, geography, and global issues are central to a functioning society. Quality learning experiences help students learn more than a body of knowledge based on facts and dates; they help them develop character, a sense of connectedness, and civic responsibility.

PRINCIPLES FOR PROJECT PLANNING

Project design methods are described in Chapter 5, but before you launch into planning, let's examine fundamental qualities of the social studies and let three planning principles guide your work.

Planning Principle 1: Make Certain Projects Reflect Values of the Social Studies

The values and intentions underpinning the social studies can serve as organizers for planning projects. If the purpose of learning social studies isn't reflected in work we ask students to do, then their toil has no return for the individual, nor for society in which each can have an impact. Let's return to the rationale for having students learn the subjects of the social studies.

The National Council for the Social Studies (1994) describes the intentions of teaching the subject this way. Social studies is the

integrated study of the social sciences and humanities to promote civic competence. The primary purpose of social studies is to help young people make informed and reasoned decisions for the public good as citizens of a culturally diverse, democratic society in an interdependent world. (p. 3)

Think back to Neil Stephenson's Cigar Box Project. As his students learn history, they also are learning whose stories are most prominent in Canada's historic narrative. Their civic competence continues to grow beyond the project as they encounter more building blocks of culture. They might continue to ask whether there is validity to the old maxim, "History is told by the victors."

Planning Principle 2: Align Projects With Students' Personal Concerns

If, as we've said, social studies are based in the human experience, then why do many students turn off and tune out during social studies?

Factoid 1. There are nine Facebook fan pages called, "I Hate Social Studies."

Factoid 2. On Twitter, teachers discuss ways to make social studies pertinent to students' lives so they will care and learn. Follow their conversations by filtering tweets using the hashtag #sschat.

Making social studies meaningful is imperative, both as a starting point and as a through line for projects. If a course of study is inert, if it isn't made relevant to their personal interests and concerns, students can't learn, remember, use, appreciate, or build on what they've been taught.

Think of one social studies lesson, unit, or project you teach that always goes over well with students. Why does it resonate and "stick"? Is it because it taps into your students' interests or concerns?

A position paper of the National Council for the Social Studies (1991) recommends aligning curriculum and instruction with what kids care about—"unifying motifs" that represent developments in children's social and emotional intelligence. The motifs include

- Concern with self: development of self-esteem and a sense of identity
- Concern for right and wrong: development of ethics
- Concern for others: development of group- and other-centeredness
- Concern for the world: development of a global perspective

Each of the 10 themes of the social studies (summarized on pp. 94–95) can be associated with one or more of these developing intelligences. Attend to these as you design projects to make sure students' experiences really count.

"The most upsetting realization I had . . ."

In Chapter 1, Diana Laufenberg's government class mimicked the actions of average people navigating bureaucratic processes. Remember Grace, the student who applied for a green card? Her reflection makes it clear that the work drew on and developed her concern for right and wrong and her concern for others, especially immigrants whose English language skills put them at a disadvantage.

Planning Principle 3: Have Students Adopt the Mantle of the Expert

Learning experiences are most powerful when they mirror authentic experiences that occur outside of school. Authenticity is important because, without it, students have limited access to the perceptions and skills capable people meaningfully and purposefully employ. Neither can they appreciate the relevance of their learning to them or their future. As we discussed in principle 2, subject matter becomes inert if it lacks meaning.

The positive effect of authenticity on achievement was recently documented in an experimental study of differential instruction in Advanced Placement economics courses. In the control group, classes of students learned through conventional lecture-and-textbook study. In the experimental group, students learned the skills of economists as they solved close approximations of real-world problems.

One project example? Teams of economic leaders from two island nations pursue the possibility of trade by analyzing data on the hours it takes to produce goods, identifying economic benefits that occur with specialization of production and trade, and calculating comparative advantage.

Students from high-performing schools did well on the AP test regardless of method. Students in low-performing schools fared better if they had taken the PBL course. Additionally, on a separate test of problem solving, all students in the PBL course outscored their peers in the traditional course (Finkelstein, Hanson, Huang, Hirschman, & Huang, 2010).

An added bonus? Teachers scored higher in satisfaction with PBL teaching materials and methods than those in the control group!

Learn From Capable Adults

Both professional people and engaged citizens work in the realm of the social studies, and students can learn from the practices of those who contribute to the human narrative or have an impact on how society functions.

Let's hear from one who has made history his professional focus.

Expert Thinker: H. W. Brands, Historian, personal interview

How does the world work? That big, open-ended question seized the interest of H. W. "Bill" Brands long before he became a historian. Reading news accounts of the Vietnam War as a teenager, he found himself pondering, "How did this happen? Why did we do this? How can we make sure we don't do something like this again?" He came up with a plan: "After I figure out how the world works, I will explain to other people how the world works, and maybe then we will figure out how to improve the working of the world."

In hindsight, he admits, "that's a remarkably naïve question. The world works in complicated ways, and everybody has a different explanation."

A prolific author, and twice a finalist for the Pulitzer Prize, Brands often tackles questions that get at human nature. Or, as he puts it, "What is it that makes people do what they do?" His biographies have explored the lives and times of Teddy Roosevelt (*T.R.: The Last Romantic*), FDR (*Traitor to His Class: The Privileged Life and Radical Presidency of Franklin Delano Roosevelt*), and Benjamin Franklin (*The First American: The Life and Times of Benjamin Franklin*), to name a few.

Not by accident, writing biographies has enabled Brands to connect with a larger audience. "Earlier in my career, when I would tell people I was writing a history book, I could see their eyes glaze over. They remembered a really boring history class in high school. But if I'd say, I'm writing a biography of Andrew Jackson, people would say, oh, biography! I really like people. That told me something," he adds. "We all want to know about other people's lives."

A high school teacher for a decade before shifting to higher education, Brands considers his readers to be "an extension of my classroom." At the University of Texas at Austin, where he is the Dickson Allen Anderson Centennial

(Continued)

(Continued)

Professor of History, he teaches both undergraduates and graduate students. Teaching and writing are "quite closely connected. I think of my readers as students I just haven't met yet."

Engaging young people in the study of history can be a challenge. For a teenager to be thinking about history "is relatively unnatural," he admits. "They're thinking about the future, not the past. The older we get, the more history of our own we have, the more naturally history comes to us." When Brands lectures to public audiences, it's not unusual for the average age to be 70.

How might we help history come alive for the current generation of students? What helps young people learn to think about problems in the way that historians do? Brands offers some pointers.

Start with the present. "I have a better chance of engaging students' interest if I talk about something that's happening today. I often teach from today's headlines. It's relatively easy to go from the events of the day to ask: So how did this situation come about? How did we get here?"

Make it personal. "If I can get students to read old diaries or old letters, if they can see that people in history were people like them, then they may find that engaging. A student might read the letters of young Abraham Lincoln and realize, here was somebody who was also dealing with issues of, Who am I? What career should I follow?"

Evaluate information. "With so much information available on the Internet, we can access materials today that weren't available 10 years ago except to people with specialized credentials and research budgets. This also means that evaluating of evidence is more important than it used to be. There's so much stuff online, and much of it is noisy and can be self-interested. There's almost no expense to publish it. I encourage students to ask: How reliable is this? Is the source somebody with an ax to grind? Even with an authoritative-looking published book, you still just have the author's word to go on. Do you require corroborating evidence? Is there a reason to believe it?"

Talk it out. "Sometimes students get stuck. They don't know what topic to research. But there's got to be something that interests them. So we'll talk. I'll ask, 'What brought you into this class?' Maybe they have an interest in a particular president. If I can get them talking about their interests, they'll realize that there was more in their head than they knew was there. That helps if they're having a hard time getting ideas down on paper, too. Almost no one has a speaking block."

Be inspiring. "Information is the death of interest in history if information comes first. I tell my students, if I fill you with information but bore you, you'll start to forget your information as soon as you walk out of the final exam. On other hand, if I inspire you with interest in history, then you will continue to teach yourself history for the rest of your life. History is a very accessible subject. It's not like chemistry or physics. If you're interested in history and you can read, the world is open to you."

Brands doesn't expect all his students to go into what he calls "the history business." What they gain from studying the discipline are reasoning and communication skills that will serve them well in life, regardless of their career choices. "If you can think and communicate, then you'll have a leg up."

What else belongs in a historian's toolkit? Here are four tools Brands considers essential:

1. **Curiosity:** "History is for the curious. If you want to know why the U.S. is the way it is, if you want to know why the position of women in Africa is the way it is, if you want to know why this world exists, then history is for you."

2. **Empathy:** "If you're going to understand the past, you have to be able to put yourself in the position of people who lived in the past—the people you're studying. If you simply go to the past seeking confirmation for your current prejudices, you might find the confirmation but you're certainly not going to understand the past."

3. **Facility with reading:** "If reading is a chore, then you're probably not going to make a very good historian. You have to read through lots of stuff. And if you take this on as a job, you can't read every book from start to finish. There will be parts that have information you need and parts that do not. In fact, you'll find yourself putting down books that you find interesting because you have to work to do!"

4. **Love of writing:** "I have some colleagues who don't particularly like to write. The fun part for them is tracking down the information. Then it's like pulling teeth getting them to write. But the rest of the world can't evaluate the kind of research you did until you write it down. I'm often asked, how is it you do so much writing? The simple answer is, I like doing it. Every morning, I get to get up and do this thing I like to do."

FOCUS ON BIG IDEAS

The National Council for the Social Studies organizes the topics of the social studies into 10 thematic strands. Looking at the big questions that relate to each should lead you to driving questions for projects that will be rigorous, meaningful, and engaging. In Table 8.1, we've offered a project snapshot that relates to each theme. What additional project ideas come to mind for you? (See Appendix A for more project examples and resources.)

Table 8.1 NCSS Thematic Strands With Project Snapshots

Thematic Strand	Big Questions	Project Snapshot
Culture	*What role does culture play in human and societal development? What are the common characteristics across cultures? What is the role of diversity and how is it maintained within a culture? How do belief systems, religious faith, or political ideals influence other parts of a culture such as its institutions or literature, music, and art?*	Through oral histories, students tell the stories of their community's newest immigrants.

(Continued)

Table 8.1   (Continued)

Thematic Strand	Big Questions	Project Snapshot
Time, Continuity, and Change	*How do we learn about the past? How can we evaluate the usefulness and degree of reliability of different historical sources? What are the roots of our social, political, and economic systems?*	Students contrast present and past with the help of digital photography. (See Project Spotlight, page 95.)
People, Places, and Environments	*Why do people decide to live where they do or move to other places? How do people interact with the environment and what are consequences of those interactions? How do maps, globes, geographic tools, and geospatial technologies contribute to the understanding of people, places, and environments?*	After examining and comparing globes and maps from different eras, students debate whether political boundaries will ever stop changing.
Individual Development and Identity	*How do individuals grow and change physically, emotionally, and intellectually? Why do individuals behave as they do? What influences how people learn, perceive, and grow? How do social, political, and cultural interactions support the development of identity? How are development and identity defined at other times and in other places?*	Students investigate the significance of youth voice in political uprisings (including Arab Spring, U.S. Civil Rights Movement, and others).
Individuals, Groups, and Institutions	*What is the role of institutions in this and other societies? How am I influenced by institutions? How do institutions change? What is my role in institutional change?*	Students evaluate local nonprofits and determine which one to support with a social media awareness-raising campaign.
Power, Authority, and Governance	*What are the purposes and functions of government? What are the proper scope and limits of authority? How are individual rights protected and challenged within the context of majority rule? What are the rights and responsibilities of citizens in a constitutional democracy?*	After an incident of cyberbullying in their school, students develop their own code of conduct for life online.
Production, Distribution, and Consumption	*What factors influence decision making on issues of the production, distribution, and consumption of goods? What are the best ways to deal with market failures? How does interdependence brought on by globalization impact local economies and social systems?*	After investigating the carbon footprint of out-of-season produce, students develop prototypes for an app that helps shoppers make informed choices at the grocery store.
Science, Technology, and Society	*What can we learn from the past about how new technologies result in broader and sometimes unanticipated social change? Is new technology always better than what it replaces? How can we manage technology so that the greatest numbers of people benefit?*	After studying instances of citizen revolt around the world, students become experts on "smart mobbing" using cell phones and advise heads of state on ways to harness smart mobbing for the good of the people and quell its use for doing harm.

Thematic Strand	Big Questions	Project Snapshot
Global Connections	*What are the different types of global connections? How have these changed over time? What are the benefits from and problems associated with global interdependence? How should people and societies balance global connectedness with local needs? What is needed for life to thrive on an ever-changing and increasingly interdependent planet?*	Students connect with classes in two other countries to produce an online news magazine with a global perspective on youth issues.
Civic Ideals and Practices	*What is the balance between rights and responsibilities? What is civic participation? How do citizens become involved? What is the role of the citizen in the community and the nation and as a member of the world community?*	Using the Civic Action Project framework from the Constitutional Rights Foundation (www.crfcap.org), students address an issue that concerns them and take civic action.

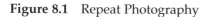

→Project Spotlight: Look Into the Past With Repeat Photography

A bloody battlefield becomes a tranquil pasture. A muddy toll road yields to an eight-lane freeway. A city's centennial celebration is revisited as its sesquicentennial nears. Imagine students interpreting how "then" became "now" as they compare historic photos alongside contemporary views of places in which important events took place.

NCSS Standard Two, Time, Continuity and Change, calls for students to conduct just such analysis. To see how the big questions of the social studies lead naturally to projects, read the following project sketch and then consider how you might put it into action.

Figure 8.1   Repeat Photography

Source: Photo by Jason E. Powell, www.jasonepowell.com.

LOOK INTO THE PAST

Subject(s): History, geography, language arts, photography

Driving Question: How can we document change?

Photograph by Jason Powell

Original taken 1920

Courtesy Library of Congress

Project Sketch: As students prepare for a history tour of Washington, D.C., their teacher presents them with a challenge: Each team is to find an illustration or photograph of a pivotal period or event in D.C. history, visit the site where the event took place, shoot a picture (or even a picture-in-a-picture as shown here), and write an essay describing the significance of the event in its time and its relevance today. When complete, students compile photo essays into a book published for inclusion in the school library (to inform future tour groups) and submitted to the D.C. Historical Society.

Imagine students studying city or state history in this way. What resources and skills might they need as they begin? Consider how you might take advantage of:

Resources

- Access to photography archives. See local or state historical societies and museums, the Library of Congress (http://www.loc.gov/pictures), and the National Archives (http://www.archives.gov).
- Experts: historians, archivists, photographers
- Maps, reference books, online materials
- Collaborative projects such as HistoryPin (www.historypin.com/)
- GPS devices
- Digital cameras

Skills

- Database and other Internet research
- Photography, photo editing
- Navigation using maps and GPS devices
- Visual storytelling

Experts

- Photographers
- Historians
- Archivists
- Docents, tour guides

Do you see opportunities for interdisciplinary connections? Which subjects might you want to include in such a project?

→Tech Spotlight: Making Meaning With Wolfram Alpha, the "Computational Knowledge" Engine

We talk a lot about helping kids do investigations where they make new meaning, but it's challenging to design learning experiences in which they actually do this. The computational knowledge engine Wolfram Alpha (www.wolframalpha.com) is a great resource for students who are investigating social studies topics that involve data. Students hone their critical thinking skills as they learn to craft good questions and evaluate and synthesize information they get from Wolfram Alpha.

Café Coffee Day

Let's explore how to conduct a social studies investigation using Wolfram Alpha. Imagine: An eighth-grade teacher in India wants her students to learn about countries in South Asia. She has students pretend they are business owners in India who want to expand their companies to nearby countries. At heart, this project asks students to compare and contrast to make an informed judgment as they learn about South Asia. To add more student choice to the project, the teacher might give students options to act as philanthropists wanting to support charitable causes or as professional sports executives wanting to expand cricket to more cities. One team selects Café Coffee Day, a popular Indian coffee chain, as its expanding business. The team members make queries in Wolfram Alpha that help them decide on a new country in which to expand.

What would they need to know to make such a decision? They think: If you want to sell a lot of coffee, you should have a lot of people to sell it to, so they start by comparing populations. In Wolfram Alpha they enter, "compare the populations of Bhutan, Sri Lanka, Pakistan, and Bangladesh." Wolfram Alpha returns this table.

Bhutan 708,000

Sri Lanka 20.4 million

Pakistan 185 million

Bangladesh 164 million

They notice that Bhutan has as many people as a mid-sized Indian city, Sri Lanka is comparatively small, and Pakistan and Bangladeshare big.

Next, they wonder about the economic health of the countries. With help from their teacher, they identify per capita income, gross domestic product, and other comparative data that are indicators of economic health. A search of per capita income shows

(Continued)

(Continued)

Bhutan $1,930 per person per year

Sri Lanka $2,020 per person per year

Pakistan $930 per person per year

Bangladesh $497 per person per year

Interestingly, Sri Lanka and Bhutan have greater per capita income but they are much smaller than Pakistan and Bangladesh in sheer numbers of people. The team wonders how this compares to their country. India comes in the middle at $1,077 per capita income per year, and it has a lot of successful Café Coffee Day franchise stores. They note this, and then move ahead.

They make this query in Wolfram Alpha: "Compare GDP of Bhutan, Sri Lanka, Pakistan, and Bangladesh." It returns this information:

Bhutan $1.327 billion per year

Sri Lanka $40.56 billion per year

Pakistan $164.5 billion per year

Bangladesh $79.55 billion per year

So far, Pakistan seems to be a good choice. It's the most populous country, and its GDP and per-capita income are high compared to Bangladesh, the second-most-populated country.

A question occurs to the team: Do people in these countries drink coffee? They type: "Compare coffee consumption of Bhutan, Sri Lanka, Pakistan, and Bangladesh." The search returns this result:

Bhutan (data not available)

Sri Lanka 6,873 sh tn/yr (short tons per year)

Pakistan 899.5 sh tn/yr

Bangladesh 1,141 sh tn/yr

They wonder what these numbers mean. Does any one person drink a lot of coffee or only a little? They wonder if they can use these numbers to calculate per capita coffee consumption. Wolfram Alpha is a step ahead. Scrolling down the same search page, students find:

Percapita coffee consumption

Bhutan (data not available)

Pakistan 0.1764 oz/person/yr (ounces per person per year)

Sri Lanka 11.08 oz/person/yr

Bangladesh 0.2469 oz/person/yr

Sri Lanka might deserve a second look! Or maybe Café Coffee Day should expand its tea offerings. What should the team do next? What else have they to consider in making an informed decision? (Think: supply chains—transportation, roads, fuel costs; business climate—policies around foreign business, civil strife, government, and economic stability.)

Not all of aspects of business climate can be understood using Wolfram Alpha, but you can see how it gives students a start in constructing an argument for selecting a new business location.

Imagine their next step is to present a case for their choice. They can download the data from Wolfram Alpha in the form of a spreadsheet and use a visual display tool like Many Eyes (www-958.ibm.com/software/data/cognos/many-eyes/) or Tableau Public (www.tableausoftware.com/public/) to represent these data graphically so they tell a story.

After they make their case for locating the business in another country, their next task might be to investigate cultural issues to understand what kind of marketing campaign would work best in that country.

Database and Computing Engine

Wolfram Alpha has two major functions. One is responding to queries with information from its vast databases, as in the Café Coffee Day example. If you want to know the properties of a specific star cluster, the cost of a gallon of gasoline in Minnesota, or what languages are spoken in Sierra Leone, you can find out. As you saw in Café Coffee Day, Wolfram Alpha can make comparisons of like data. It can also draw from disparate data sets to derive an answer. For instance, if you want to find out whether there is a correlation between gas prices and the number of cars on the road in Minnesota, you might write: "Minnesota passenger cars in use vs. price of a gallon of gasoline," to which Wolfram Alpha responds with a graph showing the relationship of those data over time.

Wolfram Alpha is also a powerful computing tool. It can simplify an algebraic expression, plot a reciprocal polynomial, or compare a set of ions. It has a type pad for scientific notation and returns graphical representations when those are indicated.

Getting queries right is a bit of a challenge at first, but Wolfram Alpha provides a helping hand. After you submit a query, the engine shows how it interpreted your input. In its way, it lets you know how it "thinks," which makes writing interpretable queries easier with practice. Explore Wolfram Alpha at www.wolframalpha.com and try out its functions. Visit the Examples page and learn how it handles calculus, weather, people and history, engineering, socioeconomic data, words and linguistics, chemistry, sports and games, colors, money and finance, and assorted other topics—many of which connect to the big and interesting universe of the social studies.

WHAT'S NEXT?

Chapter 9 focuses on inquiry in science, a rich domain for project investigations. We'll hear from a prominent scientist whose curiosity about how the world works began at a young age. Once again, we encourage you to come along for the journey even if you don't teach science. Your own curiosity may be sparked by the interdisciplinary project examples ahead.

9

Science

"To a person uninstructed in natural history, his country or sea-side stroll is a walk through a gallery filled with wonderful works of art, nine-tenths of which have their faces turned to the wall. Teach him something of natural history, and you place in his hands a catalogue of those which are worth turning around."

—Thomas Henry Huxley 1825–1895

Projectile motion is one of the fundamental physics concepts that teacher Frank Noschese wants his students to learn at John Jay High School in Cross River, New York. Physics and math teacher John Burk has similar goals for his students in Delaware.

"Projectile motion really is a wonderful topic to study," Burk explains on his *Quantum Progress* blog. "The motion of footballs, golf balls, and astronauts all, on a fundamental level, are controlled by the same single force, and [the fact that] their motion evolves in the same predictable way is very powerful" (Burk, 2011).

Interested in connecting physics with students' interests, these creative teachers set up an investigation of projectile motion around a favorite medium. Can you think what it was? Unless you've been under a bushel for a while, the digital game Angry Birds probably comes to mind.

Instead of starting with units of measurement, kinematics, and vectors, Noschese asks students, "What laws of physics hold in Angry Birds World?" From here, students design investigations to answer questions like these (Noschese, 2011):

- Does the white bird conserve momentum when it drops its bomb? Why would the game designer want the white bird to drop its bomb the way that it does?

- The yellow bird changes velocity with the tap of a finger. Analyze more than one flight path to answer this: What are the details of its change in velocity?
- Based on a reasonable estimate for the size of an angry bird, determine the value of g in Angry Bird World. Why would the game designer want to have g be different than 9.8 m/s²?
- Shoot an angry bird so that it bounces off one of the blocks. What is the coefficient of restitution and the mass of the angry bird?

To investigate these questions, students first make screencasts of game play using Jing, Screencast-O-Matic, or Camtasia Studio. Then they do analysis. To support their scientific thinking, students use tools for data analysis and modeling, such as Logger Pro and Tracker Video. As Noschese explains in an interview about Angry Bird Physics with CUNY-TV's *Science and U!* show, "My goal is to show kids that physics is all around us. They don't have to be rocket scientists to do physics" (Demillo, 2011).

Given the enthusiasm students show for this approach, it won't be surprising if some do become rocket scientists!

A DISCIPLINE FOR THE CURIOUS

Do you consider yourself a scientist? If not, you should. From the time you became aware of your surroundings, you have been investigating—observing, making conjectures, thinking through what might happen in different scenarios, testing hypotheses, weighing evidence, and drawing conclusions. If science lessons always drew on and fueled our inquisitive nature, more of us might think, yes, in my way, I AM a scientist.

Science invites us to discover and appreciate how the world works. Meaningful science projects engage students' curiosity and immerse them in investigations that lead to discovery. As importantly, good projects get at the *nature* of science. That is, they help students understand that science is a particular way of making sense of the world. Projects also give students a forum for communicating their understanding, building their confidence as people who can talk knowledgeably about science.

Recognizing how science works helps us appreciate how we know what we know and how we can learn what is still to be known. Understanding the nature of science helps us grapple with controversial topics such as climate change, food irradiation, or cloning. It helps us distinguish science from nonscience, too, and detect junk science if it's offered to support an argument. These habits of mind help us think more critically and communicate more precisely about a wide range of topics. Science is exacting. Methods are codified so we can arrive at objective results that hold up under rigorous testing. At the same time, science calls for great creativity. This tension between method and imagination makes teaching science a challenge—and an opportunity. It is easy to stay on the safe side, teaching the scientific method and constraining student "discoveries" to predictable labs, but this approach makes it less likely that students will appreciate how science works as a creative human endeavor—an endeavor they can participate in.

By bringing project-based learning into the science classroom, we increase opportunities for students to do the real work of scientists.

Projects invite students to think as scientists do from a young age. Second graders from Conservatory Lab Charter School in Brighton, Massachusetts, applied their scientific know-how to improve the image of reptiles that often get a bad rap. Their interdisciplinary project was aptly titled Don't Be S-s-scared: The Truth About Snakes. One of their products was a music video that students wrote and starred in, set to the tune of Lady Gaga's hit, "Born This Way." It's delightful, to be sure, but the clever lyrics include scientific facts that students discovered during their in-depth investigation of snakes. Students also produced a richly illustrated book, *What Snake Am I? A Clue Book of Snakes From Around the World*, and donated copies to the Harvard Museum of Natural History and a local wildlife sanctuary for use in educational programs.

Here's how teacher Jenna Gampel explains the purpose behind this project that turned her students into young herpetologists: "The focus on snakes was designed to challenge students to think beyond their initial conceptions and misconceptions and to use scientific inquiry to dispel the myths behind people's aversion to this universally feared creature. As students deepened their knowledge, they felt the need to become 'snake ambassadors' and to share the truth about these reptiles with the world" (Gampel, n.d., p. 1).

Opportunities for deep learning expand when we encourage students to investigate scientific questions in the wider world and across disciplines. This doesn't mean that science labs go out the window or that teachers no longer have a hand in guiding investigations. For the snake project, Gampel had students perform a number of specific activities, including observing, questioning, conducting and analyzing surveys, researching, inferring, taking notes, and drawing scientific sketches. With the right approach, we can design projects to balance student-driven and teacher-directed inquiry.

SCIENCE AND THE "EDUCATED PERSON"

Do you ever wonder how we came to teach what we teach? Why "hands-on" learning is something we have to make a case for, and why physics is in the typical curriculum but engineering, the practical application of physics, is not? In the United States, anyway, we are living with decisions made a long time ago about what it means to be an educated person.

In 1893, the National Education Association (yes, the NEA was around back then!) convened a group of academics known as the Committee of Ten and charged it with identifying *the* definitive U.S. secondary school curriculum. At the time, there were 43 states in the union, the majority of the population was spread out among small, rural communities, and education was local in every sense. The movement toward compulsory education was still 30 years away.

The Committee of Ten sought to bring coherence and rigor to education across the nation. Chaired by Harvard University President Charles Eliot, the Committee drew a line separating education into two domains: the studies of school that prepared students for a classical university education, and the practical learning that occurred in home occupations and the trades—that is, hands-on learning.

Their report urged high schools to adopt Latin, Greek, English, modern languages, mathematics, physics, astronomy, chemistry, biology, zoology, physiology, history, civil government, political economy, and geography as the core curriculum. These were the subjects of scholars who worked with *ideas,* not *things.*

The distinction the Committee of Ten made 120 years ago has had a lasting influence. Engineering back then was viewed as a concern of farmers, manufacturers, and machinists, not gentlemen.

Today, proponents of engineering and its modern ally computer science fight to squeeze these subjects into the K–12 curriculum. Why should it matter whether these subjects are taught? Both are central to modern life. We need the power of engineering and computer science to solve long-prevailing problems and confront new ones. As importantly, both subjects offer the "hands-on, minds-on" experiences that develop our intellects.

One bright spot is the "maker" movement, a rapidly growing subculture of tinkerers, inventors, hackers, crafters, and hobbyists who take the do-it-yourself credo to heart. Schools would do well to adopt the maker ethos by giving time to making and outfitting a maker space with design software, 3-D printers, sewing machines, shop tools, and good old twine and wire.

> *Worth noting:* Students whose teachers conduct hands-on learning activities on a weekly basis outperform their peers by more than 70% of a grade level in math and 40% of a grade level in science (Wenglinsky, 2000). Hands-on learning experiences develop hand–eye coordination, spatial reasoning, and problem-solving abilities. Such experiences, once part of everyday life outside of school, are less common now. As inexpensive and disposable goods become the norm, activities like tinkering in basement workshops and sewing from patterns have become practically extinct.

WE LIVE IN AN ENGINEERED WORLD

Ioannis Mioulis, president and director of the Museum of Science, Boston, and former dean of the School of Engineering at Tufts University, asks us to think about engineering's role in education and in life.

Beginning in preschool, students learn about rocks, bugs, the water cycle, dinosaurs, rain forests, the human body, animals, stars and planets, chemical reactions, and physics principles. These are all important topics, but they only address a minute part of our everyday experience.

Take a moment to look around. Imagine how your environment would look without any human-made things. Almost nothing you see or experience would be present—no electricity, no chair, no walls, no book, and maybe no YOU. Without human-made pharmaceuticals and sanitation processes—all engineered—your life expectancy would be 27 years.

How have we reached the ridiculous point where one may be considered illiterate if she does not know how many legs a grasshopper has, yet is considered perfectly fine in not understanding how the water comes out of a faucet? Students in middle school can spend weeks learning how a volcano works, and no time understanding how a car works. How often will they find themselves in a volcano?" (Grasso & Brown Burkins, 2010)

Just as engineering is essential to modern life, so too is computer science. Think of one aspect of your daily life that is not influenced by computing. We have a colleague in computing education who speaks about the integral role of computing and why more (and more kinds of) people should get involved. She challenges her audiences to come up with any aspect of modern life that does NOT involve computing in some way. One audience member thought she had her stumped when she shouted out, "Nail salon!" The presenter, in rapid-fire delivery, came back with: "Point-of-sale systems in cash registers to manage purchasing and inventory, instrumentation used in the formulation of nail polish, graphic design for advertising, business systems for payroll and appointment calendaring, computer chips in the massage chair controllers, shall I go on?"

While computing is ubiquitous, it is also, in many of its manifestations, fairly invisible. Getting kids involved in computing (as more than consumers) has societal benefit and is a 21st-century means of building good brains.

COMPUTERS AS THINGS (FOR EVERYONE) TO THINK WITH

When we think of hands-on learning, we usually focus on the manipulation of physical "stuff." Seymour Papert, deemed by many to be the father of educational computing, thinks of computers as "stuff you think with." Just as a pendulum is a wonderful tool to think with as you explore properties of time and motion, a computer allows you to apply precise logic. Robotics, phone apps, diagnostic tools, networks, and computer-generated imagery are just a few of the expressions of computer logic. Papert considers computers as tools to develop the intellect and invented the LOGO computer language so children could get started with a dead-simple user interface to learn formal logic as it is applied in computing to make things happen.

Papert's constructionist philosophy, situated solidly in constructivism, holds that learning to program a computer is learning not just by doing but by *making*. Being able to pose a problem in such a way that a computer can help you solve it is the cornerstone of computational thinking.

You might not think of participation in fields like engineering and computer science as a social issue, but it is. Jobs in these professions are growing, but few of our students are being prepared for them.

Looking just at computer science, consider this: the U.S. Department of Labor projects that between 2008 and 2018, 1.4 million computing jobs will have opened in the United States. For those jobs that require a bachelor's degree in computing, only 29% can be filled by U.S. computing-degree earners (Bureau of Labor Statistics, 2012b). Too few students study computer science and computer engineering at the college level, and rigorous computing that gets kids ready for these majors is seldom taught in K–12 schools. And, among those who do study computing and go on to technical careers, very few are women and minorities.

Why does this matter? For one, everyone benefits when the pool of people innovating is as diverse as the people using the products of those innovations. Point in fact: the first digitized voicemail system was calibrated to the male voice. Women trying to leave messages were hung up on because their speaking voices were of higher register than the technology was designed to capture. Had women been part of the design team, this issue might not have been overlooked.

Second, computing jobs are plentiful and lucrative, and it is unfair that few of our children are either exposed to computing or encouraged to participate. (The median starting salary for a computer science major in 2012 was $56,000, just below that for the highest-paying job, engineering, at $59,000.)

Fortunately, from the president's *Educate to Innovate* initiative to the National Science Foundation's effort to train 10,000 new computer science teachers by 2015, change is afoot. Look for opportunities to expose your students to computing through projects that incorporate Scratch visual programming, Arduino electronics prototyping, or LEGO robotics (to name a few). These are low-bar approaches that teachers with no background in computing can introduce.

MOVING TOWARD "EXPERT" UNDERSTANDING

A confluence of factors supports doing project-based learning in the sciences as well as interdisciplinary projects that deal with scientific issues.

A call for reconsidering how students learn science comes from the Next Generation Science Standards (NGSS). NGSS represent the continuation of efforts to improve science education that started with the 2061 Science for All Americans initiative in 1985. The intent of reform, then and now, is to promote a constructivist approach that has students investigating as scientists do. This is how they will build a foundation of core concepts and at the same time come to understand the nature of science.

NGSS are organized around core ideas and crosscutting concepts—the basic principles and theoretical constructs of science. Development of the NGSS by the National Research Council has coincided with the debut of the Common Core State Standards. The two sets of standards are mutually reinforcing. CCSS describe what it means to be scientifically literate; NGSS describe the science experiences students should have and the core concepts they should know.

The rationale for focusing on a few core concepts instead of a multitude of discrete pieces of information has to do with how experts and novices differ in their science understanding. Experts understand core principles and the theoretical underpinnings of their subject and rely on these to make sense when faced with new information or a novel challenge. Novices, on the other hand, tend to hold on to many bits of isolated and sometimes contradictory knowledge. Without a firm foundation of core concepts or a sense of how they connect, novices have difficulty grappling with new or complicated ideas.

NGSS recommend that students build their foundation of core concepts by spending less time studying science content and more time operating as scientists do—observing patterns, proposing explanations, developing models based on hypotheses, designing investigations to test their models, gathering and analyzing data, and constructing explanations using evidence-based arguments. Such engagement helps them become less like novices and more like experts. Open inquiry can lead science students to better retention, improved problem solving, and a greater appreciation for what science allows us to accomplish (National Research Council, 2000). Of course, open-ended questions are also what drive learning in PBL. With teacher support and facilitation, students can engage in projects that allow them to adopt the mantle of the scientist.

Expert Insights: Chemist Katie Hunt (personal interview)

How do expert scientists develop their thinking skills? Let's hear from Catherine Hunt, PhD, in a personal interview with the authors. She is the director of innovation sourcing and sustainable technology for Dow Chemical and former president of the American Chemical Society.

Growing up with six siblings, Catherine "Katie" Hunt had a surefire strategy for earning the undivided attention of her father, a chemist. "I asked questions," she recalls, "challenging questions that didn't have simple answers."

She remembers inquiring, at about age 7, "Why do they put salt on the roads in the winter?" Her father would respond to such questions with "full, complete, deep answers." That meant he sometimes used terms she didn't understand—yet. If she looked perplexed when he used a phrase like "freezing point depression," they would walk to his bookshelf, pull down his copy of *Lange's Handbook of Chemistry*, and together compare freezing points for various solutions. Without

(Continued)

(Continued)

talking down to her, he would break down concepts to make them understandable. She reflects, "He had a way of thinking that made you ask: Why does that happen? How does that work? And where else could you use that in something you're trying to do? It's all about connecting."

Not surprisingly, Hunt has followed in her father's footsteps by becoming an accomplished chemist herself. She has also followed the family tradition of encouraging good thinking in budding scientists. As soon as her son started preschool, she began paying classroom visits to help students understand what scientists do and how they think. She engages students by relating new concepts to something familiar, often something they can see or touch. She encourages good questions that get to the heart of how things work.

Baby diapers, for instance, offer a good example of super-absorbent polymers. During one classroom visit to middle school students, Hunt challenged them to think about the properties of super-absorbent polymers. A discussion about what causes the material in disposable diapers to soak up liquids led to a conversation about pH. And that sparked a good question: "How can you change the pH?" One seventh grader suggested, "You let the baby pee in the diaper." Hunt replied, "Exactly!" Next, she got them thinking about using super-absorbent polymers to release water instead of holding it. Where might that be useful? And they were off and running, thinking in the way thatscientists do.

At any age, good science comes from asking good questions.

"You have to constantly put yourself into situations where you don't know what's going on," Hunt recommends. "That's the only time you're going to learn." She follows her own advice. When she goes to professional society meetings, Hunt forces herself to get out of her comfort zone and attend sessions that deal with unfamiliar topics.

She encourages students to study broadly, "because you don't know all the things you'll need to know." She can hold her own in discussions about biotechnology, for example, because years ago, as a postdoc, she audited courses in biochemistry. "I was laying a foundation, even though it didn't have a direct application to what I was doing back then."

Along with curiosity, what else belongs in a scientist's toolkit? Being able to use technology is important, but specific tools are ever changing. More stable are the habits of mind that serve scientists well throughout their careers. Here are a few that Hunt considers essential.

Finding your focus. When Hunt arrives for a school visit, she makes a point of wearing street clothes. "I ask the students, do I look like a scientist? No!" She morphs into a chemist by donning her lab coat, gloves, safety goggles. Like a baseball pitcher going through pregame rituals, she's also getting her mental muscles ready for the work ahead. "It's about moving yourself, getting yourself ready so you can focus and learn and do whatever it is you have to do." Part of focusing is clearing your mind of day-to-day clutter so that you're ready to think. "You have to free up your brain, whether it's through yoga or writing down the things you need to remember, or whatever you do. You need to free your mind so you have room to process new things."

Risk taking. "You have to be able to take chances. You have to be willing to be wrong," Hunt says. "Everything in life doesn't come with directions." She was reminded of this when her son's Montessori teacher advised her, "You can't help your son do everything right the first time." Hunt says she promptly replied, "Why not? I know how to do it right." The teacher wisely said, "Good point! Remember, your son's in third grade. Is there ever a better time to fail, and then learn from your mistakes? There's no down side." (When Hunt's son entered college, he followed the family tradition by pursuing a degree in chemistry.)

Critical thinking. The work of science often involves gathering data, but it takes critical thinking to recognize which results are "garbage data" and which are reliable. Hunt asks herself, "How do you know that it was good data? How do you know that you asked the right question?" She describes one of her favorite strategies as "zooming in, and then panning out." She'll zero in on a question she wants to research by applying the scientific method. Then she pans out for a broader perspective, testing her hypothesis in a variety of ways. "Panning out might be by peer review, or seeing if someone else can repeat your experiment, or reading things others have written, or challenging what others have done."

Mystery loving. Unsolved mysteries suggest new frontiers for science. When she talks with lay audiences, they sometimes mistakenly assume "that we have it all figured out," Hunt says. "It's important to talk about all the things we haven't solved yet." Tomorrow's scientists can anticipate no shortage of good questions to investigate.

COUPLED INQUIRY

While learning though inquiry holds a lot of promise, in practice, student-driven investigations can have uneven results. Teachers, understandably, want to maximize learning in their classrooms and worry that student investigations might be ineffectual and waste time. A brand of instruction called "coupled inquiry" strikes the balance between teacher-directed and student-driven inquiry, providing the right amount of structure and guidance to assure success.

Coupled inquiry is a sequence of teaching and learning activities that leads to solid student-driven science investigations. The approach constrains student activity (in a good way) so it stays focused on the learning objective the teacher has in mind and, at the same time, encourages critical thinking and creativity (Dunkhase, 2003).

Coupled inquiry and PBL go well together. Both begin with the invitation to inquire. The project approach couches the science in a realistic context, and the coupled inquiry method ensures students engage in effective processes of inquiry.

In the example that follows, students study wind power and the function of turbines through the coupled inquiry method. It's easy to imagine expanding from the six steps of this structured inquiry experience into a full-blown project by involving experts and introducing real-life applications and issues around wind power.

Laura Humphreys (2011), fourth-grade teacher in Las Cruces, New Mexico, designed this investigation. The six steps described here show the typical phases of coupled inquiry. We have annotated her plans (in parentheses) to show how such an inquiry exercise could expand to become a project.

1. Invitation to inquiry: The teacher presents a wind turbine she has constructed. Students make predictions about how it will function. They watch the turbine in operation and discuss the attributes they think a wind turbine must have to collect wind energy. (In PBL, this step would come after an entry event, a "grabber" that focuses student attention and situates the learning in a realistic context.)

2. Guided inquiry: Teams recreate the teacher's wind turbine design and test it. In the process, they learn to calculate rotational velocity, record results using a table, and derive average rotational velocity by recording multiple trials. (In PBL, this would be a planned activity to build background knowledge about key concepts before students launch into their own investigations.)

3. Open inquiry: The class reconvenes to discuss the results of the guided inquiry. Students discuss new design possibilities and decide which are testable within classroom constraints. Before proceeding with their open investigations, they decide on an operational definition for effectiveness. They define this as the design that rotates the fastest while maintaining its stability. Teams then choose a question to investigate, focusing on a variable such as surface area, blade length, materials, or number of blades. They present a research plan and then proceed with their investigations. (This is heading in the direction of PBL, as students identify what they need to know to be successful. At this stage, they might also be considering a potential audience. Who would benefit from their investigation? What are the real-world applications for what they are learning?)

4. Inquiry resolution: Teams share their claims and findings from the open-inquiry investigations. Additional material is provided in the form of a grade-level reading or websites about harnessing wind energy using wind turbines. This may lead to a second cycle of inquiry (revisiting step 3) in which teams construct and test new or improved turbines. (In PBL, this leads into the in-depth inquiry phase, when students are engaging in iterative cycles of modeling, testing, and refining their solutions. They might consult with experts at this stage to gain authentic feedback on their models.)

5. Assessment: At this stage, the teacher can assess students' learning based on observation, research logs, presentations, and other means. Or she can give a test in which students examine a variety of wind turbine diagrams or photos and explain which designs would be most effective. Alternatively, she can present a performance task, asking students to choose new variables to test. (In PBL, formative assessment is happening throughout the project, giving

the teacher information to adjust instruction and address misunderstandings. Students' final products—including their public presentations—are formally assessed at the conclusion of the project.)

6. More inquiry: Students might proceed with additional investigations of wind turbines or shift to studying other mechanical devices that operate when a force moves a blade or a shaft. Turbines powered by water (waterwheels, hydroelectric dams) might be one path, and propellers, which operate with power to the shaft, might be another. (In PBL, student interest in related topics might provide the direction for a future project.)

As a coupled inquiry activity, the wind turbine example focuses squarely on physical science. If it were expanded into a project, you can imagine the scope expanding to address environmental science or economic issues. Students might find themselves in the role of experts who are advising a community on whether to consider a wind farm development or where best to site such a project to mitigate danger to wildlife. In such projects, students would need to deeply understand and be able to communicate the science behind their arguments.

→ Project Signpost 8: Beware Recipe-Like Labs

Lab exercises are a useful adjunct to inquiry-based science. Conducting a just-in-time lab can be just what students need to move to a new stage of an investigation. Alan Colburn, professor of science education at California State University at Long Beach, recommends making labs less recipe-like so that they draw on and develop students' critical thinking skills. A first step? Get rid of the data table that accompanies most labs. Have students think about what they are quantifying, the units of measurement they will record, and the way they will structure their data tables. From here, Colburn advises a continued, gradual dismantling of the scaffolds that structure labs, taking students closer to designing their investigations (Colburn, 1997).

SKETCHING A SCIENCE PROJECT

The following sketches demonstrate the wide range of projects that can result from bringing PBL strategies to the science classroom. As you read these five sketches, consider how each example incorporates characteristics of high-quality science projects:

- Realistic task that gets at fresh understanding
- Connects to the science community or those affected by that which is under investigation
- Blends structure and openness as students design investigations
- Develops understanding of the nature of science and contributes to students' development as critical consumers of science information

If a particular project example appeals to you, think about how you might modify it for your grade level or connect it with other disciplines.

THE GREAT CARBON RACE

Sue Boudreau teaches science to eighth graders in Orinda, California. She links class projects, one to the next, so that students see the connections in science content. In a project called The Problem with Oil, students investigated how we extract, transport, and fuel the world with oil. A next logical project focused on greenhouse gases, an issue related to the combustion of oil. In The Great Carbon Race, students were challenged with the question "Who can save the most carbon from entering the atmosphere?" and defend their results using clear, credible evidence for the class courtroom? Students were graded by the quality of their evidence, and the biggest footprint reducers were crowned Carbon King and Carbon Queen. Learn about Boudreau's Take Action Projects at http://takeactionscience.wordpress.com.

CHECKS AND BALANCES

In a physics and engineering project, seniors at Technology High School in Sonoma, California, use engineering methods to study technical failures that lead to real-world disasters. Before diving into a final performance task—an investigation of the 2003 Space Shuttle *Columbia* accident—students learn to pick apart a problem using root cause analysis. They probe issues of workplace culture that interfere with the discovery of engineering problems using Harvard University's corrective and preventive action method. These are the real checks and balances that govern the practices of engineering. You might think this is awfully complex for high school students, but these seniors have been preparing for the challenge since they built working Rube Goldberg machines their freshman year. Technology High takes a systematic approach to its project-based curriculum, providing experiences that increase in complexity and authenticity as students go through school. Learn more about project-based learning at Technology High at http://crpusd.schoolwires.net/Page/622.

WORLD TREE WATCH

Students in Grades 4 and 5 in the United States and Japan observe the role of trees in their communities. They do tree surveys to identify the numbers and kinds of native and cultivated trees. They meet with city arborists to learn about the growing conditions necessary for healthy trees in their location and compare those criteria. Students exchange photos, artistic renderings, haiku poetry, and descriptions that help them compare trees, geography, and climate in the two countries. They each find a tree that can be grown in the other school's environment and send these to the partner school as part of Planting Day ceremonies.

WHY HERE AND NOT THERE?

A second-grade teacher presents students with a world map and monarch butterfly and Australian stick insect specimens. He poses a challenging question: Why here and not there? Why there and not here? How can we find out? He has registered his class in the Square of Life, an Internet-based collaborative project (http://ciese.org/curriculum/squareproj) that has students investigate their local environment and share information with students from around the world. Students examine a square yard of local ground and organize what they find into categories they define themselves: living and nonliving, plants and animals. Through close examination, they organize small creatures into groups by shared characteristics and learn to discriminate between classes of animals, including insects and isopods. They theorize about the role of habitat and niche in insect distribution. They pose questions to their Australian counterparts, share their findings, and report their conclusions about: Why here and not there? Why there and not here?

LOW ENERGY AT THE FITNESS CENTER

A nearby fitness center wants to conserve energy. The director appeals to students to analyze the center's energy usage and propose recommendations. Students study alternative energy sources, complete cost/benefit analyses, examine government weatherization incentive plans, and create and explain graphs to substantiate their findings.

FROM INTERESTS TO OPPORTUNITIES

As you read the previous project sketches, you may have found yourself thinking, "I wish I'd had a chance to learn science this way!" One of the benefits of bringing the project approach to science is the heightened student engagement that PBL delivers. Students who develop an early interest in science are more likely to choose advanced science courses that can lead to career opportunities.

Like Dr. Katie Hunt, the expert chemist introduced on page 107, many people who grow up to be scientists can recall being relentlessly curious as children. They often recall being encouraged in their interests by parents and other adults. Four factors are known to predict students' education and career choices (Dick & Rallis, 1991). Think about these factors as you plan project experiences. Your influence may increase the likelihood that your students will pursue further studies in the sciences, preparing them to become tomorrow's experts.

Access to quality experiences. Use constructivist methods, take students on field trips, involve them in real-world science, and introduce them to camps, clubs, competitions, and classes outside of school.

Exposure to role models. Connect students with people who do science. Students are especially responsive to "near peers," those not too different from them in age or life experience. Get role models to tell their stories.

Encouragement. Acknowledge achievement and compliment hard work. Sometimes a breakdown precedes a breakthrough, so compliment students who take risks and persist. Help students see where their interests today might lead in the future.

Recognition. Shine a light on students' achievements and science projects. Brag about a student in front of other teachers or to the student's parents. Hold science celebrations, invite the media to highlight their science achievements, nominate students for scholarships and awards.

One way to encourage young scientists is to steer them toward science competitions. Such events hold students to expert-level standards when it comes to doing research and presenting their findings. At the same time, students receive feedback on their investigations and, often, gain access to positive role models (both adults and "near peers").

Recent award-winning projects in the Intel International Science and Engineering Fair offer a window into how young scientists think about problems. In many cases, student researchers are motivated by circumstances from their own lives. Science inquiry offers them a way to satisfy their curiosity and also take action on issues that matter to them. For example:

- A girl whose grandparents are visually impaired develops a traffic control system that improves safety for blind pedestrians.
- Students from Thailand develop recyclable packaging material from fish scales, putting to use a material they have in abundance and, at the same time, potentially reducing their country's reliance on petroleum-based plastics.
- News that tin shields meant to protect workers at a local nuclear power plant actually cause a scattering of radiation led two students to develop a possible treatment for cancer.

How else might you build on (and spark) students' interests to plan meaningful, engaging projects? Consider these strategies:

- **Play off the news.** Encourage students to share stories of technical innovation, natural disaster, global issues, science conflicts and controversies—any news around which to have science conversations. Whenever a science innovation is in the news, discuss how it came about. A little research often reveals that it is part of a long chain of accumulating innovations. Encourage students to predict which subsequent developments are likely to come out of the innovation at hand.

- **Connect to students' lives.** A teacher introduces thermodynamics by having students investigate the cooling and heating systems in cars. Another starts an investigation into memory by showing a clip of characters in the movie *Men in Black* using a mind-erasing gadget. Both approaches connect the study with students' lives and interests, making the subject more inviting while showing that you care about students' interests.

- **Encourage speculation.** Flexibility leads to better thinking. Ask thought-provoking questions and encourage imaginative conjecture about what might be going on. Whether it leads to an investigation or not, always ask: *How could we find out?*

- **Foster aspirations.** Celebrate the characteristics your students share with great thinkers, such as curiosity, persistence, and outside-the-box thinking. Plan projects in which students explore the lives of scientists and discover that all kinds of people "do" science.

- **Present the grand challenges.** Make a poster of the big problems or "grand challenges" our world needs scientists to solve, such as providing universal access to clean water, preventing pandemics, or addressing climate change. (Better yet, have students research grand challenges and make their own posters.) Discuss the ways classroom experiences connect to and might even be precursor experiences that lead to the solution of these grand challenges.

→Project Signpost 9: Connect Students With Scientists

Projects that address cutting-edge issues in science may cause students to go in search of expert help. Anticipate the expertise that students may need and help them make connections with knowledgeable people. Make sure students do the prep work so that they know what they want to ask and can make the best use of busy experts' time.

To make connections with experts, think about the scientists who work in your local community (don't overlook parents). To extend your search, tap networks such as:

- National Lab Network (www.nationallabnetwork.org), an online matching service that connects teachers and/or students with scientists for research experiences and discussions.

- On Twitter, scientists and students use the hashtag #scistuchat to organize their conversations. Discussion often revolves around science issues in the news, such as genetically modified food, cloning, stem cell research, space exploration funding, evolution, and other hot topics.

- Connect with scientists who don't call themselves scientists. Science is in action every day in your community. Someone at the wastewater treatment plant can teach students a great deal about aquifers, pollutants, and purification. Amateur astronomers would love to share what they know about astronomy and optics. Fish and wildlife professionals, hunters, and fishermen understand species distribution, animal life cycles, and ecology. Master gardeners know about botany and soil chemistry.

CITIZEN SCIENCE

As we have discussed in previous chapters, students are more motivated when they see their projects as relevant and having a purpose. By setting the stage for students to be citizen scientists, you will help students learn science, learn how scientists conduct research, and appreciate how public efforts contribute to scientific discovery.

Several clearinghouses connect scientists with the public so that they conduct research together. In many such projects, scientists need access to real-time data that widely dispersed citizens can help to gather.

Consider this sampling to get a sense of the kinds of projects your students might take part in as citizen scientists.

Ancient Lives

Suitable for high school students, this archaeology project has citizen scientists measuring and transcribing 500,000 digitized fragments of one-thousand-year-old texts from Greco-Roman Egypt.

Benefit to science: The data will help scholars understand the literature, culture, and lives of Greco-Romans in ancient Egypt.

Benefit to students: They learn history and methods of archaeology. They get to correspond with researchers at Oxford University and other international groups. See: http://ancientlives.org.

Target Asteroids!

Citizens use their own telescopes (or view from remote telescopes on loan to them) to track asteroids, cataloging the position, motion, rotation, and changes in the light they reflect.

Benefit to science: Astronomers learn about the characteristics of asteroids similar to one they will collect a sample from during a space mission in 2019. The theoretical models needed to accomplish the space mission improve with direct-observation data contributed by citizens.

Benefit to students: Students learn astronomy and observation and data-collection skills. They learn about the long-range planning that goes into space missions and participate in one that will be in the news for years ahead. See: http://osiris-rex.lpl.arizona.edu.

NoiseTube

Researchers need help tracking noise pollution. A free mobile app on a smart phone is all participants need to measure the level of noise in their areas.

Benefits to science: These data help researchers understand the effects of noise on humans and animals.

Benefits to students: They learn how noise contributes to changes in predator–prey relationships, migration patterns, and human health. They can map local data and take action with an appeal to civic officials and the public to reduce noise. See: www.noisetube.net.

Consider, too, the many projects from Cornell Lab of Ornithology. Since 1960, Cornell Lab has relied on contributions from citizen scientists to study problems from global climate change to avian health. Your students can join what is possibly the world's largest scientific research community. Current projects involve citizens in collecting distribution and abundance data for five endangered migratory bird species (see the project: Priority Migrant eBird); identifying breeding behaviors by tagging photos captured by "nestcams" (Cam Clickr); counting birds at feeders to help ornithologists understand population and distribution trends (Project FeederWatch); and many others. See: http://www.birds.cornell.edu/citsci/.

→Tech Spotlight

Remember Frank Noschese and Angry Birds physics? He incorporated technology tools to help students analyze data and make sense of their observations. Follow his lead and look for technologies that will support the scientific thinking and problem solving that you want students to be doing in a project.
For example:

- Data gathering, a fundamental skill in science investigations, is enabled by a variety of digital devices. Smart phones can be used for taking photos embedded with GPS information to pinpoint the location and time data were gathered. Add an app like Leafsnap (http://leafsnap.com) for plant identification, and students now have an electronic field guide at their fingertips.
- Models and simulations are important ways that scientists make their thinking visible. Familiar models help us understand the solar system or visualize the double helix of DNA. Using tools of digital gaming, scientists might draw on large data sets to simulate the spread of pandemics. Students can learn to represent their thinking using 3-D modeling software such as Trimble SketchUp (http://www.sketchup.com/). STELLA software (http://www.iseesystems.com/) has an easy-to-use graphical interface for building models of complex systems.
- Scientists need to keep orderly research notes and lab records. Help students organize their work (and share it with team members) using tools like LiveBinders (www.livebinders.com), the online equivalent of a three-ring binder.
- When students are presenting their research findings, an online tool like Glogster (http://www.glogster.com) enables them to turn the old-school trifold poster into a publishable, multimedia presentation.

WHAT'S NEXT?

In Chapter 10, we examine the role of inquiry in the study of mathematics. A computer scientist explains how her career direction was influenced by an early love of puzzles and math games. Once again, we encourage nonmath teachers to read along and look for project opportunities to connect math to your subjects in authentic ways.

10

Math

"Mathematics is a study of patterns and relationships; a science and a way of thinking; an art, characterized by order and internal consistency; a language, using carefully defined terms and symbols; and a tool."

—North Central Regional Educational Laboratory

Think back to your years as a math student. Does this definition resonate with you? If not, it may be because you spent a lot of time on the procedural rather than the conceptual aspects of math. Math projects flip this around, making math concepts important to the resolution of a problem or challenge. The procedures of math develop in the context of projects and are undergirded by a developing conceptual understanding and need to know.

Picture an eighth-grade class that is deciding how to spend fundraising money to help stock a local food pantry. The pantry is committed to distributing food boxes to low-income families every week. As they plan, it becomes clear to students that that certain questions must be explored mathematically. Students ask:

- *Should we contribute food over the long term or buy it all at once? What are the merits of each strategy?*
- *Where should we shop, and how often?*
- *A can of beans is less expensive than a can of tuna, but is it as nutritious? How do we balance food cost and nutritional value?*
- *Large packages can be cheaper per pound, but buying large packages means we must buy fewer, so what sizes of packaged foods should we buy?*

As these questions arise, students begin predicting, estimating, modeling, and calculating, using whatever prior experiences and mathematical means they have. After a time, an approach takes shape and formal math procedures—such as algebra to address the packaging question—become necessary, and now students are ready to learn them in context.

Contrast this example with mathematics education described in the Trends in International Mathematics and Science Study (Mullis, Martin, & Foy, 2008). TIMSS shows that more than 90% of mathematics class time in United States eighth-grade classrooms is spent practicing routine procedures, with the remainder of the time generally spent applying procedures in new situations. Little time is spent in conceptual "messing about," conjecturing when a problem presents itself and then determining which mathematical approach and procedures are called for to solve it.

PROJECTS PUT CONCEPTS FIRST

Let's examine another project in which students' conceptual work precedes and propels their procedural understanding.

Imagine Grade 8 students attempting to answer this ill-structured question: *Which places on Earth are most prone to bad earthquakes?* They form small groups and share what they know and wonder about earthquakes and the instruments and methods of earth science. One student knows that the devastating earthquake in Haiti in 2010 was shallower than others. Several know that seismographs are used to measure earthquakes. All wonder how seismographs work. Another student says there seem to be a lot of earthquakes in California. Another asks, *Could an earthquake happen here?* As each student contributes, the team's conceptual understanding grows. They begin to establish common footing for the investigation ahead. They are particularly captivated by the question, *Could an earthquake happen here?* They are eager to dive in.

Before the project work gets underway, the team has to decide what "bad" means in earthquake terms. Is it the greatest magnitude? The most destructive? A combination? They make conjectures and settle on several lines of inquiry. One has them investigating which kinds of earthquake data yield information about frequency and magnitude. They learn that magnitude is a measure of seismic wave energy that is recorded as horizontal amplitude on the Richter scale. They learn that earthquakes are measured on a curious scale, and their teacher presents a just-in-time introduction to exponents and logarithms.

As they refine their interpretation of the driving question, one team decides to collect data from real-time seismic monitors over a period of time. Students grapple with ways to collect, organize, and analyze the data. They examine how geophysicists operate (and maybe seek their advice). As they plot recent earthquakes on a map, they begin to see patterns to the distribution of earthquakes.

At times, students find that their procedures let them down or they hit a conceptual snag, such as how to represent logarithmic data in a graph. Their teacher asks questions that help them clarify what they are trying to accomplish, such as: *What are you trying to display? Why isn't this representation good enough? How could you learn more about representing logarithmic data?* She shows them how to create a logarithmic graph by formatting the axes using the "scale" tab in their digital spreadsheet. With new information, technical skill, and encouragement, they return to their work. The interplay of the conceptual and procedural strengthens both kinds of knowledge.

Remember the TIMSS that showed more than 90% of time in eighth-grade math classrooms is spent practicing routine procedures? (It's possible that the emphasis on procedures is less extreme at other grades, but it's likely not far off.) What's wrong with teaching math procedures in a straightforward way? It turns out that learning procedures outside of rich contexts in which their use is necessary makes the learning less "sticky."

Research suggests that students who develop conceptual understanding early perform best on procedural knowledge tasks later (Grouws & Cebulla, 2000). The project is one more opportunity for the students to develop lasting skills—and autonomy—as mathematical thinkers.

Students without conceptual understanding are able to acquire procedural knowledge when the skill is directly taught, but they need more massed practice (Grouws & Cebulla, 2000). To put it another way, it's hard to learn to drive when you can't see over the steering wheel!

Teachers Speak: Dan Meyer on *Concepts First*

Dan Meyer, aka blogger *dy/dan,* uses math exercises in the textbook as an adjunct to students' real-life experiences.

In an algebra lesson, students roll a tapered glass on the floor. (Try this yourself or imagine the action. What does it do?) Kids roll more tapered cups of different dimensions and observe their action. Meyer describes his approach (Meyer, 2009):

> There is math here, certainly, but I have made it a goal this year to *stall* the math for as long as possible, focusing on a student's intuition before her calculation, applying her internal framework for processing the world before applying the textbook's framework for processing mathematics.

Next, he encourages students to ask questions. Jason is first and he asks, "Why does it roll in a circle?" (Meyer, 2009). From here, conversation proceeds along interesting lines. Students speculate about how the dimensions of the cup affect the circumference of the circle it traces. Students start to imagine ways to test their conjectures. They draw the kind of cup they think would roll the largest circle using a fixed amount of plastic. They make their ideal cup from a page of card stock and draw a diagram of their cup and its path. Meyer challenges his students to find the invisible center of the circle the cup traces and describe their method for deriving it.

Meyer (2009) says, "We do all of this before we start separating triangles, before we write up a proof, before we generalize a formula. We ask for all this risk-free student investment before we lower the mathematical framework down onto the problem."

Follow dy/dan's lead. List several major topics you will introduce in math class. For each, how might you (Meyer, 2009)

- Focus on students' intuition before their calculation?
- Apply their internal frameworks for processing the world before you "lower the mathematical framework" onto the problem?

Mathematicians Work This Way, but Most Math Students Don't

Mathematicians use their intuitions, explore, and try a variety of approaches as they work, too. In the 1950s, Gyorgy Pólya studied the methods of mathematicians to learn how they approach and solve difficult problems. He learned that they generally follow these phases of problem solving:

Understanding the problem

Devising a plan

Carrying out the plan

Looking back

Notice how conceptual understanding in phases 1 and 2 precedes the procedural work of phase 3. Notice, too, how these phases parallel the inquiry cycle of PBL.

In *How to Solve It* (1957), Pólya argued that, within the phases of understanding, planning, implementing, and reflecting, mathematicians use deliberate strategies, or heuristics, to solve problems. These include

- Breaking a problem into parts
- Relating a problem to one solved before
- Constructing a simpler version
- Working backward
- Making a drawing, diagram, or table
- Looking at use cases
- Changing the representation

Pólya's investigations led to a long progression of research activity and new pedagogical thinking relating to the teaching of math (Perkins, 2008). It turns out the approach and problem-solving methods of mathematicians could be codified and taught to young people.

Over the years, math teachers attempted to teach their students to use the problem-solving phases and strategies Pólya described, but they had limited success. Why didn't learning the ways of mathematicians make students better at math problem solving? Was there a missing ingredient?

Projects Supply the Missing Ingredient

In the 1980s, Alan Schoenfeld puzzled over this problem and conducted a series of investigations to arrive at a profound conclusion. It turns out students' understanding of the methods tended to be "inert." Students could learn the methods and use them successfully when presented with straightforward word problems, but when presented with any unfamiliarity, ambiguity, or complexity, they lacked the self-regulation that experts use when they choose one strategy over another, or, depending on the result, decide when to reexamine a problem, make a new conjecture, or choose another path (Schoenfeld, 1992).

Schoenfeld found that, regardless of the level of difficulty, students tended to choose one approach and stick with it.

Examine Figures 10.1 and 10.2 below. When given the same unfamiliar problem and twenty minutes to work, a college student and a mathematician operate quite differently.

In the first graph, it's clear the student interacts with the problem in a limited way, by only reading and then exploring:

Figure 10.1   Timeline Graph of a Typical Student Attempt to Solve a Nonstandard Problem

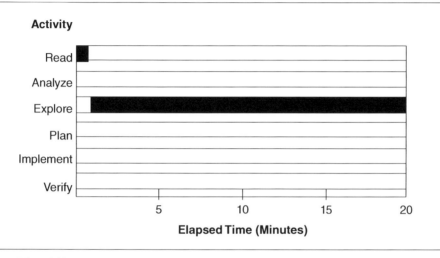

Source: Schoenfeld, 1992. Used with permission.

Looking at the mathematician's process in the second graph, it appears that about 7 minutes in, he foundered, then took another tack and kept working—analyzing, planning, exploring, and solving in iterative ways. The example doesn't make it clear what methods the mathematician used (i.e., whether he broke the problem into parts, related it to a

Figure 10.2   Timeline Graph of a Mathematician Working a Difficult Problem

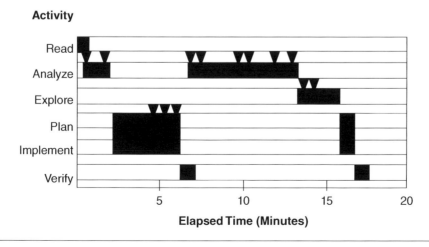

Source: Schoenfeld, 1992. Used with permission.

problem he'd solved before, or worked backward, or a combination of these), but it's apparent that he had developed methods he could use flexibly to ultimately solve the problem and check his solution.

Problem solving in traditional math classrooms frequently calls for a straightforward procedure that yields one right answer. Would the student have interacted with this problem differently had he tackled a variety of messy, ill-structured problems before? Table 10.1 shows two sets of problems. Which would be more engaging and ultimately more satisfying to solve? Which would more likely result in learning that sticks?

Table 10.1 Problem Sets

a. If the 1:20 model boat is 15 cm wide, how wide is the actual boat? b. If the boat has a mast of height 4m, how high is the mast on the model?	Toy time! Bring in Barbies, GI Joes, and similar dolls and action figures and compare them to real people. a. If each were the height of an average woman or man, what would their body proportions be? b. Design a doll or action figure with the proportions of an actual human (interdisciplinary extension: advise how to market it so it will outsell Barbie and Joe).

LEARN FROM MATHEMATICIANS BIG AND SMALL

All kinds of people make meaning with math. The smallest are young children who express their innate mathematical tendencies as they explore and manipulate their world. The biggest come up with new kinds of math such as non–Euclidian geometry, which was instrumental to the formulation of the theory of relativity, and in turn made the development of nuclear energy possible. Somewhere in the middle—and it's where most math happens—are those who use math every day.

Early in life, children take part in play that builds a critical foundation for math learning.

Child development and mathematics scholar Constance Kamii (2000) sees math in all kinds of play. A child playing with wet sand and buckets, for instance, is also exploring patterns. When children are putting objects in and out of containers, they are learning to classify and understand spatial relationships. When they build with blocks, they develop number sense.

Self-directed play nourishes the math mind all through life—if we encourage it. Think about your classroom. How might you enrich the environment with toys, games, puzzles, and brainteasers? How might play serve as an entry event, downtime activity, or even a mode of problem solving during projects?

As adults, many of us continue to employ math in our daily lives. According to the U.S. Bureau of Labor Statistics (Torpey, 2012), people use mathematical theory, computational techniques, algorithms, and the latest computer technologies to solve economic, scientific, engineering, and business problems. Consider just a few examples:

Creating the Designed World

Ergonomics engineers adjust workplace conditions and job demands to suit the physical capabilities of workers.

City planners advise on housing densities and urban growth boundaries.

Inventing New Technologies

Nanotechnologists create "gecko tape" that grips a load in one direction and releases its grip when the direction is reversed.

Aeronautic engineers design collision-avoidance systems in airplanes.

Representing Data

Public utility analysts graph customers' monthly power and water usage.

Pollsters collect and report voter preference prior to an upcoming election.

Modeling and Making

Actuaries use probability, statistics, and economic theory to determine the likelihood of future events, such as flooding.

Traffic engineers model interactions between vehicles, drivers, and infrastructure to develop optimal road networks.

Art directors use models, scale, and measurement for set design.

Chefs convert temperatures and imperial/metric units and calculate to scale recipes up or down.

Calculating and Decision Making

Nurses use dimensional analysis, a type of proportional reasoning, to determine medicine dosages.

Mechanics solve multivariant equations when repairing hydraulic systems.

Meteorologists interpret synoptic scales to calculate movement of large-scale fronts and weather systems.

Along with the many fields of applied mathematics listed above, we can also find theoretical mathematicians who are interested in expanding and clarifying mathematical theories and laws. These mathematicians may not be concerned with the practical uses of their findings, but their work is essential to many developments in applied math, science, and engineering. For example, research into the properties of random events made it possible to improve the design of experiments in the social and natural sciences. Conversely, in trying to solve the practical problem of billing long-distance telephone users fairly, mathematicians made fundamental discoveries about the more theoretical mathematics of complex networks.

Thinking about ways math is studied and used outside of the classroom will open your eyes to possibilities for authentic projects. Any real-world projects that mirror professional work in these domains will cause students to call on math in ways that experts do. An economist relies on statistics and modeling to do her work, and so should students engaged in an economics project.

In project design, think of how you might frame scenarios and plan projects that mirror professional work. Learn how math is used and let that knowledge inform your planning.

Expert Insights: Jeannette Wing, Computational Thinker (personal interview)

Let's hear from an expert thinker who has been fascinated by problem solving since childhood.

When Jeannette Wing was a child, her favorite pastime was to tackle puzzles and brainteasers. She remembers being delighted when her father gave her a math workbook as a gift. "I worked those puzzles over and over and asked for more. I just had a love of mathematics from early on," Wing recalls.

Her early fascination with problem solving set the stage for an illustrious career in computer science. Currently a professor of computer science at Carnegie Mellon University, Wing was formerly assistant director of the National Science Foundation's Computer and Information Science and Engineering Division. A consultant for some of the nation's leading technology companies, she focuses her current research on cybersecurity.

Wing is also a passionate champion of emphasizing computational thinking in K–12 education, especially at the high school level. Whether today's students follow her career path into technical fields or head in other directions, she argues that they will be well served by learning to think logically and analytically. "When you think about the difficult policy decisions people have to make in any number of fields, you want people in those roles who can look at the evidence and draw rational conclusions. When you have two arguments side by side, you need to be able to figure out which one is sound. That kind of reasoning involves logic, analysis, sometimes math, and it can carry you far beyond computer science," she says.

In hindsight, Wing can see how her parents helped her develop the habits of mind that continue to serve her well. Her father, an electrical engineering professor, encouraged her to pursue her love of math. He provided a positive counterpoint to a high school counselor who tried to steer her away from male-dominated career fields. Meanwhile, her mother instilled confidence, encouraging Wing to take risks and explore new interests.

As an undergraduate at MIT, Wing initially studied electrical engineering but soon found herself attracted to the then-relatively-young field of computer science. "My father assured me that computer science wasn't a fad. I could count on it being around for a while," she says with a laugh, "and I never looked back."

Key traits and thinking habits are part of Wing's toolkit as a computational thinker. These traits also need to be encouraged in today's students if we hope to prepare them to meet tomorrow's challenges:

- *Forward thinker:* "When I'm deciding which problems to research, I try to think far out in the future. What is a problem that's going to manifest itself in 10 years that's going to need a solution? Then I can start working on that problem now. One of the reasons I'm interested in cybersecurity is because we need to anticipate the threats of the future. The kinds of attacks we can expect may be much more extreme and sophisticated and complex than we can imagine. If we can imagine potential vulnerabilities many years out, then we can start to think about solutions."

- *Collaborator:* "I've always collaborated with colleagues and students across computing. Now, with my research interests in the science of privacy, I'm starting to look beyond computer science to understand how the social sciences think about this issue. What are the legal and ethical issues? When I was at the National Science Foundation, I was a great advocate for interdisciplinary research. The grand challenges that society faces—energy, education, health care—will require interdisciplinary thinking and collaboration. It takes time and effort to collaborate across fields, but we're seeing this happen more and more. The next generation of Ph.D.s are coming out with degrees like computational biology. It's not that one is a computer scientist doing biology or a biologist doing CS. It's an honest-to-goodness merger of the two fields. That's happening across many disciplines. We'll see many more computational X's in the future."

- *Risk-taker:* "In research, it's always about taking risks. In my own research career, I've been willing to start on one trajectory, learn what I need in that area, and then move into other areas. I'll work on a problem that's perhaps not popular or doesn't get published easily. But I'll stick with it if I believe in it. I have sufficient confidence in knowing that it's a hard problem, that the approach I'm taking is a reasonable one, and that the community may not be ready for it but that's OK; I still believe in it and in myself for working on it."

- *Good communicator:* "I guess being a communicator is part of who I am. In computer science and in many other science and engineering disciplines, the people doing the research in these areas are often not the best communicators of the importance of what they do. When I was at the NSF, I had to explain and argue to congressional staffers why funding research translates into economic impact, innovation, and societal good. Your typical scientist or engineer may not be good at translating what some technical research is good *for* in the eyes of the public. The science and engineering community needs to have people who are able to do that. So I guess I'm known for being logical and analytical, and also quite passionate."

> ### →Project Signpost 10: Find Math Experts for Projects
>
> Seek expertise from the pros as you plan. Mathematicians, actuaries, statisticians, and math-y people of all sorts belong to scholastic or professional societies that invest time and resources in education. These organizations and their members are your allies. They, too, want to strengthen the pool from which the next generations of economists, astrophysicists, biologists, and engineers come. To find them, refer to Weddle's Association Directory (http://www.weddles.com/associations). The Directory categorizes nearly 100 professions and, for each, lists several member organizations, some with regional affiliates near you. (Economists alone have seven societies and associations.) Once you identify a professional society, look to their education or outreach committees for the expertise you seek. Don't overlook chapters on college campuses to connect your students with "near peers."
>
> Consider, too, where you are most likely to find corollaries between math professions and the K–12 curricula.
>
> - Accountants—calculus, business statistics
> - Actuaries—statistics, finance, and business accounting
> - Computer scientists, software engineers and programmers—calculus, algebra, trigonometry
> - Economists—statistics, modeling, accounting, calculus
> - Engineers—algebra, geometry, modeling, trigonometry, and calculus
> - Financial analysts—finance and business statistics
> - Market and survey researchers—statistics, sampling theory, modeling
> - Physicists and astronomers—calculus, differential equations, probability theory and statistics, linear algebra
> - Statisticians—calculus, algebra, probability, and statistics

TEACHING WITH MATH PROJECTS

There are four functions to master in order to teach with projects involving math: strengthening mathematical understanding, making the world safe for math, designing quality projects, and facilitating learning in artful ways.

1. Strengthen Mathematical Understanding

It's always good to deepen understanding and hone your craft, and especially as you begin teaching math through projects. Consider these opportunities for professional growth:

Join or create a Math Teachers' Circle. This is different from the Math Circles you may know about, in which mathematicians meet with students to explore engaging, open-ended math problems. A Math Teachers' Circle brings math teachers together with mathematicians in order to strengthen their own problem-solving skills, share ideas about pedagogy, and develop a professional support network. The American Institute of Mathematics sponsors Math Teachers' Circles (learn more at www.mathteacherscircle.org).

Start reading and interacting with reflective, blogging PBL math teachers. Here are three to begin with:

- Jackie Ballarini, *Continuities* (http://continuities.wordpress.com). Ballarini teaches high school math and blogs about her effort to improve her practice.
- John Pearson, *Learn Me Good* (http://learnmegood2.blogspot.com). Anecdotes, observations, and the occasional rant from a former design engineer turned third-grade math teacher.
- Dan Meyer, *dy/dan* (http://blog.mrmeyer.com). Meyer taught high school math before starting doctoral studies. He reflects on math teaching and describes how he applies his interests in graphic design, filmmaking, motion graphics, and infographics in teaching. (Follow him on Twitter @ddmeyer.)

Join Math Chat discussions on Twitter. Follow hashtag #mathchat to follow the stream of comments of math teachers and join real-time chats each Monday and Thursday.

2. Make the World Safe for Math

Learning math fills some students—and adults—with self-consciousness and dread.

Factoid: *Two-thirds of American adults fear and loathe math* (Burns, 1998).

After years of failure or frustration, too many students take the first exit ramp off the math highway. Good projects revive interest in math and increase purposeful engagement. Meaningful projects help students see that their efforts add up to something significant. Projects help students recognize that they can interact with the world mathematically.

Because attitudes influence achievement, it makes sense to attend not only to math curriculum and pedagogy but to the social and affective aspects of math as well.

Many students (and parents) believe mathematicians are born, not made. Imagine: Parents of an eighth grader attend conference night early in the school year. The algebra teacher explains that their daughter is struggling in math. The parents say, "Oh, that runs in the family. None of us is good at math." What does this tell us about the context in which their child is learning math? Let's recast the scenario. Same parents, same child, but the language arts teacher is explaining that their child is struggling to read. The parents show great concern. They *don't* say, "Oh, that runs in our family. None of us can read!" Culturally, it is permissible to be poor at math, but who admits to not being able to read? Low expectations lead to low achievement in math (Flores, 2007). It takes expert teaching, encouragement, and sometimes a serious marketing campaign to turn that thinking around.

Turn around parents' thinking. Help parents understand your intentions for teaching math through projects. Explain that, through projects, their children will develop the capacity to define and solve problems with reason, insight, inventiveness, and technical proficiency. Tell them students' learning will mirror authentic work in which math is important and that makes math relevant now and useful in the long term. Math proficiency is a gateway to rewarding professions such as medicine, computer science, engineering, and finance. Let parents know that through projects, students will build on and make connections among mathematical concepts and find the connections between math and other subjects.

Present examples of projects the class will do. Deconstruct one to show its rigor and the concepts and skills students will learn through doing it. Present a rubric so parents can see how your expectations for learning map to the school curriculum. Help parents become as excited about your projects as their children will be.

Invite parents into projects. Ask them to participate as experts, classroom helpers, and field trip chaperones. Send updates and encourage parents to talk with their children about projects at home. Post announcements, student testimonials, and pictures to a project blog.

Reshape students' thinking, too. Some students believe only certain people have an aptitude for math and that a natural affinity or love for math is necessary for moving ahead in the subject. Let students know they don't have to be "math whizzes" to do well in it. Hard work, rather than some inborn talent, is the true discriminating factor that leads to success in math (and all the doors that math ability opens).

The very act of adopting the project approach upsets the old paradigm in which math is a strictly structured activity that yields single right answers and is done on one's own. For many students, math projects represent a new chance at math. Any math anxiety or defeatist attitudes they come in with are erased when students are presented with an engaging project and encouraged to proceed in inventive and collaborative ways. High-achieving students benefit from projects too. Because projects have no upper limit, it is less likely that accomplished students will go unchallenged and become bored or disinterested in math.

Many small acts can make your classroom safe for math. Consider these:

- Bring current events with math connections into the classroom. (*Did you hear? An iceberg the size of Connecticut calved off a glacier in Greenland.*) Encourage students to do the same and marvel with them.
- Tell math jokes, show math comics, and present math puzzles.
- Make math visual (see information about *infographics* later in this chapter).
- Tell life stories of mathematicians. (Eratosthenes, Gauss, and Fibonacci are a good start.)
- Muse aloud about the nature of things mathematical, especially those that can be investigated, such as: *I wonder if all green lights in town stay green for the same amount of time.* Encourage students to wonder, too. Post these "wonderings" in a visible place so students can ponder them over time.
- Don't rush students when they are explaining their thinking.
- Acknowledge effort, not smarts.

- Encourage inventive approaches.
- Discourage speed. Encourage deliberate, iterative effort instead.
- Encourage students to ask for help and praise them when they do.
- Model thinking aloud. Show dead ends and redirections in your thought processes, too.
- Allow students to teach one another.
- Present students' work so others can appreciate and acknowledge it.

3. Design Quality Math Projects

As you start planning, you may go online looking for projects to emulate. Your search of PBL + math will return both *problem*-based learning and *project*-based learning. As discussed in Chapter 1, these are similar but distinct approaches.

You may have good reasons to include problem-based lessons that last for one or a few class periods, but also plan for project-based learning that connects a number of math concepts in a comprehensive and realistic or real-life experience. Math projects may last several days or even weeks.

From textbook problems to math projects. Let's get a flavor for math projects that are a definite contrast with textbook math. Listed in Table 10.2 are pairs of textbook problems contrasted with projects and students' refinement of each prompt in the parentheses that are more authentic, engaging, and challenging. Note that these projects likely differ in duration, from one or two periods to some time each day over several weeks.

Math textbooks often include good seed ideas for projects. Look in the "extensions" section at the end of each chapter and imagine how these "seeds" might grow into a project that drives key learning.

Table 10.2 Textbook Math and Project Math

Textbook Math	Project Math
Birthday math! Make a picture graph showing our class birthdays.	Birthday math! Two of us were born on September 7! (How could we find out whether other kids in our school were born on September 7? Could we find all the birthday buddies in the school?)
Forty-three of us are traveling to the museum. We will rent 10-passenger vans at $84 apiece. How many vans will we need and how much will they cost?	Forty-three of us are traveling to the museum. We need to rent vans. How should we go about this to arrive at the most affordable and safe rental? (How do we compare rental agreements and policies around driving and accidents?)
High and low temperatures over 5 days are 77/54, 72/54, 73/50, 68/48, and 65/44. What was the average high and low temperature?	Our garden needs a steady soil temperature of at least 55° for 3 days before we plant peas. What do we do? (When should we start recording daily soil temperatures? What will we need?)

(Continued)

Table 10.2   (Continued)

Textbook Math	Project Math
Examine this family's diet against the USDA Food Pyramid. Where does their diet fall short?	Here are *Time* magazine pictures of families from around the world with the food they eat in a week and how much they spend. (What proportion of their income do these families spend on food? What is the caloric and nutritional value of each family's food? Who's healthiest?)
Measure the dimensions of two juice boxes. If filled to the top, how many cubic centimeters will each hold?	How strange. These juice boxes have different dimensions but hold the same amount of juice. What is going on? (We could measure different brands of juice box boxes to find out which has the greatest amount of juice while using the least amount of packaging material. We could compare prices to figure out who's making more money, too!)
Examine this architectural drawing and identify these geometric solids: rectangular-based pyramid, square-based pyramid, triangular-based pyramid, cone, cylinder, cube, rectangular prism, and triangular prism.	Where do geometric solids show up in architecture? (Examine famous architecture from around the world and identify as many different geometric solids as we can. Design our own significant buildings in SketchUp using geometric solids and tell their "stories.")
a. If the 1:20 model boat is 15 cm wide, how wide is the actual boat? b. If the boat has a mast of height 4m, how high is the mast on the model?	Some dolls and action figures seem to have extreme body proportions. Could toys with human proportions capture the market? (Toy time! Bring in Barbies, GI Joes, and similar dolls and action figures and determine: a. If each were the height of an average woman or man, what would their body proportions be? b. Design a doll or action figure with the proportions of an actual human, and figure out how to market it so it outsells Barbie and Joe.
Examine this map showing bicycle thefts in Appleville during one year. In which square mile do the most thefts occur? The fewest?	The newspaper says bike thefts are on the rise. Should everyone worry? (Examine local police records for monthly bicycle theft data and create a public service announcement and posters to inform the community about the best and most risky places to keep a bike.)
Using this table of fees from several cell phone companies, create an algebraic expression that reflects the billing of services.	Phone plans are complicated and families are trying to cut corners. (Help each of our families choose the best cell phone plan for its needs from among three local providers. Write a letter to Mom and Dad justifying our recommendations.)
Determine how the graph of a parabola changes as a, b, and c vary in the equation $y = a(x - b)2 + c$.	Do ball skills come down to technique or talent? (Examine the projectile motion of a ball used in a favorite sport. Explain mathematically and practically how to adjust its parabola for best scoring results.)

Textbook Math	Project Math
How much interest will you pay on a loan of $350 at 12% APR if you pay it off the loan in 6 months?	College freshmen carry an average of $1,585 in credit card debt, the *cost of three iPads!* (Create a scenario that shows we understand what it takes to manage our own credit cards.)
Find a, b, and c included in the definition the sine function f given by $f(x) = a \times \sin(bx + c)$ such that the maximum value of $f(x)$ is 6, $f(0) = 6$, and the period of the graph of function f is equal to π. a, b, and c are positive and c is less than 2π.	Let's pick the perfect evening for an outdoor wedding! (In pairs, we collect temperature and sunset data for a major U.S. city and model the averages using sinusoidal functions. We present the data in a way the couple understands so they can make an informed choice.)

Two Approaches to Project Planning

As you begin planning, consider two approaches to designing math projects. Either start with math and seek life connections or start with life connections and map back to math.

Math first. Identify several high-level math standards that naturally fit together and plan a project that encompasses them. Here is an example of several West Virginia standards that fit together. In Grade 5, students will

- collect, record, estimate, and calculate elapsed times from real-world situations (with and without technology);
- determine the actual measurements of a figure from a scale drawing using multiple strategies; and
- solve real-world problems involving whole numbers, decimals, and fractions using multiple strategies and justify the reasonableness by estimation.

What project might address these standards? West Virginia Teacher Lisa Moody designed California, Here We Come! in which fifth-grade "travel agents" plan a customer's air travel, taking into account time zones, distance, in-air and layover times, amenities, fares, taxes, baggage fees, and more. They present their customer with a proposal that includes a scale map and cost comparison table she needs to make an informed decision.

As you design, consider how standards can be "batched" so learners get the most out of each project. West Virginia teachers design projects using Power Standards, which get at the "big ideas" of each subject.

Life connections first. In the travel agent example, the teacher might have arrived at the same project starting from a geography angle or with inspiration from the Travel Channel. Many subject-matter and life connections are ripe for the math projects treatment. Take the project called An Eye-Opening Experience, in which students across the United States and around the world joined Connecticut fifth-grade students to count the number of metal eyelets on their shoes. Shoes and eyelets? What kind of math project could this be? In it, students engaged in prediction and estimation; data collection, representation, and analysis; review of variables; and calculating mean, median, and mode. In addition, they met new friends around the world and learned about geography, culture, and differences and similarities (for instance, no matter where laced shoes come from, the eyelets are set in multiples of four!).

MATHEMATICAL PRACTICES

Make Sure Students Operate as Mathematicians

Whichever route you take into project planning, make sure your plan prompts students to operate as skillful mathematicians. The *Common Core State Standards* initiative combined NCTM Process Standards with the National Research Council's Strands of Mathematical Proficiency to arrive at one set of Mathematical Practices. Mathematical Practices describe "processes and proficiencies" students should develop as they learn math. These practices have longstanding importance in mathematics education and have parallels in the capabilities of mathematicians that Pólya described.

Your project should cause students to

1. Make sense of problems and persevere in solving them

2. Reason abstractly and quantitatively

3. Construct viable arguments and critique the reasoning of others

4. Model with mathematics

5. Use appropriate tools strategically

6. Attend to precision

7. Look for and make use of structure

8. Look for and express regularity in repeated reasoning

Facilitate Learning in Artful Ways

Diving into math projects. Imagine how students will respond to the project, and consider the different ways the project may play out. Multiple lines of inquiry may emerge, and that's a good thing!

Plan a "hook." Think back to the fifth-grade travel agents. How would you introduce that project with an entry event? Imagine arranging chairs into four long rows with an aisle down the middle. When students are seated, speak into your "microphone" and thank your "passengers" for their patience with the boarding delay. Thank them again for being patient with the lack of air conditioning—that will get better after takeoff, which should only be delayed another 30 minutes due to thunderstorms in the area. Ham it up, encourage a little disgruntled behavior, and then break scene. Ask kids what they know about air travel horror stories and then introduce the idea: Even if some things are outside our control, many aspects of travel can be managed with good planning. As "travel agents," they get to plan a trip for a customer.

Remember, the entry event is not a rundown of tasks and timelines. Introduce those later, after students are engaged and excited to get to work.

Once the project is underway, be aware that math facilitation is a bit different from other project facilitation. There are more landmines to avoid (crushing confidence, getting bogged down in procedures), and specific questioning techniques ala Pólya that can prompt good thinking at different stages.

Encouragement. What kinds of encouragement will help math students persist when problems get tough or in the face of confusion or miscalculation? Remember to encourage effort (not smarts), and use encouragement as a gateway into asking clarifying questions that help students learn.

Questioning. In *How to Solve It* (1945), Pólya organized the problem-solving cycle into four parts and provided questions teachers or mathematics students themselves could ask while solving challenging problems.

Pólya's terminology is a bit antiquated and less than kid friendly. As you read his language in the box below, consider rewriting his questions in language you would use and your students can understand. One caution: Retain significant math terms. For instance, if you teach students to approach every problem by identifying the *unknown*, the *data*, and the *condition*, the consistent use of those terms will strengthen their approach to math problem solving.

How to Solve It

Four Phases of Problem Solving and Questions to Drive Each

1. Understanding the problem

   - What is the unknown? What are the data? What is the condition?
   - Is it possible to satisfy the condition? Is the condition sufficient to determine the unknown? Or is it insufficient? Or redundant? Or contradictory?
   - Draw a figure. Introduce suitable notation. Can you use pictures or math notation to represent the problem?
   - Separate the various parts of the condition. Can you write them down?

2. Devising a plan

   Find the connection between the data and the unknown. You may be obliged to consider auxiliary problems if an immediate connection cannot be found. You should obtain eventually a plan of the solution.

   - Have you seen it before? Or have you seen the same problem in a slightly different form?
   - Do you know a related problem? Do you know a theorem that could be useful?
   - Look at the unknown! And try to think of a familiar problem having the same or a similar unknown.
   - Here is a problem related to yours and solved before. Could you use it? Could you use its result? Could you use its method? Should you introduce some auxiliary element in order to make its use possible?
   - Could you restate the problem? Could you restate it still differently? Go back to definitions.

(Continued)

(Continued)

If you cannot solve the proposed problem, try to solve first some related problem.

- Could you imagine a more accessible related problem? A more general problem? A more special problem? An analogous problem?
- Could you solve a part of the problem? Keep only a part of the condition, drop the other part; how far is the unknown then determined, how can it vary?
- Could you derive something useful from the data? Could you think of other data appropriate to determine the unknown?
- Could you change the unknown or data, or both if necessary, so that the new unknown and the new data are nearer to each other?
- Did you use all the data? Did you use the whole condition? Have you taken into account all essential notions involved in the problem?

3. Carrying out the plan
- As you are carrying out your plan of the solution, check each step. Can you see clearly that the step is correct? Can you prove that it is correct?

4. Looking back, examine the solution obtained
- Can you check the result? Can you check the argument?
- Can you derive the solution differently? Can you see it at a glance?
- Can you use the result, or the method, for some other problem?

Ideas Presented in Writing and in Pictures

I can no longer imagine teaching math without making writing an integral aspect of students' learning.

—Marilyn Burns (2004), math educator

Writing in mathematics gives me a window into my students' thoughts that I don't normally get when they just compute problems. It shows me their roadblocks, and it also gives me, as a teacher, a road map.

—Maggie Johnston, ninth-grade
math teacher (Urquhart, 2009)

During math projects, get ideas out in the open through discussion, writing, and graphical representations. The acts of speaking, writing, and representing ideas shape the ideas themselves. Model the expression of ideas that you want students to emulate.

Writing shapes students' thinking and helps you interact with that thinking. Do your math students write every day—about mathematics?

NCTM *Principles and Standards for School Mathematics* (2000) state that "written communication should be nurtured" and that math instruction should include writing so students learn to:

- Organize and consolidate their mathematical thinking through communication
- Communicate their mathematical thinking coherently and clearly to peers, teachers, and others

- Analyze and evaluate the mathematical thinking and strategies of others
- Use the language of mathematics to express mathematical ideas precisely

Researchers have examined strategies for introducing writing in math (Woodard & Baxter, 1999). Let's look at them in a school-year sequence, but imagine how they fit into the beginning, middle, and end of a project, too.

Make math journal writing a part of everyday practice. Introduce writing in math at the beginning of the school year (and at the beginning of a project) and start with affective, open-ended questions that prompt students to write about their feelings and opinions. Ease students into writing with failsafe questions. Ask for their opinions about using calculators in math class or about their favorite experiences in math. As a project begins, ask them what they are excited to find out or what they've been mulling over. As you read and respond to their writing, encourage students to use the language of mathematics.

Next, ask students questions about concepts with which they should be familiar and are on firm footing. These prompts fit in well during the fall and at the start of a project when you are assessing prior knowledge.

As the year and projects proceed, ask students to write about more complex math topics. Writing prompts at this stage reinforce and extend students' understanding of the mathematical concepts they are learning. Their written expression, now that they have gained writing fluency, is a rich source for formative assessment.

Finally, use students' written explanations of their strategies and math understanding at the end of a project as one aspect of your final assessment. Ask them, too, to reflect on what they learned and how they felt about the project. This final, more affective writing can cement positive feelings and make students ready for challenges ahead.

→Tech Spotlight: Infographics

Many projects, especially those that ask students to quantify and make sense of the real world, involve data collection, analysis, and visual representation.

NCTM Focal Points state that instructional programs from prekindergarten through Grade 12 should enable all students to:

- create and use representations to organize, record, and communicate mathematical ideas

- select, apply, and translate among mathematical representations to solve problems

- use representations to model and interpret physical, social, and mathematical phenomena

(Continued)

> (Continued)
>
> Most math teachers are familiar with common representations in math, such as charts, tables, and graphs. One form of visual representation that is growing in use outside of school is the *infographic*. Let's look at infographics and imagine how students might work with these interesting visual displays of quantitative data.

Imagine Utah students charged with designing a promotional poster that will convince visitors that Utah's slogan, "The Greatest Snow on Earth," is true. They must create an *infographic* that both quantifies and illustrates the ski scene in Utah in an accurate and appealing way. The Ski Utah infographic in Figure 10.3 was created by Michael Greenberg when he was a high school junior.

Figure 10.3   Ski Utah Infographic

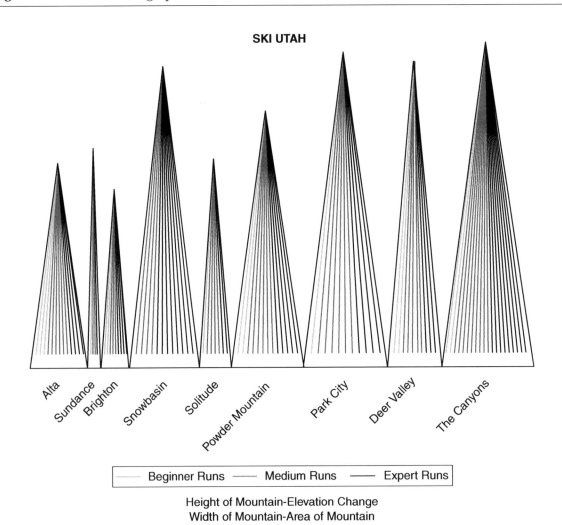

An *infographic*—or information graphic—is a visual representation of data. The representation can be pictorial, showing the very thing under consideration—as in the Ski Utah infographic that shows mountains where one can ski—and it can also show dynamic processes. An early example of the latter is the famous 1869 Minard Map, which shows Napoleon's troops as a river of 442,000 men that diminishes as it marches on—and then retreats from—Moscow.

Here is a partial translation that helps with interpreting this map: *"The numbers of men present are represented by the widths of the colored zones at a rate of one millimeter for every ten-thousand men; they are further written across the zones. The lighter color designates the men who enter into Russia, the black those who leave it."*

Infographics can be more compelling than tables, charts, or words. They tell stories and raise questions. In the Minard map, 6,000 troops split off and later rejoined the retreating army. It leads us to wonder, *What circumstances and decisions led to this development?* The lower portion of the graph, reading from right to left, shows the temperatures on different dates on the army's retreat from Russia in degrees below freezing on the Réaumur scale. *Is –30° Re cold? How cold? Might weather conditions have anything to do with the diminishment of the army?*

Learning to read infographics. Consider using infographics as a teaching tool. Visual representations of data foster all kinds of mathematical thinking. As students examine them, they engage in analysis and interpretation to derive meaning. They might ponder dynamic systems, relational data, or change over time.

Imagine examining Greenberg's Ski Utah infographic together. You might ask students what they know about skiing in Utah based on Greenberg's pictorial representation. You might ask what they can infer about the mountains that get the most or least business. Ask, too, how they could represent other data of interest to someone contemplating a Utah ski vacation, for example, showing distance from the airport. Ask them to make conjectures about how many data sets are represented and how they were derived.

Present good and bad charts, graphs, and infographics (aka "chartjunk") for students to examine. Help them determine when statistics reflect value judgments, are presented in a distorted scale, or otherwise "lie." As future consumers and citizens who are presented with statistical data all the time, learning to understand graphical representations of data is an important form of math and information literacy.

Sources for infographics abound. *The New York Times* website publishes many, as do the sites listed below. Present infographics regularly for data analysis, and consider decorating and enriching your classroom with them, too. Many infographics are available for download. Select ones that follow the "rules" below(Figure 10.5; Yau, 2010), and make your own inexpensive posters on Zazzle (www.zazzle.com). Imagine students pondering a visualization of time travel plots in films and TV programs or making sense of the largest bankruptcies in history in an infographic showing bankrupt companies as sinking ships of relative size.

Figure 10.4 Figurative Map of the Successive Losses in Men of the French Army in the Russian Campaign 1812–1813. Drawn up by M. Minard, Inspector General of Bridges and Roads in Retirement. Paris, November 20, 1869

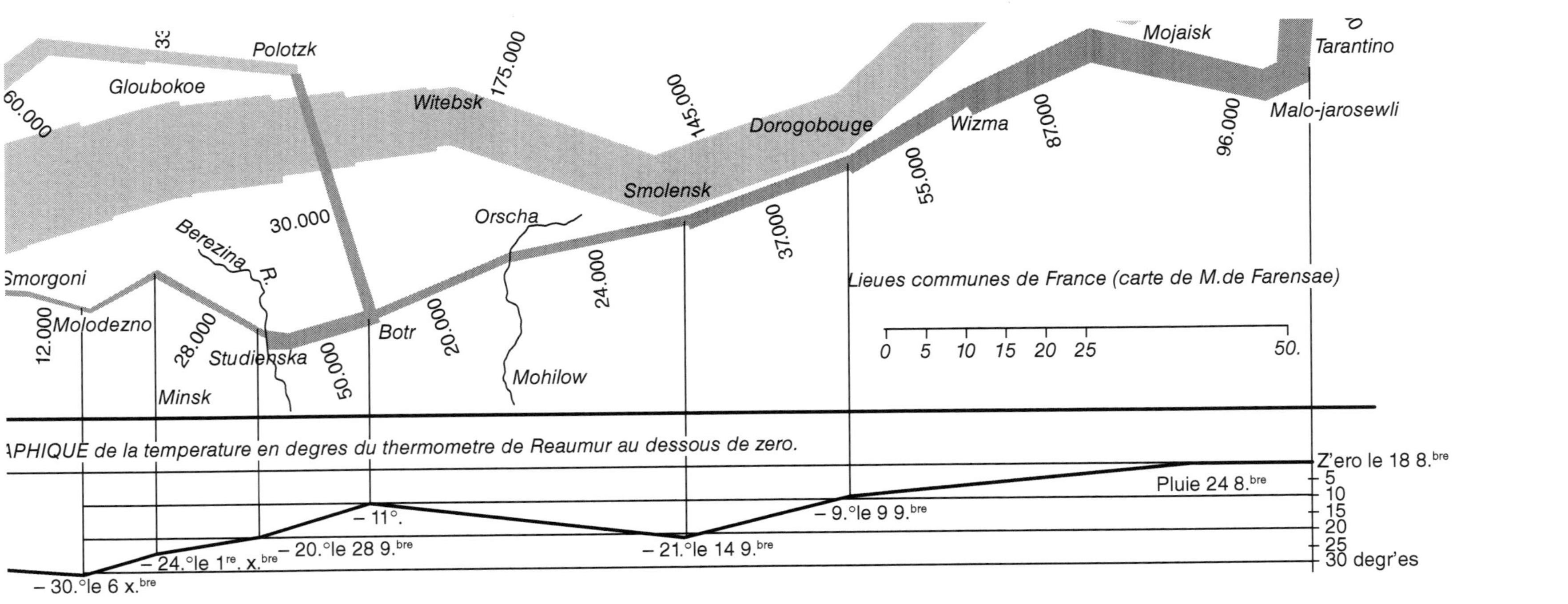

Some infographics sites to inspire you:

Cool Infographics: http://www.coolinfographics.com

Floating Sheep: http://www.floatingsheep.com

Flowing Data: http://flowingdata.com

GOOD/Transparency: http://www.good.is

Information Aesthetics: http://infosthetics.com

Information Is Beautiful: http://www.informationisbeautiful.net

Learning to make infographics. The National Council of Teachers of Mathematics advises that students at every grade undertake investigations in which they collect and represent data graphically. They are also to make sense of statistical data by representing the important features of a data set and the relationships *between* data sets. In their pictorial "narratives," the data have to be valid and the representation *true.* By making infographics themselves, students learn that the ways they represent data are as important as the data themselves.

Imagine how students might express their project learning in infographics in this example: A middle school class is studying livability in their town. One project has them responding to the driving question "Can everyone get where they need to go?" Students notice many sidewalks are broken, making them impassable for people using strollers, wheelchairs, walkers, and canes. They survey their neighborhoods, recording their neighbors' mobility challenges and identifying sidewalks that present the worst impediments. Imagine the data they collect. Imagine how they might present their information pictorially to tell a story and make the case for fixing the worst sidewalks. What might their infographic look like?

Envision your classroom walls, school halls, or even the city council chambers adorned with infographics your students make. Several sets of guidelines are available to help your students represent data accurately and convincingly in infographics. High schooler Greenberg came up with his own: Get an idea, sketch it out, collect the data sets, start doing proof-of-concept, then do layout work ("fun").

Nathan Yau, blogging for *Flowing Data,* offers seven rules for making infographics (Yau, 2010).

7 BASIC RULES FOR MAKING INFOGRAPHICS

To put it simply: tell your story clearly and communicate the data accurately.

1. **Consider your audience and purpose.** Take into account who and what your graphs and charts are for, and design accordingly. Imagine how the viewers will take it in. Design a graphic to be super-detailed for a poster that people can stare at for hours. But limit complexity if it's for a presentation.

2. **Check the data.** If your data sets are weak, your infographics are weak, so make sure the data are accurate and make sense. Verify or correct any data that do not make sense.

3. **Keep geometry in check.** If geometry or scale is wrong, the graphics won't tell a true story.

To eliminate the need for any guesswork from the reader

1. **Explain encodings.** Maybe you use a color scale to indicate magnitude or the size of a square to represent values. Maybe it's a combination of both. Explain what these encodings are supposed to indicate. The most common ways of explaining encoding are to provide a legend, directly label shapes, or describe the graphic in a lead-in paragraph.

2. **Label axes.** Label your axes so that readers know what scale points are plotted on. Is it logarithmic, incremental, exponential, or per 100 flushing toilets? Also, in most cases, you'll want your value axis to start at zero.

3. **Include units.** Indicate what numbers reference. Is it percentage, volume, miles, or the number of chickens that crossed the road?

4. **Include sources.** Always include where the data come from. Put it directly in a graphic, or if it's part of an article or report, the source can be specified in the copy.

In the end, all of these rules can be broken for specific cases. You'll learn where you can bend with practice.

Infographic design tools. A variety of technologies are useful for making infographics. In his blog about creating Ski Utah, student Michael Greenberg describes how he used graph paper, spreadsheets, and InDesign, a desktop design software program, to create his infographic.

Greenberg uses Photoshop and Illustrator for infographics, too. These, along with InDesign, are graphic design programs commercial artists use that may not be in of the suite of tools used in most classrooms.

Luckily, free, Web-based tools are available. Consider using Google Spreadsheets for data collect and manipulation. Because their spreadsheet lives in the "cloud" (on Google servers), students in a team can use it at the same time and get to it from any computer. For design software, give Science Pipes, Tableau Public, and Inscapes a try. Finally, if your students want to represent multiple data sets as individual elements in an infographic, they may want to use Glogster, interactive "poster" software with lively text, graphic, and background options.

Glogster: http://www.glogster.com

Google Spreadsheets: http://www.google.com/drive/start/apps .html#product=sheets

Inkscape: http://inkscape.org

IBM Many Eyes: http://www-958.ibm.com/software/data/cognos/manyeyes/

Science Pipes (for biodiversity data): http://sciencepipes.org/beta/home

Tableau Public: http://www.tableausoftware.com/public

PROJECT IDEAS

Finally, remember that math reaches beyond the math classroom, and projects in other subject areas will use math in significant ways. See the Project Library in Appendix A for more ideas for projects, including ones that incorporate math in interdisciplinary studies.

WHAT'S NEXT?

Now that we have explored inquiry in the four core content areas, let's see what happens when a project takes off in unexpected directions. Chapter 11 helps you anticipate the "project spiral." That's what happens when projects expand beyond the classroom, engaging the community and perhaps even the larger world. Are you ready for your project idea to go big?

11

The Project Spiral

Heather Hanson is always looking for material that will engage her students at Todd County High School in South Dakota. That's why she took the risk of screening a network television documentary that she knew would draw a strong emotional reaction from her students, nearly all of whom live on the Rosebud Indian Reservation. *Children of the Plains*, narrated by Diane Sawyer of *20/20*, focused on the hardships of growing up on the reservation, including alcoholism, poverty, and family dysfunction.

How did students respond? Some cried. Some were outraged at what they saw as stereotypes of their Lakota Sioux culture. Others shrugged off the one-sided portrayal as "the way they always talk about us." Hanson, who teaches speech and communication, challenged students to do something productive in response. That challenge was the entry event for a project that took students places they couldn't have imagined, including two trips to Washington, D.C., to use their newfound voice to speak up for their community—and for themselves.

Project-based learning enables students to become active participants in their world. Through projects, students may discover that they have the ability to influence others, make meaningful contributions, or even right wrongs. Such opportunities may not happen with every project, but savvy teachers are ready to let a worthy project "spiral" out in new directions.

What do we mean by the project spiral? It's what happens when students' projects "go big," creating a buzz in their community or a greater impact than anyone expected. It's what happens when their project video goes viral on YouTube (as happened for the students from South Dakota). The project spiral takes learning beyond the classroom and inspires the larger community to ask questions, reflect, consider alternatives, or take action.

The project spiral is also a way to describe the infectious energy that good projects generate. An engaging project experience in one classroom has the potential to spread interest in PBL across grade levels or across content areas, potentially influencing the culture of a school. The project spiral fosters professional growth, too, as PBL veterans share what they know with peers—in person or through ever-expanding online networks.

FOLLOW THE LEADERS

Several years back, when we were conducting research for *Reinventing Project-Based Learning*, we happened to hear of two teachers who were connecting their classrooms across great distances for something called the Flat Classroom Project. That was the first year of global collaboration by the creative teaching team of Vicki Davis from rural Georgia in the United States and Julie Lindsay, an international teacher then based in Bangladesh. Their students used Web 2.0 tools to overcome distances and explore real-world topics raised by author Thomas Friedman (2005) in *The World Is Flat*.

That first collaboration has since spiraled in many directions, including the development of several more global education projects, professional learning events, and a book, *Flattening Classrooms, Engaging Minds* (Lindsay & Davis, 2012), that captures the insights gained from 5 years of collaborative project work. They even offer teacher certification for educators who demonstrate proficiency in designing and managing global education projects using social media. (Learn more about Flat Classroom projects, events, and resources at www.flatclassroomproject.net/.)

The success of the Flat Classroom "brand" may be unusual, but there is plenty we can learn about the project spiral from Davis and Lindsay's example. From the start, they have emphasized high-quality, technology-rich projects. Learning is personalized and relevant, focusing on issues that matter to students and giving them opportunities to be media creators. Students connect with other students and leave the "silos" of traditional classrooms. As more educators take part in these projects, they connect via social media to exchange insights with their growing professional network. That's how a good idea shared by two teachers has grown to become a global phenomenon.

PREPARE TO SPIRAL

Let's look at three ways you can be ready for the project spiral:

- Go bigger: Extend projects in directions you didn't anticipate.
- Go public: Broadcast your students' project results.
- Connect with your network: Share insights with your professional network to grow the culture of PBL.

Go Bigger

When Heather Hanson challenged her students to respond to that television documentary, she knew she wanted them to apply what they were learning in speech class and think critically about media messages. She didn't tell students what to produce; that was left up to them.

Before students decided on the medium and message for their project, Hanson led them through a critical analysis of the documentary. As if they were doing a close reading of a text, they analyzed the piece for point of view, bias, and audience manipulation through words and images. For instance, students timed the number of minutes in the documentary that showed Native American children crying. The data helped them think about deliberate decisions by videographers to get an emotional reaction from viewers.

Students decided to produce their own video in response, countering with more positive images about growing up Native American. After writing a script in speech class, they teamed up with a media arts class to produce a YouTube video titled *More Than That (Falcon Daily,* 2011). In the tightly edited black-and-white video, filmed on their campus, students have written words on their own bodies. While students enact short vignettes, close-ups show words such as *family, determination, pride, honor, peace, bravery, creativity, resilience.* These are terms that more accurately describe who students say they are and convey what they care about.

They uploaded their video to YouTube, hoping to inspire dozens or, with luck, hundreds of people. Instead, the video quickly went viral, with hits topping 80,000 as a national audience responded to their positive, creative message.

Then Hanson got a call from a nonprofit organization, the National Association of Federally Impacted Schools, inviting her to bring students to speak to their national conference in Washington, D.C. During their trip to the nation's capital, National Public Radio interviewed students about their project and why it mattered. Students put their speaking skills to authentic use when they addressed the conference and, later, lobbied Congress to fund programs in their community.

Of course, the original project plan included none of these activities. As the project spiraled in new directions, Hanson welcomed each opportunity for her students to engage with the wider world. "They have discovered the power of words. They know how to use their own voice to get their message across," Hanson said in an interview with the authors, "and now they know how it feels to be motivated."

Keep your eyes open for unexpected opportunities to take your students' projects in new directions. At the end of a project, when students reflect on what they have learned, you might ask them to imagine next steps. A final reflection prompt might ask: "If you have the chance to keep going with this project, what will you do next?" Their answers might point you in unexpected directions.

Go Public

In the previous example, the press arranged to interview South Dakota students during their trip to Washington, D.C. Some teachers make a point of inviting the media into the classroom to learn more about students' projects.

Remember George Mayo, the middle-school teacher whose *Transitions* project was described in the chapter on language arts? He lets the media know when his students are doing newsworthy work. "When I listen to them answer a reporter's questions about what inspires them to write their stories, their answers blow me away. This is a real-world way to encourage reflection," he said in an interview with the authors.

On the day that his young authors received their *Transitions* books from the printer, for instance, a camera crew from the school district was on hand to record the occasion. The resulting video allowed students to share their learning experience with their families and gave other teachers in the district a window into a project-based classroom.

Mayo also plans an event each spring when his young filmmakers share their best work in a documentary showcase. They hold the event at an historic movie theater and even roll out a red carpet for student filmmakers. Such grand gestures inspire students to do their best work. That doesn't mean that the weeks leading up to the premiere are free of challenges. "It gets crazy," Mayo admits, as students work furiously to edit material they have been gathering for months. But the extra effort is worth it when students see their final cuts presented in a professional space.

To go public with projects, look for allies at your district public information office. Invite reporters from local media to consider writing about noteworthy student projects. Encourage students to issue press releases about their culminating events (developing their real-world marketing and public relations skills), or find other ways to let the public know what they have accomplished—and why it's worth knowing about.

Connect With Your Network

Throughout this book, we have encouraged you to connect with colleagues who share your interest in project-based learning. Connecting with your network will help good ideas spiral and build the culture of PBL in the larger education community.

Look for these opportunities to grow your network and exchange ideas about PBL:

- *In your own building:* Find a colleague (or several) who shares your interest in PBL. Rely on each other as sounding boards when you are designing projects. Offer critical feedback to improve on each other's ideas. Examine student work together. Are students meeting the quality standards you hope to achieve, or does student work reveal places where you need to focus improvements? Ideally, your school culture will support these professional conversations with dedicated time for teacher collaboration. Make sure school leaders see the results of student projects and enlist them as your PBL allies.

- *In your online network:* Thanks to social media, there are more networks than ever for making connections with colleagues. Here are a few with a PBL flavor: On Twitter, follow the hashtag #pblchat and take part in anytime discussions as well as weekly conversations about a specific aspect of PBL. On Edmodo, join the PBL community and tap online colleagues for ideas or inspiration. On Edutopia, take part in the PBL discussion group. On Classroom 2.0, join the group PBL: Better with Practice. Join the group Project Based Learning on Diigo, an online bookmarking site, and learn what others are tagging as useful on the web.

- *At special events:* PBL advocates tend to be active participants in the "unconference" movement. These loosely structured gatherings, sometimes called Edcamps, give educators opportunities to meet face-to-face for peer-led conversations.

- *In publications:* Look for opportunities to reflect on what has worked well or what's been challenging in projects. For example, the *Digital IS* site of the National Writing Project is a storehouse of rich teacher reflections. High Tech High produces an online, peer-reviewed journal called *Unboxed*, where teachers reflect on their project experiences. The Buck Institute for Education invites teachers to contribute project plans to its ever-expanding online project library.

CLOSING THOUGHTS

In our own experiences as PBL advocates, we have enjoyed the spiraling effects of working with—and learning from—teachers from around the globe who are interested in improving learning through engaging, meaningful projects. We've seen projects grow more ambitious as teachers gain confidence and get better connected through professional networks. We've seen the real-world connections grow, too, as experts and other community members become willing partners in the project-based learning enterprise. The biggest beneficiaries, of course, are the students who are taking a more active role in learning experiences that will stick with them for years to come.

We look forward to staying connected and hearing about the exciting, memorable learning opportunities that projects create for you, your community, and your students.

Appendix A

Project Library

PROJECT SKETCHES

Many projects are described in *Thinking Through Project-Based Learning*. Here they are again in an easy-to-scan digest, interspersed with additional project sketches that will get your imagination flowing.

Projects are loosely organized by grade band under the subject matter headings of Social Studies, Science, Math, and Language Arts. Because good projects extend into the "real" world, and because real life seldom happens in content-specific silos, most sketches describe interdisciplinary projects.

We encourage you to read with an open mind. If you see a project that strikes your fancy but is a grade band below or above what you teach, ask yourself, "How could I scale this up? Down?" If a project has an emphasis in a subject you do not teach, consider doing it anyway. Ask yourself, "How could I adjust this project so it's sure to address significant instructional aims for my subject? Who from other disciplines might want to collaborate?"

If you are reading this book as a staff activity, gather in groups of five or six and divide up the projects for close reading. In your groups, have each person share two or three projects that he or she thinks deserve the group's attention. Discuss. Together, ask yourselves, which projects resonate the most? Why? How might we adopt or adapt these projects for our classes?

SOCIAL STUDIES

1. Come Fly With Us: p. 59 (Grades K–2)

Driving Question: How do people work together to get a big job done?

After a commercial pilot visits school, a second-grade class designs its own airport. Their challenge is to get all the parts working together so

---

Note: To read more about projects that are described in more detail elsewhere in the book, see corresponding page numbers.

"passengers" make their way through ticketing, security, and boarding and get to their seats in time for a scheduled "flight." Along the way, they come to understand how different jobs and different functions of an airport all work together to create a system that puts people on the move.

2. Let's Be Fair (Grades K–2)

Driving Question: How can we share and be fair?

When faced with an issue of scarcity, first graders learn firsthand how rules and laws help people get along. Their teacher sets up a situation in which students are faced with a problem of scarcity—six handheld game consoles are distributed randomly among 25 eager students. After a period of chaos, students feel compelled to construct rules that govern individuals' actions for the good of the group. Their teacher draws on this experience later as students study how communities function. Credit: Kathy Cassidy, Moose Jaw, Alberta, Canada.

3. What's in a Name? (Grades K–5)

Driving Question: Does our school's name say who we are?

In this schoolwide and cross-school project, students plan a celebration of the source of their schools' names. (Note: They could investigate their city's namesake or the name given to a significant natural feature as well.) In the process, they answer: How does our name reflect who we once were and who we are today? How does our identity compare to that of other schools? Each grade takes on different aspects of the celebration, from doing research and producing multimedia at Grade 5 to writing songs and painting murals in Grade 1. Each school's celebration is filmed and shared with participating schools and their larger communities.

4. A Week in the Life: p. 168 (Grades 3–5)

Driving Question: How do our lives compare?

What can we learn from one another that we couldn't learn alone? A Week in the Life is a project for third through fifth grades. Over 6 weeks, kids from around the world build cultural understanding and awareness as they study how people in different places live and communicate. Credit: Flat Classroom Project. Join A Week in the Life at the Flat Classroom website: http://www.flatclassroomproject.org.

5. California, Here We Come! p. 133 (Grades 3–5)

Driving Question: How can we provide service that meets others' needs?

Fifth-grade "travel agents" plan a customer's air travel, taking into account time zones, distance, in-air and layover times, amenities, fares, taxes, baggage fees, and more. They present their customer with a proposal that includes a scale map and cost comparison table the client can use to make an informed decision. Credit: Lisa Moody, Point Pleasant, West Virginia.

6. Families Around the World: p. 132 (Grades 3–5)

Driving Question: How do the lives of families compare?

Students study a *Time* magazine photographic essay that shows families from around the world surrounded by the food they eat in a week and come up with these questions to investigate: What proportion of their income do these families spend on food? What is the caloric and nutritional value of each family's food? Who's healthiest? How can we help those with the most meager diet? See the "What the World Eats" photogallery here: http://www.time.com/time/photogallery/0,29307,1626519,00.html.

7. Plotting History (Grades 3–5)

Driving Question: How does the past share its stories?

Although they never leave the school grounds, students' "field trips" kick off significant history investigations. Before students study a pivotal historic period or event, teachers superimpose scale maps of the region of study over the school grounds, stash "artifacts" in locations relative to real historical sites, and retag each cache. For example, for the study of Lewis and Clark Corps of Discovery, Fort Mandan, the headwaters of the Great Falls in the Rockies, and Fort Clatsop are geotagged with a bit of history hidden in each place. An arrowhead, bullet casing, or a candle mold finds its way into caches, as well as raw materials such as deer hide and antler. Equipped with historical maps, geographic coordinates, and GPS devices, students set to work, puzzling out each item's significance to the era or events they are studying. History experts are on call to discuss students' theories and guide their investigations. As their studies conclude, students plan historical reenactments to share during a community celebration. In short dramas, each student stars as a historical figure and relates a true tale from the past. In preparing their dramas, with the help of experts, students transform cache materials into their own props, and in the process learn about tanning hides, flint napping, taxidermy, and dugout canoes.

8. Arkansas: Shape of Things to Come? (Grades 3–5)

Driving Question: Is our presence here inevitable?

Students learn about their state's geography, people, and pivotal turns in history up to statehood through two related projects. The first has them working from a landforms map and examining political maps from different periods prior to statehood to document the role of geography on human settlement and to show change over time. They tag major developments in cultural geography and history on a timeline and make judgments about which developments have had the greatest influence on society as we know it today. They look at factors that led to key events along with the impact of those events and write scripts for historic reenactments that are vetted by historians and history enthusiasts. Their reenactments demonstrate understanding of the causal nature and dynamism of history.

9. Let's Remember (Grades 3–5)

Driving Question: It was important then; is it important still?

A teacher brings a neglected local monument to students' attention and gets them thinking, *How has our community commemorated what it cares about over time?* A search of newspaper and historical society archives reveals a trove of documentary evidence of ribbon cuttings, statue unveilings, and more. Some memorials no longer exist and others are in poor repair. Some students create a virtual tour using Google maps for a kiosk at the local visitors' center. Others research the stories that have gone untold and recommend ways to commemorate people and events deserving recognition. Still others campaign for a day of recognition for unsung heroes who walk among us.

10. Bike Theft: p. 133 (Grades 3–5, 6–8)

Driving Question: How can we make our community safe?

The local newspaper reports that bike thefts are on the rise. Should everyone worry? Students address this question by examining local police records for monthly bicycle thefts, plotting the data on maps, and creating public service announcements and posters to inform the community about the best and most risky places to keep a bike.

11. Make Me Care: p. 58 (Grades 6–8)

Driving Question: Where should we focus our efforts to do the most good?

Student advisors help community members select local charities to support. They identify problems in their community and do a gap analysis to determine the nature and severity of the problems in relation to efforts to resolve them. They plan a night of persuasive "lightning" talks to garner support for charitable causes. They advertise the event using Twitter and Facebook, set up FirstGiving accounts (www.firstgiving.com) to collect donations, and, on show night, watch as donations roll in.

12. State of the City (Grades 6–8)

Driving Question: How does a town operate?

After initial local government studies, student teams create an organizational chart of their town, showing how the city functions and how decisions are made. Teams analyze each other's charts and ultimately settle on one collective chart. Next, they identify people holding key roles in different sectors of civic life. They ask the city manager to examine the chart and recommend adjustments. Now pairs of students select a job role, research it thoroughly, write a short paper, and prepare to interview the person who fills that role. Student interviews lead them to understand general civics and challenges unique to their city, as well as problems facing cities nationwide (such as an aging workforce and lack of career pipeline leading to city hall). They investigate ways to improve their city and decide which executive, legislative, or community actions are in order. Students present their "mayor" with critical issues and viable solutions to include in an upcoming State of the City speech.

13. Café Coffee Day: p. 97 (Grades 6–8)

Driving Question: How do our neighboring countries compare?

A middle-school teacher in India wants her students to learn about neighboring countries in South Asia. She has students pretend they are business owners who want to expand their companies to nearby countries. (She's setting up a task in which students compare and contrast to make an informed judgment as they learn about South Asia. She also could have asked them to act as philanthropists wanting to support charitable causes, or as professional sports executives wanting to expand cricket to more cities.) They use Wolfram Alpha and other sources to study socioeconomic data and draw conclusions about life and economy in other countries.

14. Sim City: p. 21 (Grades 6–8)

Driving Question: How do we make a place livable?

Using the simulation game Sim City, students build a virtual city in order to investigate urban design principles and growth patterns. Game-generated graphs and moment-in-time screenshots at various decision points serve as the basis for assessing their decisions around urban planning. This foray into systems thinking helps students as they go on to examine the built environment around them. As they consider their own city, they ask, Why were bridges built where they were? Why are high-rises luxury housing in some cities but low-income housing in others? Experts in land use and city planning help them understand how decisions were made in the past and how present thinking shapes decisions around livability. Credit: Julie Robison, Portland, Oregon.

15. Cigar Box Project: p. 87 (Grades 6–8)

Driving Question: How does the imagery we choose reflect who we are?

Students operate as historians do to understand Canada's colorful history by studying the commercial art on cigar boxes. They research the people and events portrayed and seek to interpret the stories the panels illustrate. They meet with a museum curator and historian to share their interpretations and ask questions and then go deeper, designing cigar boxes of their own drawn from the memories and perspectives of those whose stories are infrequently told. Credit: Neil Stephenson, Calgary, Alberta, Canada.

16. Granny Em on the Move (Grades 6–8)

Driving Question: How can we all get where we need to go?

Recently, a student's grandmother fell on a broken sidewalk and fractured her hip. Kids expressed concern about mobility and safety in the community. Groups craft "need-to-know" questions and investigate the needs of different citizen constituencies (elderly, disabled, bike commuters, parents with strollers, joggers, young pedestrians, etc.). They develop reasoned solutions to mobility concerns for those groups, develop an action plan, and campaign for change.

17. Look Into the Past: p. 96 (Grades 6–8, 9–12)

Driving Question: To what degree can we see the past in the present?

As students prepare for a history tour of Washington, D.C., their teacher presents them with a challenge: Each team is to find an illustration or photograph of a pivotal period or event in D.C. history, visit the site where the event took place, shoot a picture (or even a picture-in-a-picture), and write a photo essay describing the significance of the event in its time and its relevance today. When complete, students compile photo essays into a book published for inclusion in the school library (to inform future tour groups) and for submission to the D.C. Historical Society.

18. Mingling at the Renaissance Ball (Grades 6–8, 9–12)

Driving Question: Does "greatness" endure?

After a brief study of the Renaissance Period, students form affinity groups based on their interest in different fields that advanced during the period (medicine, architecture, science, arts, literature, etc.). Each group determines who the greats were in their area and then each student in the group studies one. Next, they pool their understanding and the team writes an operational definition of "greatness." They write a justification for their definition and present it to an expert for vetting or improvement. Once the definition is solid, each student makes a case for why his or her notable figure best exemplifies the definition. Ultimately they rank the figures, design an award that signifies the qualities of the field, and present it in character at their Renaissance Ball.

19. Civil War Then and Now: p. 60 (Grades 6–8, 9–12)

Driving Questions: Is war inevitable? Do civil wars share common roots?

History students examine events and conditions that contributed to the Civil War in the United States and compare these to factors influencing contemporary civil wars. Along the way they meet a newly minted citizen of South Sudan over Skype.

20. Deserts in Rainy Seattle? p. 9 (Grades 6–8, 9–12)

Driving Question: Is healthy food a right or a privilege?

In this project, students ponder issues of access to healthy food. After examining USDA nutrition guidelines, they discuss how easy or hard it is to meet them. They decide to investigate one barrier to good nutrition: access to healthy foods. Using government data (http://www.ers.usda .gov/data/fooddesert), teams identify local "food deserts" (defined as

Appendix A

neighborhoods in which fresh and affordable food is lacking) and attempt to "shop" for a week's menu using the USDA thrifty food budget (http://www.cnpp.usda.gov/usdafoodcost-home.htm). Using Google maps, spreadsheets, phone calls, grocery store advertisements, and actual visits to "desert" neighborhoods, students analyze food availability and afford-ability, interview residents, draw conclusions about issues of food access, and recommend ways to solve them.

21. Digiteens: p. 179 (Grades 6–9)

Driving Question: What does citizenship mean in the digital age?

In the Digiteens project, eighth- and ninth-grade students explore their rights and responsibilities as digital citizens. Teams from across the globe partner to study and then teach others about topics as wide ranging as cyberbullying, Internet fair use, and balancing security and personal free-dom. Credit: Flat Classroom Project. Join this year's project on the Flat Classroom website: http://www.flatclassroomproject.org.

22. Eracism: p. 179 (Grades 6–9)

Driving Question: How can our diversity be our strength?

Eracism is a global student debate that joins diverse cultures with the intention of building global competence and international-mindedness. Schools selected for the project enter a four-person team to debate other teams, and the remaining students in each class act as researchers around the topics of debate. The topic statement debated in 2012 was "Government regulation requiring immigrants to adopt the beliefs, habits, and language of the dominant culture does more harm than good." Credit: Flat Classroom Project. Join this year's project on the Flat Classroom website: http://www.flatclassroomproject.org.

23. Slavery in the Third Millennium: p. 79 (Grades 6–8, 9–12)

Driving Question: What can we do to address modern-day slavery around the world?

After reading a novel about a girl who was trafficked, students launch a social media campaign to speak out against modern-day slavery. They incorporate research on human rights to add authority to what could oth-erwise have been a strictly emotional appeal. Credit: Shelley Wright, Moose Jaw, Saskatchewan, Canada.

24. It's All About the Benjamins (Grades 9–12)

Driving Question: Does money really make the world go 'round?

Starting with the story of Argentina's currency collapse in 2002, stu-dents explore the role of money, currencies, commodities, and trade. After "news" of the collapse of the U.S. dollar, students invent alternative methods of trade (these may include bartering, gift economics, time banks) and test them through commerce for feasibility and fairness. Next, students study the history of money, work in groups to design their own national currencies, and then establish an exchange rate with other countries' currencies by calibrating against the value of a common basic good such as a loaf of bread. Tariffs, embargoes, and other mitigating factors are introduced during a final trade simulation designed by students.

25. Government for and of the People? p. 3 (Grades 9–12)

Driving Questions: How do everyday people engage with the government? Could government serve its people better?

High school students interact with federal functions as anyone might who navigates a bureaucratic process. Students explore government functions by "applying" for federal student aid or a green card, making a request permitted by the Freedom of Information Act, or submitting a complaint to the Better Business Bureau. Along the way, they analyze each process, present it in a diagram, and recommend ways the process might be improved. As students share their investigations, the class comes to understand the myriad ways in which citizens interact with government. Credit: Diana Laufenberg, Philadelphia, Pennsylvania.

26. Work the System, Change the World (Grades 9–12)

Driving Question: In what ways can citizens make a difference?

Using the Civic Action Project framework from the Constitutional Rights Foundation (http://www.crfcap.org), teams address an issue that concerns them and take civic action. In the process, they explore the relationships between the issue, their proposed actions, and the public policy they need to work within or attempt to change to make civic action possible. Students develop a cogent argument for their position, study opposing views, defend their solution, and rally others to their cause. Civic concerns students addressed in the past include: high school start times, coyotes in the park, euthanasia, increased funding for cancer research, sin tax on junk food, elder abuse, advocacy for "real size" models in fashion, crime against immigrants, and texting while driving.

27. Roll the Presses (Grades 9–12)

Driving Question: In what ways is information power?

Students investigate all aspects of the written word that affect the exchange of ideas, from innovations such as Johannes Gutenberg's 15th-century invention of the printing press to societal rules governing that exchange, such as legal protections and censorship. Students also examine the American constitutional guarantee of freedom of speech and consider ways it has been protected or compromised over time. Credit: Intel Education.

SCIENCE

28. Blue Fender Defender: p. 79 (Grades K–5, 6–8)

Driving Question: Can we make a difference?

Students learn that a butterfly species relies on a prairie habitat that is rapidly diminishing. Their research leads to a letter-writing and leafleting campaign that gets the community's attention, and part of a local park is returned to prairie.

29. The Square of Life: p. 8 (Grades K–2)

Driving Question: Why do some creatures live in one place but not another?

Primary classrooms studying life science team up over Skype to explore diversity, habitat, and niche. They are registered in the Square of Life, an Internet-based collaborative project in which students investigate their local environment and share information with students from around the world (http://ciese.org/curriculum/squareproj/). Student teams select a square meter of local ground to examine. They organize what they find into categories based on shared characteristics and learn to discriminate between living and nonliving, plants and animals, insects and isopods, and more. They theorize about and investigate the role of habitat and niche in the distribution of organisms. They share their findings through Skype with Australian students and report their conclusions about *Why here and not there? Why there and not here?*

30. Don't Be S-s-scared: The Truth About Snakes! p. 103 (Grades K–2)

Driving Question: Where would we be without snakes?

In this project, second-grade students root out truths about snakes' place in the world and speak up for these often-maligned reptiles. One of their products is a music video they write and star in, set to the tune of Lady Gaga's hit, "Born This Way." The clever lyrics include scientific facts students discovered during their in-depth investigation. Students also produce a richly illustrated book, *What Snake Am I? A Clue Book of Snakes From Around the World,* and donate copies to the Harvard Museum of Natural History and a local wildlife sanctuary for use in educational programs. Credit: Jenna Gampel, Brighton, Massachusetts.

31. Be Prepared (Grades 3–5)

Driving Question: How can we prepare for a natural disaster in our area?

Student groups study the instances of natural disaster in their region over time and identify the best ways to avoid, prepare for, and react to different disasters. They seek advice from first responders, city management personnel, and others as they create brochures and public service announcements for the community. This scenario could be expanded to imagine living in other places in the world where a different assortment of natural disasters occur.

32. World Tree Watch: p. 112 (Grades 3–5)

Driving Question: What conditions influence where and how trees grow?

Students in Grades 4 and 5 in the United States and Japan observe the role of trees in their communities. They do tree surveys to identify the numbers and kinds of native and cultivated trees. They meet with city arborists to learn about the growing conditions necessary for healthy trees in their location and compare these criteria. Students exchange photos, artistic renderings, haiku poetry, and descriptions that help them compare trees, geography, and climate in the two countries. They each find a tree that can be grown in the other school's environment and send these to the partner school as part of Planting Day ceremonies.

33. The Landmark Game (Grades 3–5, 6–8)

Driving Question: How do landmarks tell the story of who we are?

In this global game, classes choose landmarks anywhere in the world and become experts on them. They compile nine interesting clues and dole out three at a time as other classes try to guess the landmark by asking questions for which a simple "yes" or "no" must suffice. Along the way, students refine their writing, problem solving, critical thinking, map reading, and organizational skills. At the end of 3 weeks, the team guessing the most landmarks is declared the winner. The Landmark Game project runs each year in February. Join at http://www.kidlink.org/project/landmark. Credit: Terry Smith, Macomb, Illinois.

34. The Garden Project: p. 132 (Grades 3–5, 6–8)

Driving Question: How does a garden grow?

Students break into research groups to study different considerations for growing a garden. One subset of questions students investigate relates to determining when to plant: *If tender plants require a steady ground temperature of 55°, when should we start recording daily soil temperatures? What instruments or materials will we need? What patterns might historical temperature records reveal? Is there a way to speed up the process?* Other research teams look at selecting crops suited for the local climate, calculating the expense of gardening relative to yields, and lining up experts such as the county extension agent, farmers, and gardening grandparents.

35. The Great Carbon Race: p. 112 (Grades 6–8)

Driving Question: How can I change my carbon footprint and tread more lightly on the world?

After completing a project called The Problem with Oil, eighth-grade students focus on greenhouse gases, an issue related to the combustion of oil but related to other emissions, too. In The Great Carbon Race, students are challenged with the question: Who can save the most carbon from entering the atmosphere? They have to defend their results using clear, credible evidence for the class courtroom. Students are graded by the quality of their evidence, and the biggest footprint reducers are crowned Carbon King and Carbon Queen. Credit: Sue Boudreau, Orinda, California. See more Take Action Projects at http://takeactionscience.wordpress.com.

36. Water, Water, Everywhere? (Grades 6–8)

Driving Question: What problems does the world face with its water supply?

In this collaborative project, students research the world's water problems, particularly relating to fresh water, and focus on how their personal water use affects aquatic ecosystems in their communities. Students participate in email exchanges as they explore the global importance of water. See ePals http://www.epals.com/projects/info.aspx?DivID=Water_over view. Credit: ePals.

37. Energy Diet: p. 63 (Grades 6–8)

Driving Question: Can we spend money to save money?

Student consultants advise their city council, director of a retirement home, business owner, and other ratepayers on ways to invest in improvements (i.e., solar panels, insulation, regulation sensors) that will save them energy and money. On the way to proposing a plan of action, each team conducts an energy audit, evaluates options for saving energy, and calculates investment costs, loans, and payback based on their client's budget. They seek advice from a nonprofit that helps utility customers save energy and run their proposals by experts here before sharing them with clients.

38. Low Energy at the Fitness Center: p. 113 (Grades 6–8)

Driving Question: How can we conserve energy?

A nearby fitness center wants to conserve energy so it can keep club prices low. The director appeals to students to analyze the center's energy usage and propose recommendations. Students study the center's energy bill, investigate alternative energy sources, complete cost/benefit analyses for competing innovative ideas, examine government weatherization incentives plans, and create graphs to substantiate their recommendations.

39. Life in the Balance (Grades 6–8, 9–12)

Driving Question: What causes an ecosystem to hang together or fall apart?

An ecology class considers factors of regulation and equilibrium by modeling population dynamics in a desert ecosystem. Students plot data and look for relationships among populations (example: coyote and desert hare) over time as they investigate the question "What causes an ecosystem to hang together or fall apart?"

40. Los Rayos X: p. 61 (Grades 9–12)

Driving Question: How can we put energy from the electromagnetic spectrum to work safely?

Physical science students investigate electromagnetic waves and differences and similarities between kinds of waves as a means of transmitting energy by examining consumer products that put electromagnetic waves to work. They write consumer manuals that explain how products function and advise on their safe use and disposal. Some of the products and devices include X-rays, MRIs and other imaging technologies; compact fluorescent, incandescent, and LED bulbs; ultraviolet light-protecting products like house paints and sunscreen; laser beams; digital, plasma, and LCD televisions; wifi, radios, microwaves, satellites dishes, repeaters, and antennas for telecommunications; surgical gamma ray knives and Geiger counters; infrared and radio-frequency remote controllers such as automobile key fobs, garage door openers, TV remotes, and Bluetooth devices; and bombs that create an electromagnetic pulse.

41. Checks and Balances: p. 112 (Grades 9–12)

Driving Question: What systems do pros use to ensure quality work?

In a physics and engineering project, high school seniors use engineering methods to study technical failures that lead to real-world disasters. Before diving into a final performance task, an investigation of the 2003 Space Shuttle *Columbia* accident, students apply real checks and balances that govern practices of engineering. They learn to pick apart a problem using root cause analysis and probe issues of workplace culture that interfere with the discovery of engineering problems using Harvard University's corrective and preventive action method. Credit: Technology High School, Sonoma, California.

42. Phys Newtons: p. 70 (Grades 9–12)

Driving Question: How can we best represent Newtonian physics?

An art and physics project has students researching one of Newton's Laws (motion, gravity, energy, circular motion, or projectiles) and then painting images to illustrate the law. They design a page for a book called *Phys Newton*, using a combination of images and text. A page explaining Newton's Second Law, for instance, features a series of images showing a baseball player going through the motions of pitching. Accompanying text explains the relationship between force and acceleration. In an authentic performance assessment, students use their book to teach their peers about Newton's laws. Credit: Andrew Gloag and Jeff Robin, San Diego, California.

43. Microbes Ate My Driveway (Grades 9–12)

Driving Question: How does bioremediation work to keep the environment safe?

Equipped with a basic understanding of the hazards of motor oil to the environment, ecology students study microbes, bioswales, and other bioremediation methods and plan investigations that ultimately lead to recommendations for ridding the pavement of the school parking lot of motor oil before it runs off into the water system.

44. Kinetic Conundrum (Grades 9–12)

Driving Question: How does art move us?

After investigating and documenting public art in their community, students set out to create their own kinetic sculptures. Working in teams, they design and build prototypes for sculptures that move or change in response to the environment. Developing their plans involves researching art and engineering, making mathematical calculations, learning about the history of public art projects, and using language arts to write artists' statements explaining their intent. They share their prototypes at a community art showcase where attendees vote on a "best in show" that will be produced for a park in the community. Credit: King Middle School, Portland Maine. Watch a video about the project at Edutopia: http://www.edutopia .org/stw-maine-project-based-learning-kinetic-art-video.

MATH

45. Birthday Math: p. 132 (Grades K–5)

Driving Question: How can we know who we are as a group?

It turns out that two students in class were born on the same day, which causes students to speculate, *How could we find out whether other kids in our school were born on September 7? Could we find and connect all the birthday buddies in the school?* Small groups propose research methods such as examining school records and surveying classes and then discuss the merits of each before settling on a plan. Once all birthday buddies are identified, students plan a social event through which all buddies become acquainted.

46. Eye-Opening Experience: p. 133 (Grades 3–5)

Driving Question: How do we compare?

Students across the United States and around the world join Connecticut fifth graders to count the number of metal eyelets on their shoes. Shoes and eyelets? What kind of math project could this be? In it, students engage in prediction and estimation; data collection, representation, and analysis; review of variables; and calculating mean, median, and mode. In addition, they meet new friends around the world and learn about geography, culture, and differences and similarities in life (and shoes) around the world.

47. Which Wheels to the Museum? p. 132 (Grades 6–8)

Driving Question: How do we balance safety, speed, and expense to get where we need to go?

A group of 43 of us are traveling to the museum next month. What forms of transportation should we consider to get where we need to go quickly, inexpensively, and safely? Students study the public transit system, van rentals, use of parent cars, bicycles, and other means of travel and examine expense, safety, and liability issues associated with each to arrive at a recommended "best" mode of transportation.

48. What's the Plan? p. 132 (Grades 6–8, 9–10)

Driving Question: How can we help consumers weigh their options?

Mobile phone plans are complicated, and families are trying to live within tight budgets. Students help families choose the best cell phone plan for their needs from among local providers. They use algebra as they analyze plans, create comparative graphs and charts, and write a letter justifying their recommendations. Credit: Telannia Norfar, Oklahoma City, Oklahoma. Learn about Telannia Norfar's treatment of this topic at: http://www.edutopia.org/economic-stimulus-education-technology-oklahoma.

49. Juice Boxes: p. 132 (Grades 6–8)

Driving Question: What are the best ways to package goods?

How strange. These juice boxes can have different dimensions but hold the same amount of juice. What is going on? Students decide to measure different brands of juice box boxes to find out which has the greatest amount of juice while using the least packaging material. They compare prices to figure out who's making more money, too! One group investigates the quality of the contents, determining which product is the healthiest. Ultimately, students select (or redesign) one product that meets the highest criteria for quality, container, and price.

50. Home Improvement (Grades 6–8)

Driving Question: How can we maximize the effort of volunteers?

In this math and service-learning project, students get on board with a Habitat for Humanity project, helping to build a home for a local family. The project manager asks them to recommend how to make interior painting more efficient. The problem? This stage of the process is popular with new volunteers but often results in wasted paint. Students calculate the interior surface areas that need to be painted in the new house and estimate how much paint should be needed to finish the job. Then they develop a quick training program to teach volunteers how to paint more efficiently. They recruit volunteers from their school community and lead them through the training. Newly trained volunteers work in shifts to complete the painting job in a timely and efficient way. Credit: Jill Sumerlin, Tillamook, Oregon. Read about the project in an archived issue of *NW Teacher* magazine, downloadable as PDF at http://educationnorth west.org/webfm_send/347.

51. A Penny Saved (Grades 6–8)

Driving Question: How can we use money wisely?

A local man wins a large amount of money in the lottery and asks for advice on how to invest his winnings wisely. Students contact local tax advisors, investment advisers, and financial institutions to understand how the financial industry works and learn from the stories and decisions of past lottery winners. Along the way, they learn investment terms, use algebra to explore compound interest, and create graphs showing how different investment schemes play out over time.

52. Human vs. Doll: p. 132 (Grades 6–8, 9–10)

Driving Questions: How do our idealized selves compare with reality? Who decides what form our play takes?

Some dolls and action figures have extreme body proportions. Could toys with more realistic human proportions capture the market? Students bring in Barbies, GI Joes, and other dolls and action figures. They determine what the dolls' relative body proportions would be if each were the height of an average woman or man. Next, they design a doll or an action figure with the proportions of an actual human and figure out how to market it so it outsells Barbie and Joe.

53. Ball Skills and Parabolas: p. 133 (Grades 9–12)

Driving Question: Do ball skills come down to technique or talent?

Student teams examine the projectile motion of a ball used in a favorite sport and explain mathematically and practically how to adjust its parabola for best scoring results.

54. Math Is Beautiful (Grades 9–12)

Driving Question: In what ways can we represent math through art?

Students create an all-math art exhibit for the local museum. They present beautiful nature photos to illustrate Fibonacci's golden mean; create harmonograms, spirographs, and Lissajous figures using the online Encyclogram (http://www.mathcats.com/explore/encyclo/ency clogram.html); and create fractal art. Their projects involve Fibonacci series, sine curves in trigonometry, and algebra and complex numbers for fractals. Credit: Wendy Petti, Washington, D.C. See: Math Cats at http:// mathcats.com.

55. Knit Me Some Math Pants (Grades 9–12)

Driving Question: How can we represent polyhedral patterns in tactile forms?

In this advanced geometry project, students explore polyhedral models as they knit hyperbolic octagon pants and three-dimensional Mobius strips called Klein bottles. Credit: Sarah-Marie Belcastro, Amherst, Massachusetts. See: The Home of Mathematical Knitting: http://www.toroidalsnark.net/mathknit.html.

56. Angry Birds Physics: p. 101 (Grades 9–12)

Driving Questions: What laws of physics hold in Angry Birds World? How do software engineers make decisions?

A best-selling video game becomes the basis for an investigation of projectile motion as physics students investigate the question: "What laws of physics hold in Angry Birds World?' Students seek answers questions like these: *Does the white bird conserve momentum when it drops its bomb? Why would the game designer want the white bird to drop its bomb the way that it does? The yellow bird changes velocity with the tap of a finger. Analyze more than one flight path to answer this: What are the details of its change in velocity?* To investigate these questions, students make screencasts of game play using Jing, Screencast-O-Matic, or Camtasia Studio, then do analysis. To support their scientific thinking, they use tools for data analysis and modeling, such as Logger Pro and Tracker Video. Credit: Frank Noschese, Cross River, New York, and John Burk, Delaware.

57. The Floor Covering Scenario 2: Waste Not, Want Not: p. 11 (Grades 6–8)

Driving Question: How can we divert usable material from the waste stream?

A hotel renovation nearby is the spark for a project on waste and reuse. Upon seeing piles of discarded carpet on the street, students estimate how much carpet, by volume, is destined for the landfill. They go on to look at issues of—and solutions to—dumping carpet and other bulky, composite waste. The project continues with students working with a reuse and recycling center to find ways to clean, donate, place, and even advertise and resell used carpeting. Learn more about diverting bulky waste from landfills at ReMade: http://www.remade-southeast.co.uk/rse/docs/bulkywaste.cfm.

58. Geometric Forms in the Built World: p. 132 (Grades 6–8)

Driving Question: How is geometry expressed in the built world?

Students investigate the driving question by examining famous architecture from around the world and identifying as many different geometric solids as they can. Next, they design their own buildings in SketchUp and tell stories of their historical or architectural significance.

59. Perfect Wedding: p. 133 (Grades 6–8)

Driving Question: How can we use longitudinal data to make a decision?

Let's pick the perfect evening for an outdoor wedding! In pairs, students collect temperature and sunset data for a major U.S. city and model the averages using sinusoidal functions. They present the data in a way the bridal couple understands so they can make an informed choice for a wedding date.

60. Buy Low, Sell High (Grades 6–8)

Driving Question: How does money grow?

In a stock exchange project, teams of students research and then select two stocks they want to follow, such as McDonald's, Toys R Us, or Great Adventure. They make a brochure for prospective investors that includes a graph of stock prices over short- and long-term periods; figure out the amount of stock they can buy with a given amount of money; and learn what decision rules investors use to decide when to buy and sell. Ultimately, they advise the purchase of one company's stock over the other.

61. 20 Years Old and in Debt! p. 133 (Grades 9–12)

Driving Question: How can we prosper and not go into debt?

College freshmen carry an average of $1,585 in credit card debt, the cost of three iPads! Students create a scenario that shows they understand what it takes to manage their own credit cards and also consider alternatives to credit cards.

62. Let's Design a Shopping Mall (Grades 9–12)

Driving Questions: How do we engineer the designed world? What considerations go into designing complex and multipurpose megastructures?

Students take on the role of architects to design a shopping mall. In teams, they research the design of malls by looking at blueprints made available by an architecture firm. They study land use considerations and research the cost of designing and building the mall. Next, teams pick features of the mall on which to concentrate. For example, one team works on parking: where to put it and how many employee, service, and customer parking spots to create. (This feature of the project focuses on linear programming and maximization: How much money does a customer space bring in at a mall? How many employee and service spaces should there be relative to the number of customer spaces?) Design teams need to work together to reconcile their contributions into a single plan, which they render in SketchUp (http://www.sketchup.com/intl/en/industries/education.html).

The end product is a presentation to a panel of architects and city planners, who will weigh in on the quality of their proposals.

63. Lockers, Schmockers (Grades 9–12)

Driving Question: How do we make our environment work for us?

As a school becomes increasingly digital and paperless, students' needs for storage space change. When it's time to install new lockers, the principal asks students to investigate all options and propose a solution. As they proceed, students study students' storage needs, geometric concepts of volume and surface area, costs, aesthetics, and alternative storage approaches on their way to making a proposal to the principal, superintendent, and school board.

LANGUAGE ARTS

64. Building Bridges to Tomorrow (Grades K–2)

Driving Question: What's life like for other children?

In a project of cultural understanding, young children from around the world use digital media to collaborate around topics such as: How We Play, Celebrating Together, Part of a Family, Making a Meal, Sharing Stories, and Our View From the Window. Credit: Flat Classroom Project. Join A Week in the Life at the Flat Classroom website: http://www.flatclass roomproject.org.

65. Global Book Club (Grades K–2, 3–5)

Driving Question: Is taste in literature universal?

Students partner with kids in other places to form book groups and read on topics of shared interest. In the process, they learn to set up and moderate group discussions, create a shared blog for each book, and negotiate time differences for real-time conversations. Conversations, not surprisingly, expand beyond the book and lead to several projects, including fundraising to put books into the hands of kids who can't afford them and collaborations on advertising of favorite books.

66. Story Like a Pebble: p. 79 (Grades K–2, 3–5)

Driving Question: How do our stories shape who we are?

Students learn about oral traditions of storytelling as they interview family members for a podcasting project called Stories from the Heart (http://blogs.egusd.net/mscheung). By making their interviews public, the class helps listeners learn from each other's stories and recognize the importance of drawing out stories from their own families. Credit: Theresa Cheung, Sacramento, California.

67. The Monster Exchange (Grades 3–5)

Driving Questions: Does communication always work? Do we all see the same thing?

Almost one-quarter of a million kids have participated in the Monster Exchange since 1995. Classes sign up for the online Monster Exchange and each is assigned a body part. Each draws and then describes its part as accurately as possible so other classes can recreate it perfectly. Their descriptions go into a shared table in a wiki so everyone can see all the parts. Each class constructs the entire monster as well as it can based on the descriptions. It turns out that writing precisely and interpreting what others describe is hard! And making a head that matches a neck that matches a body requires collaboration! Once the monsters are created, they are photographed and the photos are uploaded to a gallery for all to enjoy. Along the way, kids learn to read and write for a purpose, learn to work cooperatively and collaboratively, and make new friends. Teachers acquire new professional partners in the monster community. Credit: founders Brian Maguire, Suzie Calvert, and Terry Smith.

68. Let's Remember (Grades 3–5, 6–8)

Driving Question: If it was important then, is it important still?

A teacher brings a neglected local monument to students' attention and gets them thinking, *How has our community documented what it cares about over time?* Along with interviews with elders, a search of newspaper and historical society archives reveals a trove of documentary evidence of ribbon cuttings, statue unveilings, and more. Some memorials no longer exist and others are in poor repair. Some students create a virtual tour using Google maps for a kiosk at the local visitors' center. Others research the stories that have gone untold and recommend ways to commemorate people and events deserving recognition. Still others campaign for a day of recognition for unsung heroes who walk among us.

69. Global Peace Movie Project (Grades 3–5, 6–8, 9–12)

Driving Question: How can I make the world a more peaceful place?

The Global Peace Movie Project brings together schools in more than 20 countries for filmmaking around the message of peace. Each year, in conjunction with the International Day of Peace, fourth graders at Lafayette Regional School curate the 30-second to 1-minute film submissions into a longer film. Credit: Garret Ferguson, Franconia, New Hampshire. Join the growing community of peacemakers here: http://globalpeacemovie.weebly.com.

70. Transitions: p. 73 (Grades 6–8)

Driving Question: How can our experiences help pave the way for others?

In the Transitions project, students draw from their personal experiences and apply reading, writing, speaking, and listening skills along with visual literacy, creativity, empathy, and an understanding of media arts as they share their wisdom to help other children learn from life's challenges. The result? A book called *Transitions*, available on Amazon. Credit: George Mayo, Silver Spring, Maryland. This is one of many projects featured on the Nerdy Book Club. See: http://nerdybookclub.wordpress.com.

71. Language Comes Alive! (Grades 6–8)

Driving Question: How can we illustrate the essence of literary terms?

In this language arts and multimedia project, Wikistix, modeling clay, Legos, and action figures are all put to work as students create stop-motion animation to illustrate literary concepts, terms, and devices such as characterization, denouement, hyperbole, metaphor, literary conflict, personification, and plot. Credit: George Mayo, Silver Spring, Maryland. Learn more at The Longfellow Ten: http://lf10.wordpress.com.

72. Coming of Age in Literature (Grades 6–8)

Driving Question: What can literature set in the past teach us about how to live in the present?

Through reading *Roll of Thunder, Hear My Cry, Sounder, To Kill a Mockingbird, A Member of the Wedding, The Watsons Go to Birmingham*, and *The Legend of Buddy Bush*, students analyze, explain, and support with details from the novels seven key themes: growing up, family relationships, understanding and empathy, justice and law, racial prejudice, courage and sacrifice, and life in a place. Students create a Glogster poster that illustrates the details of each theme and contrasts them with life today.

73. The Dane's Destiny (Grades 9–12)

Driving Question: What causes a plot to go one way rather than another?

English students examine how events unfold in *Hamlet* and determine whether Hamlet's fate would have changed if his actions, such as his timing for killing Claudius, were different. In doing this project, students focus on the causal elements of plot as well as character profiles to describe alternate scenarios.

74. A Hero in My Eyes: p. 49 (Grades 9–12)

Driving Question: Who are the heroes among us?

A Hero in My Eyes is a beginning-of-the-year project in which students produce a photo portrait that captures a heroic moment. Students learn photography through trips to a local museum of photography and by working with a local photographer. For their culminating event, students present their work in a gallery setting. Standing next to their exhibits, students talk with parents and other community members about what about what defines a hero to them. This "right-sized:" event gets them ready for the larger audiences they will share their work with later in the year. Credit: Diana Cornejo-Sanchez, San Diego, California.

75. Invisibility Project: p. 13 (Grades 9–12)

Driving Question: What does it take to open people's eyes?

Students provide a public service by bringing the invisible to light through a multimedia exhibition that exposes hidden paradigms, underground cultures, and unresolved issues. Some of their topics include graffiti, rave culture, youth activism, self-mutilation, and the media. Student documentaries, photo/sound essays, and video installations showcase information gathered from on-the-street videography, expert interviews, and in-depth investigations of local professional, cultural, and institutional communities. Credit: Margaret Noble and Lacey Segal, San Diego, California.

76. Hollywood Nights (Grades 9–12)

Driving Question: How do our stories reflect what matters to us?

Through writing, storyboarding, and multiple cycles of critique, students create digital stories about a defining moment, message, or lesson learned from their own lives or the life of someone they know. In the process of creating their stories, students collect images, record voice-overs, and use digital movie-making software to produce short films. They share their presentations on the big screen for peers and parents at a Digital Storytelling Exhibition Night. Credit: High Tech High, San Diego, California.

77. Every 26 Seconds: p. 79 (Grades 9–12)

Driving Question: How can we all cross the finish line together?

Every 26 seconds, a student drops out of high school. High school students respond to this statistic by participating in "26 Seconds," a national advertising campaign in which they challenge one another not to become statistics. Student-produced videos of inspirational stories, scary statistics, and even flashmobs are designed to motivate a specific audience—their peers. See 26 Seconds at: http://www.26seconds.com.

Appendix B

Discussion Guide

*T*hinking Through Project-Based Learning introduces strategies and exercises to take inquiry deeper in PBL. The authors recommend discussing these ideas with colleagues to foster professional learning and personal reflection. This discussion guide is intended as a starting point for collegial conversations.

CHAPTER 1: THE WHYS AND HOWS OF PBL

1. Chapter 1 provides a succinct definition of project-based learning. How closely does this 25-word description match your current understanding of PBL? What would you add or change?

2. In Project Signpost 1, the authors ask you to sum up what projects accomplish in a Twitter-sized phrase (140 characters). How did the constraint influence your thinking? Now imagine having students share their understanding in a short phrase or headline. What's the value of writing extreme summaries?

3. In the end-of-chapter exercise, the authors ask you to choose from four projects. Which one do you wish you had tackled as a student? Discuss your reasoning. Now, think about what might be challenging about implementing the same project with your students. As a teacher, how will you decide if a project is worth the effort to overcome potential challenges? What else would you like to know about this project idea before attempting it yourself?

CHAPTER 2: THE INQUIRING HUMAN ANIMAL

1. Table: Applying Mind-Brain-Education Science Insights to Projects summarizes five key concepts that have emerged from the relatively young field of mind, brain, and education science. How do these

concepts influence how you think about teaching and learning? Discuss the implications of mind, brain, and education science for shaping your approach to project-based learning.

2. The exercise "Encourage Executive Skills" asks you to consider the skills and dispositions (habits of mind) that students can develop through PBL. Think about your own skills and dispositions. In the areas where you are strongest, what has helped you to develop particular skills or dispositions? How do you accommodate skills in which you are weaker?

3. What do you notice about your students' attention cycles? What are some ways you can maximize phases of peak learning?

4. Do you use predicable classroom routines that help to minimize stress for students? What do you notice about students' responses to these routines?

5. Which of the brain-based project strategies have you tried with your students? What did you notice as a result?

CHAPTER 3: MAKING THE WORLD SAFE FOR THINKING

1. Principal Richard Coote from Birkdale Intermediate School makes a strong case for building student buy-in to projects: "We know that if a project is flat at the outset, it's going to be six weeks of dragging students along." What have you done to get students engaged in projects at the outset?

2. Consider the suggestions about school design offered in *The Third Space* (such as: display learning; emulate museums; make classrooms agile). How is your classroom like a museum? How do you display evidence of learning? How easy or hard is it to reconfigure your classroom for different kinds of activities?

3. How have you reinvented learning spaces on a budget? Which of the ideas for "Putting the Pieces Together" might you try in the future? Which seem impractical for your context?

4. What's at the top of your PBL wish list? Discuss your additions to the table at the end of this chapter.

CHAPTER 4: THE THINKING-OUT-LOUD-AND-IN-VIEW CLASSROOM

1. Teacher Mike Gwaltney uses the phrase "teaching backwards" to describe how he connects students' current interests to history projects. What might you ask your students to find out about their concerns or interests?

2. Discuss the characteristics of "fertile questions" developed by Harpaz and Lefstein. What might you ask your students if you wanted to stir their thinking with an "undermining" question?

3. Compare how you modified the driving questions in the exercise Make Good Questions Even Better. Explain how your versions are improvements over those offered here. Which one would you expect to generate the most student interest?

4. Discuss the suggestions offered in the section Help Students Build a Thinking Toolkit. Which ones are you most likely to try? Why?

CHAPTER 5: DESIGNING RICH LEARNING EXPERIENCES

1. This chapter suggests two routes to project design: (1) Start with standards and plan learning experiences based on these objectives. (2) "Back in" to the standards, starting with a compelling idea and then mapping it to objectives to ensure there is a fit with what students are expected to learn. Which approach describes how you have planned projects in the past? Do you agree with the authors' assertion that the second approach may be more generative?

2. Which professions relate to your subject area(s)? How might you expand on real-life connections for projects?

3. Think about your strategies for scaffolding students' critical thinking (such as use of thinking maps or Socratic seminars). Discuss how you might incorporate these strategies into projects.

4. Share your project sketches with colleagues. How might you revise your project sketch based on critical feedback?

CHAPTER 6: THINKING ACROSS DISCIPLINES

1. The authors suggest that most work that gets accomplished takes interdisciplinary efforts. They write, "It's hard to think of a career field or profession that operates in isolation." Do you emphasize interdisciplinary thinking with your students? How?

2. If you have specific content-area expertise, how would you describe the "lenses" of your discipline?

3. Discuss the four features of interdisciplinary work described by Veronica Boix Mansilla and colleagues at Project Zero. How do you talk about the importance of "thoughtful" or "purposeful" learning with your students?

4. As a group, examine the Venn diagram at the end of this chapter. Suggest careers that are not represented here. Where would they belong? What kind of thinkers would be well-suited for these roles?

CHAPTER 7: LANGUAGE ARTS

1. George Mayo describes the kind of classroom environment necessary for students to be successful writers. He says, "Before you can get students to open up in their writing, you have to make sure they feel comfortable, that they respect one another, and that they will not be put down if they honestly share ideas." What are your strategies for creating a respectful climate for learning?

2. Nonfiction writer Rebecca Skloot offers a vivid example of how curiosity can take hold and keep us motivated to keep learning. What do you do to nurture your students' curiosity in the language arts classroom? Discuss and compare strategies.

3. The authors encourage robust discussions—between peers, among groups, and as a whole class—during the investigation stage of projects. How do you encourage "good talk" in your classroom?

4. Tech Spotlights in this chapter suggest tools for curating content and building information literacy. Which tools do you think would be most useful with your students? How do you accomplish those tasks now?

5. Common Core State Standards call for increased emphasis on nonfiction reading. How do you help readers engage with challenging text? If your content area is not language arts, how might you team up with the literacy experts in your school to support your students?

CHAPTER 8: SOCIAL STUDIES

1. The authors point out the shrinking time allotted to the social studies in U.S. schools. What is your experience with finding time in the curriculum for teaching social studies? How do you ensure that students are developing the skills and attitudes to become competent, contributing citizens?

2. What do you think of the observation by historian H. W. Brands that young people tend to focus on the future, not the past? How might you borrow his strategy of using today's events to connect the study of history with students' current interests?

3. Discuss the 10 thematic strands of the social studies. Where do you see the strongest connections to your standards? To interdisciplinary opportunities?

4. The Tech Spotlight in this chapter introduces Wolfram Alpha, a computational search engine. Have you used this as a classroom tool before? What ideas for your own projects might you borrow from the Café Coffee Day example?

CHAPTER 9: SCIENCE

1. How do you respond to the authors' question, "Do you consider yourself a scientist?" Compare your response with colleagues.

2. Don't be S-s-scared: The Truth About Snakes offers a good example of a project that goes beyond superficial understanding of science. Reread the project description and discuss what sets this project apart from more elementary science assignments (such as retelling facts about a favorite animal).

3. Chemist Katie Hunt shares some of the early life experiences that whetted her interest in science. When she learned something new, for instance, her father prompted her to ask, "Where else could you use that in something you're trying to do?" How do you help students see the connection between what they are learning today in science and what they might want to accomplish or understand in the future?

4. In their discussion of coupled inquiry, the authors suggest how this approach can be extended into PBL. Discuss a science activity that you have done in the past and imagine how you might remodel it into a project using this approach.

5. Have you ever engaged in citizen science projects—as part of school activities or on your own? What did you gain from the experience? With colleagues, discuss which of the examples could be incorporated into school projects. How might your students' attitudes change if they knew they were making real contributions to science?

CHAPTER 10: MATH

1. This chapter begins with a comparison of routine math procedures versus math concepts. Where do you spend more of your time with students? Discuss the challenges of exploring concepts before teaching procedures. How might students respond if you put concepts first?

2. Think about the finding from Alan Schoenfeld that students' understanding of math methods tends to be "inert." Have you seen students struggle to apply problem-solving strategies to new or ambiguous situations? How do you help them work through this?

3. Computer scientist Jeannette Wing traces her enduring interest math to the puzzles and games she enjoyed as a child. She also credits her parents for providing encouragement for her chosen career field. Compare her experiences as a budding computational thinker to those of your students. Who supports their interest in mathematics? Who are their math role models?

4. Discuss the idea of starting a Math Teachers' Circle. What purpose might this serve in your context? Who might be interested in joining you? How do you extend your math teachers' network with the use of digital tools?

5. What do you think of the authors' suggestion that it's "culturally permissible to be poor at math"? Have you seen evidence of this?

CHAPTER 11: THE PROJECT SPIRAL

1. Has a project of yours ever "spiraled" in directions you didn't anticipate or reach audiences you didn't expect? Share your stories. How do you think your students would react to having a project "go big"?

2. Talking about project experiences with colleagues—in person or online—can help recharge your batteries for the hard work of PBL. Where do you connect with colleagues who share your interest in PBL? Discuss the value of your personal learning networks. How has your teaching improved as a result of connecting?

3. At the end of a project, what evidence of learning do you keep for your classroom archives? How do you use these artifacts (for example, as curated exhibits of learning or as exemplars of student work for future classes to analyze)?

4. Talk about your identity as a PBL teacher or instructional leader. How does the project experience shape how you see yourself as a learner and teacher? Where do you want to go next with your professional learning?

Appendix C

Professional Development Guide

Project-based learning offers fertile ground for professional development. The project examples, exercises, and signposts included in *Thinking Through Projects* can be used as the starting point for collegial conversations about PBL, action research, project design (or remodeling), professional learning community (PLC) discussions, and more.

Here are six suggested exercises for use in facilitated professional development, PLC groups, online communities, or other groups that share an interest in taking inquiry deeper through PBL.

1. RANDOM REMODEL

Using the examples in the Project Library, randomly assign two or three projects to each participant.

After reading silently, participants discuss sketches (in pairs or small groups): How would you remodel these projects to suit your context? For example, how would you want to change a project to meet grade-level or subject-area standards? What would you keep from the sample project? What else would you like to know about a sample project?

2. GO GLOBAL

The following projects, all included in the Project Library, offer the potential to connect students with a larger, often global community:

3. What's in a Name?, p. 152

4. A Week in the Life, p. 152

21. Digiteens, p. 157

22. Eracism, p. 157

Participants discuss (in pairs or small groups): What would you need to connect your students globally? For example: Access to technology tools like Skype or webcam? Fluency in a second language or translation tools? Membership in a global education organization like iEARN? Permission from parents or school administrators? Do you anticipate any barriers that could be difficult to overcome before you are ready to tackle a global project? Where might you find help?

Select another project from the Library, or think of a project you have done previously. How would you globalize it? What benefits would you expect students to gain from adding global learning goals to the project?

3. FOCUS GROUP

Invite at least four students to serve as a focus group to review project ideas.

Participants select their favorite examples from the Project Library and share them with students in a way that's age appropriate. (For example, older students could read summaries from Project Library; younger students might benefit from having teachers describe the projects to them.) Students provide feedback about:

- Which projects appeal to them? Why?
- Have students describe what makes them most curious about the projects they like. What would they look forward to learning from the project experience?
- Are there any projects that students say they would not want to do? Why?
- Do students have suggestions to change or expand on the project ideas?

After receiving the students' focus group feedback, participants examine the same projects again. How has their thinking changed about which projects are worth implementing? Or how they might alter selected projects based on students' feedback? How might the experience of working with student focus groups inform "from scratch" project design?

Extension: Do the same activity with parents, other community members, or mixed groups of students and adults.

4. CLOSE TO HOME

Several projects described in *Thinking Through Project-Based Learning* emphasize local problem solving. For example, in the project Deserts in Rainy Seattle? (Chapter 1: The Whys and Hows of PBL, p. 3), students addressed the issue of poor access to nutritious food in local neighborhoods. In an example mentioned in Chapter 7: Language Arts (p. 73), students created an exhibit to honor the nearly forgotten civil rights heroes in their community.

In both examples, students had to thoroughly understand the issue they were solving before they could design a solution. As part of their project, they developed the skill of *problem finding.*

Participants discuss (in small groups or as a whole group): How can we find the issues in our community that could form the basis for good projects? Who might have an ear to the ground? Who can help us learn more about local issues?

After their discussion, participants develop an action plan for problem finding that might include

- Using community surveys, focus groups, data analysis, or interviews with local experts to identify potential issues
- Engaging students in the problem-finding process
- Inviting local advisers (through parent groups, business or civic organizations, professional groups, and so forth) to help with local problem identification

5. EXPERTISE EXERCISE

In this book, we have emphasized the value of disciplinary thinking, that is, getting students to operate in the manner of professionals for whom certain subject matter is central to their work. See how far you can go with identifying professions aligned to specific subjects. Start with a warm-up and ask the group to think of professional people whose work causes them to engage in the language arts (reading, writing, listening, and speaking). They will easily name many occupations, from editors to politicians to marketing executives to journalists. Now give the group a challenge. At table groups, make a list of professions for which math is central to the work. A little healthy competition adds to the fun. Stop the teams after 2 or 3 minutes and ask them to count and report on the number of occupations on their lists. Set a goal. Ask: Can anyone beat this table with 13? Encourage them to keep going and stop after 5 minutes. Ask the group with the most to read their list. Encourage others to challenge items and ask for justification. End the exercise with a reminder that this was all in fun but to remember that a generative exercise such as this is useful when they start planning projects, how their students will operate within the project, and as they seek expertise, too.

6. PROJECT SPIRAL

Several examples in *Thinking Through Project-Based Learning* exemplify what the authors describe as the "project spiral." These are projects that extend well beyond a single classroom, perhaps connecting with a wide audience, engaging with experts or learners in other communities, or extending across disciplines.

Participants discuss

a. Readiness: How prepared are our students for a project that lasts for an extended time or involves more than one content area?

b. Preparation: How can we prepare our students to tackle more ambitious projects? What precursor activities or mini-projects would get them ready to tackle larger efforts?

c. Spinoffs: Examining projects that participants have done before (or using examples from the Project Library), they discuss: Where might these projects lead? What are the possible extensions or project spirals? What would be the benefits to learners or the school community if these projects were to "spiral" in new directions?

Appendix D

Project-Based Learning Resources

PBL BOOKSHELF

Build a PBL bookshelf for your own professional reading and share titles with colleagues to promote deeper discussions about the opportunities and challenges of project-based learning. Here are several titles we recommend.

Berger, R. (2003). *An ethic of excellence: Building a culture of craftsmanship with students.* Portsmouth, NH: Heineman.

Ron Berger shares insights gained as chief program officer for Expeditionary Learning, a national network of PBL schools. Berger emphasizes the value of students producing "beautiful work" and shares three simple but powerful rules for providing critical feedback: Be kind. Be specific. Be helpful.

Boss, S., & Krauss, J. (2007). *Reinventing project-based learning: Your field guide to real-world projects for the digital age.* Eugene, OR: International Society for Technology in Education.

Designed to follow the arc of a project, this book offers an accessible introduction to PBL with digital tools. Project examples from around the world show how PBL works in diverse contexts.

Boss, S. (2012). *Bringing innovation to school: Empowering students to thrive in a changing world.* Bloomington, IN: Solution Tree.

The author showcases breakthrough projects in which students become effective community problem solvers, describes a process for emphasizing innovation in PBL, and shares strategies for encouraging more creative thinking in classroom and community alike.

Katz, L., & Chard, S. (2000). *Engaging children's minds: The project approach (2nd ed.).* Santa Barbara, CA: Praeger.

The authors combine academic insights with classroom vignettes of in-depth, student-driven investigations involving young learners.

183

They make PBL accessible by demonstrating that good questions for student investigations—*How do we build a house? How does our school bus take us places safely?*—are right at hand.

Hallerman, H., & Larmer, J. (2011). *PBL in the elementary grades: Step-by-step guidance, tools, and tips for standards-focused K–5 projects.* Novato, CA: Buck Institute for Education.

With a specific focus on PBL in the elementary grades, this book combines practical tools with classroom tips for scaffolding critical thinking, fostering collaboration, and building a foundation for other 21st-century skills. Seven project spotlights illustrate PBL from grades K–5.

Larmer, J. (2009). *PBL starter kit: To-the-point advice, tools, and tips for your first project.* Novato, CA: Buck Institute for Education.

Along with practical tools for project design, management, and assessment, this guidebook includes detailed descriptions of six spotlight projects in middle school and high school.

ONLINE RESOURCES

Buck Institute for Education (www.bie.org)

Buck Institute for Education (BIE) promotes project-based learning to improve 21st-century teaching and learning. In addition to delivering professional development and coaching to districts nationwide, the nonprofit organization maintains an online library of project plans and videos; provides downloadable tools for project planning, management, and assessment; and tracks research on the effectiveness of PBL.

Edutopia (www.edutopia.org)

Edutopia, produced by the George Lucas Educational Foundation, promotes project-based learning as a key strategy to improve teaching and learning. The website includes an extensive library of videos, articles, blogs, research summaries, and classroom guides, along with online communities where educators can connect with colleagues.

Envision Education (www.envisionschools.org)

Envision Education includes four all-PBL, college-prep high schools in California, along with Envision Learning Partners, which provides professional development and coaching. Envision Schools Project Exchange (www.envisionprojects.org) includes detailed project examples, including videotaped reflections from teachers and students.

ePals (www.epals.org)

The ePals Global Community is a collaborative space for sharing project ideas and connecting with classrooms from around the world.

Expeditionary Learning (http://elschools.org/)

A national network of PBL schools, Expeditionary Learning publishes detailed project examples in its online project showcase.

High Tech High (www.hightechhigh.org/)

A network of K–12 charter schools in Southern California, High Tech High publishes a peer-reviewed journal called *Unboxed* and shares project examples and other PBL resources online.

iEARN (www.iearn.org)

iEARN, the International Education and Resource Network, is a nonprofit global network that enables teachers and youth to use the Internet and other technologies to collaborate on projects that enhance learning and make a difference in the world.

New Tech Network (www.newtechnetwork.org)

A national network of PBL-based high schools, New Tech Network shares project success stories and other resources on its blog (www.new technetwork.org/newtech_blog). New Tech Network also facilitates a weekly Twitter chat about PBL. Follow #pblchat on Twitter.

Reinventing Project-Based Learning Blog (http://reinventingpbl.blogs pot.com)

Co-authors Jane Krauss and Suzie Boss maintain this blog to track trends, opportunities, and reflections related to project-based learning as an international trend in education.

References

Allington, R., & Cunningham, P. (2011). Developing effective reading curricula for struggling readers. In Ravinski, T. (Ed.), *Rebuilding the foundation: Effective reading instruction for 21st century literacy*. Bloomington, IN: Solution Tree.

Amaral, O., Garrison, L., & Klentschy, M., (2002). Helping English learners increase achievement through inquiry-based science instruction. *Bilingual Research Journal, 26*(2), 213–239.

Applebee, A., Langer, J., Nystrand, M., & Gamoran, A. (2003). Discussion-based approaches to developing understanding: Classroom instruction and student performance in middle and high school English. *American Educational Research Journal, 40*(3), 685–730.

Barrows, H., & Tamblyn, R. (1980). *Problem-based learning*. New York: Springer.

Boix Mansilla, V. (2006). Interdisciplinary work at the frontier: An empirical examination of expert interdisciplinary epistemologies. *Issues in Integrative Studies, 22*, 1–31.

Boix Mansilla, V., & Dawes Duraising, E. (2007). Targeted assessment of students' interdisciplinary work: An empirically grounded framework proposal. *Journal of Higher Education, 78*(2), 215–237.

Boix Mansilla, V., & Jackson, A. (2011). *Educating for global competence: Preparing our youth to engage the world*. New York: Asia Society Partnership for Global Learning and the Council of Chief State School Officers. Available for download as PDF from asiasociety.org/files/book-globalcompetence.pdf.

Boss, S. (2012, May 31). Teaching non-traditional learners. *Edutopia*. Retrieved Aug. 27, 2012, from http://www.edutopia.org/blog/supporting-struggling-students-suzie-boss.

Boss, S., Johanson, C., Arnold, S., Parker, W., Nguyen, D., Mosborg, S.; Nolen, S. . . . Bransford, J. (2012). The quest for deeper learning and engagement in advanced high school courses. *The Foundation Review, 3*(3), 12–23.

Boss, S., & Krauss, J. (2007). *Reinventing project-based learning: Your field guide to real-world projects for the digital age*. Eugene, OR: International Society for Technology in Education.

Bureau of Labor Statistics, U.S. Department of Labor. (2012a). *Occupational outlook handbook, 2012–13 edition, kindergarten and elementary school teachers*. Retrieved Aug. 26, 2012, from http://www.bls.gov/ooh/education-training-and-library/kindergarten-and-elementary-school-teachers.htm.

Bureau of Labor Statistics, U.S. Department of Labor (2012b). *Occupational outlook handbook, 2012–13 edition, sources of career information*. Retrieved *August 29, 2012*, from http://www.bls.gov/ooh/about/sources-of-career-information.htm.

Burk, J. (2011, Feb. 17). Why you should wait to teach projectile motion part 2: Introducing projectile motion using Angry Birds [web log post]. *Quantum Progress*. Retrieved Aug. 27, 2012, from https://quantumprogress.wordpress.com/2011/02/17/why-you-should-wait-to-teach-projectile-motion-part-2-introducing-projectile-motion-using-angry-birds/.

Burns, M. (1998). *Math: Facing an American phobia.* Sausalito, CA: Math Solutions.

Burns, M. (2004). Writing in math. *Educational Leadership, 62*(2), 30–33. Retrieved January 3, 2012, from http://www.pbs.org/teacherline/courses/rdla230/docs/session_1_burns.pdf

Cassidy, K. (2012, April 4). PBL in primary: Who asks the questions? [web log post]. *Powerful Learning Practice Blog.* Retrieved Aug. 29, 2012, from http://plpnetwork.com/2012/04/04/pbl-in-primary-who-asks-the-questions.

Center on Education Policy (2007, May). Educational architects: Do state agencies have the tools necessary to implement NCLB? *From the capital to the classroom: Year 5 of the No Child Left Behind Act.* Washington, DC: Author.

Cheung, T. (2010). Stories from the heart [web log post]. *Mrs. Cheung's Connection.* Retrieved Aug. 27, 2012, from http://blogs.egusd.net/mscheung/2010/12/16/stories-from-the-heart/.

Colburn, A. (1997, Fall). How to make lab activities more open ended. *California Science Teachers Association Journal,* 4–6. Retrieved Aug. 30, 2012, from www.exploratorium.edu/IFI/resources/workshops/lab_activities.html.

Conley, P. (2008, July 1). *School days in China.* Capital Public Radio. Sacramento, CA: Sacramento StoryCorps. Accessed Aug. 27, 2012, at http://archive.capradio.org/articles/2008/07/01/sacramento-storycorps-locke-native-recalls-school-days-in-china.

Coote, R. (n.d.). *Developing a thinking curriculum: Teachers' Guide.* Auckland, NZ: Birkdale Intermediate School. Retrieved Aug. 26, 2012, from http://www.bis.school.nz/thinking_learning.html.

Davis, B., Sumara, D., & Luce-Kapler. (2007). *Engaging minds: Changing teaching in complex times.* New York: Routledge.

Davis, S. (2012, Feb. 23). Collaboration, really? *Getting Smart* blog. Retrieved Aug. 26, 2012, from http://gettingsmart.com/blog/2012/02/collaboration-in-the-21st-century/?utm_source=twitterfeed&utm_medium=twitter.

Dawson, P., & Guare, R. (2004). *Executive skills in children and adolescents: A practical guide to assessment and intervention.* New York: Guilford Press.

Demillo, E. (2011, Dec. 27). *Science and U! Science, technology, and the Internet.* New York: CUNY-TV. Retrieved Aug. 27, 2012, from http://www.youtube.com/watch?v=cUoYqoM2i1I&t=10m24s.

Dewey, J. (1997). *Democracy and education.* New York: Free Press.

Dewey, J. (2011). *The school and society & the child and the curriculum.* Readaclassic.com.

Diamond, A. (2010). The evidence base for improving school outcomes by addressing the whole child and by addressing skills and attitudes, not just content. *Early Education and Development, 21*(5), 780–793.

Dick, T., & Rallis, S. (1991). Factors and influences on high school students' career choices. *Journal for Research in Mathematics Education, 22*(4), 281–292.

Didion, J. (1976, Dec. 5). Why I write. *The New York Times Book Review.*

Drake, S., & Burns, R. (2004). *Meeting standards through integrated curriculum.* Alexandria, VA: Association for Supervision and Development.

Dunkhase, J. (2003, Spring). The coupled-inquiry cycle: A teacher concerns–based model for effective student inquiry. *Science Educator, 12*(1), 10–15.

Ebbetts, J. (2012, Feb. 7). What do you know? And how well do you think? *Smith College: Insight.* Retrieved Aug. 26, 2012, from http://www.smith.edu/insight/stories/knowledgebuilding.php.

Falcon Daily. (2011, December 12). *More than that...* Retrieved January 3, 2013, from http://www.youtube.com/watch?v=FhribaNXr7A.

Felton, T. (2012, April 1) From scholars to citizen scholars: The story of Hope House. *Expeditionary Learning.* Retrieved Aug. 27, 2012, from http://elschools.org/best-practices/scholars-citizen-scholars-story-hope-house.

Finkelstein, N., Hanson, T., Huang, C.-W., Hirschman, B., & Huang, M. (2010). *Effects of problem based economics on high school economics instruction.* (NCEE 2010–4002). Washington, DC: National Center for Education Evaluation and Regional Assistance, Institute of Education Sciences, U.S. Department of Education.

Flores, A. (2007). Examining disparities in mathematics education: Achievement gap or opportunity gap? *High School Journal,* 29–42. Retrieved January 3, 2012, from http://schoolcounselconnect.weebly.com/uploads/1/0/2/4/10242617/ achievementoropportunitygap.pdf.

Friedman, T. (2005). *The world is flat: A brief history of the twenty-first century.* New York: Farrar, Straus and Giroux.

Gampel, J. (n.d.). *Don't be s-s-scared: The truth about snakes.* Expeditionary Learning Documentation Project. Brighton, MA: Conservatory Lab Charter School.

Grasso, D., & Brown Burkins, M. (2010). *Holistic engineering education: Beyond technology.* New York: Springer.

Grouws, D., & Cebulla, K. (2000). Elementary and middle school mathematics at the crossroads. In T. L. Good (Ed.), *American education: Yesterday, today, and tomorrow* (part II, 99th yearbook, National Society for Studies in Education (NSSE)), pp. 209–255. Chicago: University of Chicago Press.

Harpaz, Y., & Lefstein, A. (2000, Nov.). Communities of thinking. *Educational Leadership, 58*(3), 54–57.

Humphreys, L. (2011). *Wind turbine investigation and design challenge.* http://edu cation.nmsu.edu/projects/sc2/documents/lh-wind-inquiry-connecting-to-defining-inquiry.doc.

Jacobs, H. (1989). *Interdisciplinary curriculum: Design and implementation.* Alexandria, VA: Association for Supervision and Curriculum Development.

Kamii, C. (2000). *Young children reinvent arithmetic: Implications of Piaget's theory (2nd ed.).* New York: Teachers College Press.

Kohn, N., & Smith, S. (2010). Collaborative fixation: Effects of others' ideas on brainstorming. *Applied Cognitive Psychology, 25*(3), 359–371. Available online: http://onlinelibrary.wiley.com/doi/10.1002/acp.1699/full.

Larmer, J. (2009). *PBL starter kit: To-the-point advice, tools, and tips for your first project in middle or high school.* Novato, CA: Buck Institute for Education.

Lindsay, J., & Davis, V. (2012). *Flattening classrooms, engaging minds: Move to global collaboration one step at a time.* New York: Pearson.

Marzano, R. J., & Heflebower, T. (2012). *Teaching and assessing 21st century skills.* Bloomington, IN: Marzano Research Laboratory.

Mayo, G. (2012, February 20). Transitions: A collection of children's books. *Digital IS.* Online journal. Retrieved Aug. 27, 2012, from http://digitalis.nwp.org/ resource/3509.

Meyer, D. (2009, June 10). What I would do with this: Glassware [web log entry]. *dy/dan.* Retrieved Aug. 27, 2012, from http://blog.mrmeyer.com/?p=4018.

Moje, E., Young, J., Readence, J., & Moore, D. (2000). Reinventing adolescent literacy for new times: Perennial and millennial issues. *Journal of Adolescent & Adult Literacy, 43*(5), 400–411.

Mullis, I., Martin, M., & Foy, P. (with Olson, J., Preuschoff, C., Erberber, E., Arora, A., & Galia, J.). (2008). *TIMSS 2007 international mathematics report: Findings from IEA's Trends in International Mathematics and Science Study at the fourth and eighth grades.* Chestnut Hill, MA: TIMSS & PIRLS International Study Center, Boston College.

National Council for the Social Studies. (1991). *Social studies in the middle school: A report of the task force on social studies in the middle school.* Washington, DC: Author. Retrieved Aug. 27, 2012, from http://www.socialstudies.org/posi tions/middleschool.

National Council for the Social Studies. (1994). *Expectations of excellence: Curriculum standards for social studies.* Washington, DC: Author.

National Council of Teachers of Mathematics. (2000). *Principles and standards for school mathematics.* Reston, VA: Author.

National Governors Association Center for Best Practices, Council of Chief State School Officers. (2010). *Common core state standards English language arts.* Washington, DC: National Governors Association Center for Best Practices, Council of Chief State School Officers.

National Research Council. (2000). *How people learn: Brain, mind, experience, and school.* Washington, DC: National Academy Press.

The Nerdy Book Club. (2012, Feb. 14). Transitions: A collection of children's stories [web blog post]. *The Nerdy Book Club.* Retrieved Aug. 27, 2012, from http://nerdybookclub.wordpress.com/2012/02/14/transitions-a-collection-of-childrens-stories/.

Noschese, F. (2011, June 16). Angry birds in the physics classroom. [Web log post]. *Action-Reaction.* Retrieved Jan. 3, 2013, from http://fnoschese.wordpress.com/2011/06/16/angry-birds-in-the-physics-classroom/.

OWP/P Cannon Design, VS Furniture, & Bruce Mau Design. (2010). *The third teacher: 79 ways you can use design to transform teaching and learning.* New York: Abrams.

Parker, W., Mosborg, S., Bransford, J., Vye, N., Wilkerson, J., & Abbott, R. (2011). Rethinking advanced high school coursework: Tackling the depth/breadth tension in the AP *US Government and Politics* course. *Journal of Curriculum Studies,* 43(4), 533–559. Retrieved Aug. 27, 2012, from http://dx.doi.org/10.1080/00220272.2011.584561.

Perkins D. (2008). *Making learning whole: How seven principles of teaching can transform education.* San Francisco: Jossey-Bass.

Perry, B. (n.d.) How the brain learns best. *Scholastic* website. Retrieved Aug. 26, 2012, from http://teacher.scholastic.com/professional/bruceperry/.

Pólya, G. (1945). *How to solve it.* Princeton, NJ: Princeton University Press.

Pólya, G. (1957). *How to solve it (2nd ed.).* Princeton, NJ: Princeton University Press.

Robin, J. (2011). *Phys newtons.* San Diego, CA: author. Retrieved Aug. 27, 2012, from http://dp.hightechhigh.org/~jrobin/Projects/David_Macaulay/TitlePage.html.

Scardamalia, M., & Bereiter, C. (2003). Knowledge building. In *Encyclopedia of Education (2nd ed., pp. 1370–1373).* New York: Macmillan Reference. Downloaded Aug. 26, 2012, from http://ikit.org/fulltext/2003_knowledge_building.pdf.

Schloss, A., Franz, P., Thakur, A., & Wojcicki, E. (2012). *In search of things: A curriculum for understanding Web search strategies, copyright, bias and credibility.* Stanford, CA: Authors.

Schoenfeld, A. (1992). Learning to think mathematically: Problem solving, metacognition, and sense making in mathematics. In Douglas A. Grouws, *Handbook of research on mathematics teaching and learning,* pp. 334–370. New York: Macmillan.

Segal, L., & Noble, M. (2008, Spring). Invisibility. *Unboxed: A journal of adult learning in schools (1).* Retrieved January 31, 2012, from http://www.hightechhigh.org/unboxed/issue1/cards/3.php.

Skloot, R. (n.d.). FAQ. Rebecca Skloot website. Retrieved Aug. 27, 2012, from http://rebeccaskloot.com/faq/.

Snider, L. (2012, March 4). 11-year-old publishes 200th issue of Boulder community newspaper. *Daily Camera Online.* Retrieved Aug. 27, 2012, from http://www.dailycamera.com/boulder-county-news/ci_20092950.

Stahl, R. (1994). *Using "think-time" and "wait-time" skillfully in the classroom.* ERIC Document Reproduction Service: ED370885. Retrieved Aug. 26, 2012, from http://www.ericdigests.org/1995–1/think.htm.

Tokuhama-Espinosa, T. (2010). *Mind, brain, and education science: A comprehensive guide to the new brain-based teaching.* New York: W.W. Norton & Co.

Torpey, E. (2012). Math at work: Using numbers on the job. *Occupational Outlook Quarterly*, 2–13. Retrieved January 1, 2012, from http://www.bls.gov/opub/ooq/2012/fall/fall2012ooq.pdf.

Turckes, S. (2011, Aug. 26). What schools can learn from Google, IDEO, and Pixar. *Fast Company Co. Design.* Retrieved Aug. 26, 2012, from http://www.fastcodesign.com/1664735/what-schools-can-learn-from-google-ideo-and-pixar.

Urquhart, V. (2009). Using writing in mathematics to deepen student learning. Retrieved January 3, 2012, from http://www.mcrel.org/~/media/Files/McREL/Homepage/Products/01_99/prod19_Writing_in_math.ashx.

U.S. Department of Agriculture. The food desert locator. *USDA Economic Research Service website.* Accessed Aug. 26, 2012, at http://www.ers.usda.gov/data-products/food-desert-locator.aspx.

U.S. Department of Agriculture. (2012, June). Cost of food at home. USDA Center for Nutrition Policy and Promotion website. Accessed Aug. 26, 2012, at http://www.cnpp.usda.gov/usdafoodcost-home.htm.

Wenglinsky, H. (2000). *How teaching matters: Bringing the classroom back into discussions of teacher quality.* Princeton, NJ: Educational Testing Service. Downloaded Aug. 29, 2012, from http://www.ets.org/research/policy_research_reports/pic-teamat.

Wessling, S. (2011). *Supporting students in a time of core standards: English language arts, grades 9–12.* Urbana, IL: National Council of Teachers of English.

Wiggins, G. & McTighe, J. (2005). *Understanding by design (Expanded 2nd ed.).* Upper Saddle River, NJ: Prentice Hall.

Willis, J. (2007, Summer). The neuroscience of joyful education. *Educational Leadership* online. Retrieved Aug. 26, 2012, from http://www.ascd.org/publications/educational-leadership/summer07/v0164/num09/The-Neuroscience-of-Joyful-Education.aspx.

Willis, J. (2011, June 13). Understanding how the brain thinks. *Edutopia.* Retrieved Aug. 26, 2012, from http://www.edutopia.org/blog/understanding-how-the-brain-thinks-judy-willis-md.

Woodard, J., & Baxter, J. (1999, June 30). *Tools for understanding: A resource guide for mathematical understanding in secondary schools.* Website funded by U.S. Department of Education, Office of Special Education Programs. http://www2.ups.edu/community/tofu/home.htm.

Yau, N. (2010, July 22). 7 basic rules for making charts and graphics [web log post]. *Flowing Data.* Retrieved Aug. 30, 2012, from http://flowingdata.com/2010/07/22/7-basic-rules-for-making-charts-and-graphs/.

Index

CORWIN
A SAGE Company

The Corwin logo—a raven striding across an open book—represents the union of courage and learning. Corwin is committed to improving education for all learners by publishing books and other professional development resources for those serving the field of PreK–12 education. By providing practical, hands-on materials, Corwin continues to carry out the promise of its motto: **"Helping Educators Do Their Work Better."**